Savage Cinema

THE UNIVERSI~

Other Film Studies Titles from The Athlone Press

Whom God Wishes to Destroy
Francis Coppola and the New Hollywood
Jon Lewis

"This book will likely occupy a place of central importance in setting the agenda for thought about contemporary American film."
Richard de Cordova
0 485 30071 0 hb

Viewing Positions
Ways of Seeing Film
Edited by Linda Williams

The essays in *Viewing Positions* consider questions of
human subjectivity and the sociology of audiences in
relation to the viewing of films of different styles and
genres.
0 485 30075 3 pb

The Studio System
Edited by Janet Staiger

What it is like to work in Hollywood, within the complexities of film-making, is studied in depth in the
essays gathered together in *The Studio System*.
0 485 30074 5 pb

Silent Film
Edited by Richard Abel

The most important aspects of the silent cinema, drawing new and provocative parallels with today's postmodern films.
0 485 30076 1 pb

Movies and Mass Culture
Edited by John Belton

How films both effect and reflect changes within a society and in a nation's self-image.
0 485 30073 7 pb

Cinema and Painting
How Art Is Used in Film
Angela Dalle Vacche

Discusses how film-makers have used the imagery of
painting to shape and enrich the meaning of their films.
0 485 30079 6 pb

Savage Cinema

Sam Peckinpah and the Rise of Ultraviolent Movies

by Stephen Prince

THE ATHLONE PRESS
LONDON

First published 1998 by THE ATHLONE PRESS
1 Park Drive, London NW11 7SG

© The University of Texas Press 1998
British Library Cataloguing-in-Publication Data
A catalogue record for this book is available from the British Library
ISBN 0 485 30087 7

Printed and bound in The United States of America

For violence, like Achilles' lance, can heal the wounds that it has inflicted. —JEAN-PAUL SARTRE

If you would endure life, be prepared for death.
—SIGMUND FREUD

I'm afraid the truth, to me as I see it, is more important than entertainment for its own sake. The unfortunate thing is, I suppose, I see a certain kind of truth only too clearly. —SAM PECKINPAH

For My Parents
and Tami

Contents

Acknowledgments

WRITING THIS BOOK has been a pure pleasure, not the least of which has been due to the help and assistance I received from friends and colleagues. I must thank Tony Williams who chaired a panel on Peckinpah at the 1994 Society for Cinema Studies Conference. My paper, "Melancholy and Violence in Peckinpah's Films," which Tony kindly included on his panel, was the real beginning of this book and the start of my thinking about the issues that preoccupy this study.

The Virginia Tech Division of Arts and Sciences furnished me with a travel grant that made possible the study of Peckinpah's papers that are archived in the Margaret Herrick Library at the Academy of Motion Picture Arts and Sciences in Los Angeles. At the Library, Sam Gill, in the Special Collections Department, and research archivist Valentin Almendarez were extremely cordial and helpful in guiding me through this extensive collection that fills 95 boxes.

Jerry Scheeler, a Peckinpah fan, once again loaned me lights, viewer, and other equipment needed for making frame enlargements. Jeff Slater kindly allowed me to use pictures from his personal collection. Paul Messaris, David Cook, and Michael Bliss read the manuscript with care and offered extremely useful suggestions for improving it. Ken Long kindly offered the use of his computer equipment for making some late-in-the-game frame enlargements.

As she has on past books, Teresa Darvalics offered invaluable manuscript assistance and computer support.

Finally, though she is no fan of Peckinpah, Tami Tomasello offered the warmth, kindness and good cheer that add greatly to the pleasures of producing a new book.

Introduction

SAM PECKINPAH directed only fourteen feature films, a small number compared with the output of such prolific directors as John Ford and Howard Hawks. Peckinpah's career as a feature director was a relatively brief one, spanning just over two decades and marked by several lengthy hiatuses between productions. Measured in terms of the quantity of his output, therefore, he might appear to fall outside the circle of major American filmmakers. Part of what gives Ford and Hawks their stature is, in fact, a measure of quantity—the large number of accomplished films that they directed. If we shave from Peckinpah's career those productions where the work was chaotic and relatively undisciplined, we are left with six or seven clearly first-rate pictures.

Why, then, does Peckinpah's presence loom so large in modern American cinema? A small part of the answer lies in the folklore and legends that surrounded Peckinpah, the man. Like John Huston, he was an exceptionally colorful and interesting personality about whom friends and associates could spin an endless supply of anecdotes and tall tales. With his brawling and drinking, Peckinpah cut a wide swath through life, a life that was consistent with a peculiarly romantic notion of how an artist should live and behave. Sadly, that romantic ideal included a requisite for self-destruction as the certifier of the artist's integrity and sensitivity, and Peckinpah ably fulfilled this component as well, dying at fifty-nine after a long period of decline and abuse of his talents.

This end was consistent with the romanticism on which his career has been constructed in the media and in the public eye—a romanticism that was, to some extent, lived out by Peckinpah. Today so many movies seem utterly mechanical and prefabricated, assembled by engineers who are digital wizards but have little to say about life. Actors emote in a void, placed before a blue screen for subsequent compositing with computer-animated environments. In this climate, the intensity that Peckinpah brought to his life and art and the general (and romantic) disdain that he felt for machinery ("The Devil seeks to destroy you with *machines,*" a preacher snarls in *The Ballad of Cable Hogue*) seem a more authentic stance to occupy with regard to life and cinema. Peckinpah studied drama in college, but he was not a film-school graduate, and in temperament and spirit he belonged with an earlier generation of American filmmakers—Raoul Walsh, William Wellman, Hawks—who brought a wealth of life experience with them when they entered the movie industry. Thus, their artistic reference points included these lived experiences as well as other movies, whereas for many of today's directors the only reference points are other movies and television shows. Peckinpah was a great director of Westerns (and one of the last great ones) precisely because the West was, for him, an authentic place and experience that he had briefly encountered in his youth during visits to the Sierra Nevadas and his grandfather's ranch. The loss of that ranch haunted him as an adult and was a paradigmatic experience underlying his treatment on film of a vanishing West. Part of Peckinpah's staying power for modern filmmakers and viewers, then, lies in the legendary and mythic qualities of his larger-than-life personality and the romanticism and authenticity (as noncontradictory qualities) that he brought to his roguish films.

A second reason for his current stature is the extraordinary influence that the style and content of his films has exerted over later filmmakers. Though he did not innovate them, the slow-motion violence and exploding squibs that are closely identified with his work have now become the normative techniques for rendering screen violence. More than any other American director, Peckinpah made slow motion the requisite format for capturing and extending the action of violent gun battles, and he coupled this with an extremely kinetic mode of montage editing. To look at the action set-pieces in the films of Walter Hill, Tony Scott, or John Woo is to see a visual syntax that ties their work directly to Peckinpah's films and clearly demonstrates that the traditions his work has established are part of its legacy.

The moral abrasiveness of Peckinpah's work, particularly its tendency to place a brutal or compromised protagonist at the center of the narrative, has been a tremendous influence on subsequent filmmakers. In pictures like *The Wild Bunch* and *Straw Dogs*, Peckinpah decisively shifted the moral parameters of commercial cinema away from a clear separation of good and evil and toward the unsettling contemplation of flawed, debased behavior viewed up close and without a secure moral reference point. When in *The Wild Bunch* Pike Bishop executes a wounded comrade without feeling or hesitation, and when children, sentimental archetypes in generations of film, gleefully torture and burn a scorpion, we see that Peckinpah did not merely attach a new level of violence to screen images but exploded the moral absolutes that had given shape and meaning to screen narratives for decades.

Beyond their capacity for brutality, Peckinpah's villains and killers are memorable because he characterized them so vividly. Crazy Lee's dying dare in *The Wild Bunch* that his killers kiss his sister's black cat's ass, and Chris Cawsey's merry proclamation in *Straw Dogs* that "Rats is life" do not exactly make these no-accounts endearing, but such remarks do make these men become, through this brief poetry, unforgettably, disturbingly human. Directors like Martin Scorsese took courage from this and began to explore the creative possibilities inherent in the portrayal of evil, psychopathic, or borderline personalities. Many of the cynical and amoral characters who now populate our movie screens—and the ultraviolence they perpetrate—derive from the flawed heroes and gutter-trash losers who scrabble through Peckinpah's films.

Peckinpah's work helped propel American film toward explorations of subterranean aspects of human behavior that had been too dark or twisted for the industry to countenance in earlier decades. Recognizing this brings us to the most important feature of Peckinpah's relevance for modern American film and highlights for us the fundamental issue explored in this book. Graphic screen violence has become an obsessive feature of contemporary filmmaking. We cannot, it seems, go to the movies today and avoid for very long the spectacle of exploding heads and severed limbs, or escape the company of the screen sociopaths who perpetrate these acts. If we trace this contemporary fetish for graphic bloodletting to one of its chief sources, we arrive again at Peckinpah's films. Violence is what his work was chiefly known for in its day, and it continues to be the central attribute that many people think of when his films are mentioned. This is with good reason. We have already noted that Peckinpah showed subsequent filmmakers how to stylize scenes of graphic violence and that his techniques have become the standard tools of the trade. Moreover, the rise of ultraviolent movies is tied to the impact of Peckinpah's work on the American cinema. Violence, I will argue, is the central preoccupation of his cinema.

Does this not damn his work? If we (correctly, I believe) tie the current cinematic fascination with graphic bloodshed to his groundbreaking work of the late 1960s and early 1970s, and if we accept that contemporary movie violence is excessive and produces harmful social effects, does this not tend to invalidate any claims we might make on behalf of Peckinpah's work?

We could seek to legitimize that work by claiming that its violent content is only a secondary and lesser component of other thematic or stylistic interests that lie essentially elsewhere (e.g., the vanishing West or the vicissitudes and travails of friendship). But if we argue, as I do here, that the inquiry into violence is the most important, and basic, component of Peckinpah's work, and if we can see clearly where that inquiry has led contemporary cinema, then this might seem to foreclose on the usefulness of closely studying these films. After all, doesn't their violence make them a known quantity? But this is not the case. By confronting the violence issue directly and unraveling the volatile problems with which it is entangled, we can position Peckinpah's work more precisely and gauge its singular importance in the history of American cinema. We must try to differentiate his films' focus and moral attributes from the unfortunate tradition of movie violence that they have helped inspire. Peckinpah is a major figure and his filmmaking a major force in postwar American film, and the value we should accord to Peckinpah's work rises or falls on the violence issue. We must confront this issue to understand the work, and this task becomes more urgent given the pervasiveness of the bloodshed in recent film.

What follows, then, is a systematic and comprehensive examination of Peckinpah's use of cinema to inquire into the phenomenon of violence in human life and an analysis of the consequences of this inquiry for contemporary cinema. This focus necessarily imposes boundaries. I do not systematically cover all of Peckinpah's films in depth. For instance, in *The Ballad of Cable Hogue* and *Junior Bonner* Peckinpah notably moved away from the violent screen worlds that he more typically rendered. Accordingly, these films do not receive an extended treatment here. (The less said about *Convoy,* the better.) Of his other work, I principally examine those productions from *The Wild Bunch* in 1968 to *Bring Me the Head of Alfredo Garcia* in 1974, a period that is arguably the most significant portion of his career. Before 1968, Peckinpah was constrained by the MPAA Production Codes and could not explore the violence issue as he did in the years that followed, and after 1974, his work becomes quite checkered. These factors motivate the rationale for the principal time period covered by this study.

Furthermore, the study is organized conceptually, and individual films are examined with reference to the particular issues and problems at hand. I do not proceed chronologically, film by film; neither do I completely analyze a given film in any single chapter. Rather, I reexamine the films across the chapters according to the particular frames of reference that are important within a given topic or focal area. I trust that this method better clarifies the structural features of Peckinpah's cinematic inquiry into violence, features that transcend their incarnation within any single film.

Given the nature of this study's focus, it does not deal with other vital aspects of Peckinpah's work. His Westerns, for example, helped decisively to revise that genre, shifting it away from the chivalric and idealized West of Ford toward a more pyschopathic and mud-spattered landscape. This territory has been ably explored by Paul Seydor, and I consider it in *Sam Peckinpah's* The Wild Bunch, a collection of essays dealing with that film and Peckinpah's use of the Western.[1] Peckinpah's remarkable ability to elicit superlative performances from actors is evident in the outstanding work contributed to his films by William Holden, Ernest Borgnine, Susan George, Robert Ryan, James Coburn, and others. Furthermore, the memorable stock company comprised of R.G. Armstrong, Warren Oates, Strother Martin, and L.Q. Jones is an indelible part of his work. But assessment of these sterling performances properly belongs in a more traditional study of Peckinpah as dramatist. A detailed assessment of the production history of Peckinpah's ongoing collaboration with composer Jerry Fielding, cinematographers Lucien Ballard and John Coquillon, and editors Lou Lombardo and Robert Wolfe also falls outside the purview of this study.

To understand Peckinpah's approach to, and stylistic rendering of, screen violence, we must first grasp the social preconditions that fueled his worldview and allowed it free expression, before turning to the aesthetic properties of his distinctive mode of presentation. Chapter One examines the social preconditions, which fall into two broad areas: transformations within the film industry and changes within society at large. When Peckinpah returned to feature filmmaking with *The Wild Bunch,* he was able to take advantage of sweeping changes in the codes governing acceptable screen content and of the film industry's willingness to champion new kinds of films and filmmakers. The years from 1966 to 1968 saw a series of key economic, sociological, and artistic changes that predated Peckinpah's innovative work on *The Wild Bunch* and helped make it possible. The first chapter profiles these changes and discusses their relevance for Peckinpah's filmmaking. In style and sensibility, Peckinpah was a late 1960s filmmaker, and to understand his work, he must be situated in reference to an industry that was dramatically reorienting and reinventing itself to keep pace with a changing society.

These larger shifts in society constitute the second broad arena in which Peckinpah's work should be located. Chapter One also examines the numerous ways in which Peckinpah reacted and responded to the era's tumultuous events. Some of the responses address specific events that appalled and agitated him, such as the My Lai massacre and the murders of John Kennedy and Sharon Tate. But, more generally, Peckinpah's attitudes and views toward the nation, particularly the era's ongoing social violence, resonate with the radical, New Left critique of American culture that was being developed and applied during those years. Peckinpah was an engaged observer and commentator on the dynamic and memorable history of the period through which he lived and during which he directed his best films. To understand why Peckinpah was drawn so deeply toward exploring the violence issue in his films, we must understand him as an artist connected with and responding to his times. This has, on the whole, been an area that scholars have neglected when trying to understand Peckinpah's films, and I hope to show how essential the 1960s were for shaping and influencing his work. Peckinpah himself acknowledged that great art emerges from powerful connections between artists and the society in which they live, and he remarked that "*The Ballad of Cable Hogue* is perhaps the least obviously social film I have made. But it is a dimension which is not totally absent from it."[2] Peckinpah's use of cinema was more socially engaged and less abstracted than commentators have traditionally emphasized, and this chapter places his work on the social landscape which helped configure it.

While Chapter One helps explain *why* Peckinpah chose to explore violence in films, the three chapters that follow explain *how* he did it. They explicate the basic aesthetic structures that he utilized in representing screen violence. The unique aspect of his films is the way they super-impose these structures to provoke viewers into disturbingly ambivalent responses. Chapter Two examines Peckinpah's use of montage editing to stylize human violence according to what he considered to be its essential external, physical attributes and its internal, spiritual ones. Peckinpah used three principal types of montage construction to aestheticize violence in ways that would compel the viewer's fascinated attention. The chapter explores these in detail and closes with a consideration of the danger inherent in a montage aesthetic: namely, a glorification of violence rather than its condemnation.

Chapter Three examines the emotional and psychological attitudes in the films that attach to the violent episodes and that tend to counterbalance the spectacular visual effects of the montages. We will see that, for the most part, Peckinpah was rigorous and systematic in excoriating violence by showing the emotional pain that is its consequence. Peckinpah claimed that he wished to use cinema to warn viewers about the terrible nature of violence and to produce a cathartic experience that would have beneficial social effects. Accordingly, the viability of the catharsis theory is assessed in Chapter Three, with particular reference to the extensive social science data on the effects of viewing film violence. The chapter concludes with a discussion of the implications of these findings for Peckinpah's work.

Chapter Four examines Peckinpah's use of self-reflexive audiovisual designs as declamatory devices for emphasizing what he saw as essential principles or truths of human violence. These devices tend to impose a more emphatically intellectualized perspective on the films, and, accordingly, they inflect the work in a very different direction from the use of montage to elicit spectacle. These designs demonstrate the rigor and care with which Peckinpah pursued the violence question and his awareness of the need to control and contextualize the explosive effects of his montages.

Chapter Five orients Peckinpah's work in relation to the legacy of screen violence that it helped inspire. I emphasize this as a problematic legacy and a misleading one. Peckinpah's work belongs to a different historical period than the films of such contemporary masters of gore as Martin Scorsese, Oliver Stone, and Quentin Tarantino, and consequently Peckinpah's films embody an alternative, more humanistic moral sensibility than does the work of these contemporary directors. Peckinpah's films, then, ought to be disentangled from the legacy that they have helped to inspire, because the moral and social project that his work undertakes is incompatible with the terms by which Scorsese, Stone, Tarantino, and others today render violence. By explicating the reasons for this, I hope to show why Peckinpah's films remain valuable and important, as violent works of art, at a time when one might sensibly and in principle object to contemporary screen violence. Understanding Peckinpah's work enables us to understand the problems and limitations of the treatment of violence in contemporary film.

To help explain the complexities of Peckinpah's approach to, and representation of, violence, I have drawn extensively on his papers and correspondence, which are archived at the Margaret Herrick Library at the Academy of Motion Picture Arts and Sciences in Los Angeles. This material reveals significant aspects of his work, and of the perceptions which underlie it, which have not traditionally been emphasized in scholarly studies of his films. The Herrick Collection is extraordinarily rich, and it demonstrates that we are only yet beginning to understand the dynamic interplay between Peckinpah, his times, and his work.

In particular, this material reveals a rather different Peckinpah than the personality he colorfully presented to the press. Peckinpah's frequent belligerence when talking to the media was a creation not unlike the persona of guileless entertainer that Alfred Hitchcock adopted when talking with reporters about his work.In each case, the postures adopted by Peckinpah and Hitchcock were intended to deflect serious and extended discussion of their films—discussion which they were often reluctant to undertake. However, both filmmakers were very thoughtful about their work and approached it with intelligence and ambition. In the extensive set of interviews he granted French filmmaker François Truffaut, Hitchcock dropped his pose and revealed the seriousness with which he conducted his work. Similarly, Peckinpah candidly discussed the design and goals of his work, without the public posturing, in his private correspondence and in his working papers directed at production personnel. Peckinpah's remarks in these private papers are validated by the evidence of the films. In the chapters that follow, I therefore give more weight to the correlation between the filmic evidence and the private papers than to the more colorful pronouncements he made when posturing for the media.

Screen violence is now a largely debased and exploitative form. Despite this, Peckinpah's films are of seminal importance for the stylistics and history of recent American film. They demonstrate the enormous, if transient, creative and social potential of the cinema in the late sixties and beyond. It will take some time to show this, so, as Peckinpah's most famous character might say, a little impatiently, "Let's go."

Savage Cinema

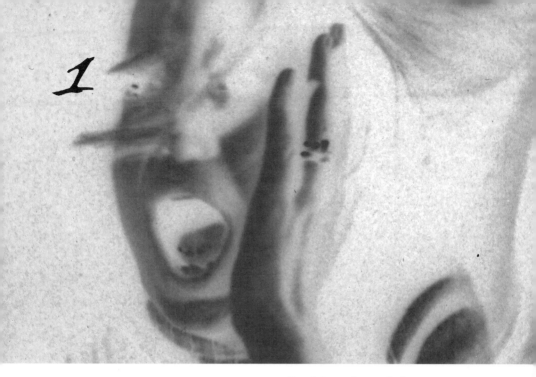

Peckinpah and the 1960s

MOVIES TODAY are saturated with blood. Beatings, shootings, and dismemberments, portrayed in lingering and graphic fashion, crowd the screen. Filmmakers like Quentin Tarantino (*Reservoir Dogs,* 1992, and *Pulp Fiction,* 1995) and Paul Verhoeven (*Robocop,* 1987, and *Basic Instinct,* 1992) have found critical and popular acclaim, in part, at least, through the outré images of violence they have fashioned. Both of these filmmakers have used explicit gore to make audiences alternately squirm with discomfort and roar with delight. The ear-cutting scene in Tarantino's *Reservoir Dogs* is quite unpleasant to watch, while the exploding head in the back of the car in *Pulp Fiction* initiates an extended comic sketch in that film. Verhoeven opens *Robocop* with the gruesome scene of the cop Murphy (Peter Weller) being literally shot to pieces by gangsters and subsequently shifts the film's violence into a more comic mode when a thug is covered with toxic waste and quickly turns into a glob of (walking) gunk.

The intense audience reactions these scenes elicit demonstrate the considerable skill and care with which they have been crafted. That each of these films was a critical and commercial hit shows, as well, how palatable graphic screen gore now is. An entrenched feature of contemporary cinema style, it extends well beyond the work of Tarantino and Verhoeven, two of its most successful practitioners. Even moronically plotted movies, careless in their handling of narrative and character, will often boast state-of-the-art blood effects. Ultraviolence is offered up by auteurs and hacks alike, and it regularly draws fire from politicians and other social watchdogs over its presumably unwholesome influence on American culture.

For those concerned about the contemporary state of American visual culture, the present fetish for explicit gore is a worrisome development, given the evidence that now exists (and which we will review in Chapter Three) about the effects on viewers of repeated exposure to violent images and narratives. Furthermore, it is highly probable that ultraviolent movies are here to stay, and that, once having turned that corner, American cinema cannot unlearn its present violent ways. Once the taboos and restrictions on movie content have come down, they prove very hard to reestablish. In addition, because ultraviolence is immensely popular, the style is likely to have considerable staying power.

We ought, therefore, to ask some questions of it. Principally, these are three: When did ultraviolence come to the American cinema and why? What are the aesthetic and ethical problems and contradictions for filmmakers and viewers that are inherent in the presentation of graphic screen violence? Must ultraviolence be a retrograde phenomenon? In other words, can it be used in a way that is aesthetically and intellectually honest and that might have progressive social consequences? We will examine these questions in a historical context. To understand the present, we shall look at the recent past.

We can gain considerable insight into the problems and shortcomings (both artistic and social) of contemporary movie gore by tracing ultraviolence back to that period when the detailed visual rendering of physical violence first became a distinct stylistic possibility in the American cinema. One figure clearly emerges from this period as the dominant and most influential practitioner of graphic movie violence. Sam Peckinpah is the crucial link between classical and postmodern Hollywood, the figure whose work transformed modern cinema in terms of the stylistics for rendering screen violence and in terms of the moral and psychological consequences that ensue, for filmmaker and viewer, from placing brutality at the center of a screen world. The cinema today is an uncommonly savage place. To understand how it got to be that way, we shall explore the genesis of movie ultraviolence in the work of its seminal practitioner, Sam Peckinpah. By looking backward, at an earlier period of filmmaking, we can

Quentin Tarantino's *Reservoir Dogs* features the graphic bloodshed and general fascination with violence that typify contemporary filmmaking. © 1992, Miramax Films.

better understand the forces that have made contemporary cinema so bloody and, most importantly, why ultraviolence is today so limited and so deadening a style.

In his day, Sam Peckinpah was one of the most contentious directors working in the American cinema and one of its most controversial. Following *The Wild Bunch* (1969) and, especially, *Straw Dogs* (1971), his work became synonymous with graphic, slow-motion violence, and it earned him the dubious sobriquet, "Bloody Sam." The controversies that swirled about his renditions of violence and the moral (or amoral) visions of his films came to overshadow his achievements, and with the rapid and sad decline of his talents after 1974, Peckinpah's critical reputation seemed thoroughly tarnished. He had his defenders and fans, but, following his death in 1984, he and his work sank into a critical obscurity that lasted for a decade. During this period, for many critics and scholars Peckinpah seemed to have become a largely discredited and forgotten figure in American cinema. But this neglect did not last. With the restoration and theatrical reissue of *The Wild Bunch* by Warner Bros. in 1995, accompanied by glowing reviews in the popular press, and with the publication of David Weddle's 1994 biogra-

Director Sam Peckinpah was the pivotal figure who transformed the stylistics of violence in modern cinema. Here, he relaxes during filming of the Agua Verde massacre in *The Wild Bunch,* an epochal and trend-setting sequence of screen violence.

phy of Peckinpah, the director reemerged into the spotlight as an authentically roguish voice in the American cinema and one in need of careful critical reassessment.

Peckinpah's detractors and admirers loathe and love him with passions equal in their intensity. That his work could so inspire such extremes of response is surely one sign of its extraordinarily rich texture, yet the existing critical discussions of his work have tended to neglect or minimize some of its most important dimensions—namely, the precise ways in which it connects with the era during which Peckinpah worked and the importance it gives to the moral and stylistic inquiry into violence. Peckinpah's critics have tended to extrapolate the films from the period that nourished his work and to identify and attach the moral, ideological, and artistic content of the films to broader and more abstract currents or categories of social thought and artistic tradition. On the negative side, his work has been labeled "fascist"[1] and a vicious celebration of primal masculine instinct.[2] By contrast, sympathetic critics place Peckinpah securely within established, and honorable, intellectual and cultural traditions. Paul Seydor finds Peckinpah to be part of a solidly American philosophical and artistic tradition that abhors conformity, is fascinated by wildness and criminality, and seeks a code of conduct to keep the terrifying void of existence from overwhelming the fragile self. Seen thus, Peckinpah joins the esteemed company of Melville, Emerson, Twain, Hawthorne, Hemingway, and Mailer.[3] Kathleen Murphy concurs, placing Peckinpah in the "anachronistic company" of

During the Agua Verde massacre, Pike Bishop (William Holden) forsakes his six-gun for an automatic weapon, thereby amplifying the scale of the slaughter. By introducing a machine gun into the climax of his Western, Peckinpah shifted the genre into newer, more lethal territory.

these writers who "fished dark waters, from Moby Dick's domain to the Mississippi to the Big Two-Hearted River."[4] She continues, "The American artist is most often a confidence man who plies his trade in dangerous, uncharted waterways rather than on the settled shorelines where the yea-sayers squat."[5]

Michael Bliss finds Peckinpah to be "the last of the great American directors in the tradition of Stroheim and Ford, larger-than-life figures who left an indelible stamp on their films and who were ready to do battle with studios and producers who dared to compromise the integrity of their productions."[6] Robin Wood writes that Peckinpah is the true heir of John Ford by virtue of the two directors' equal commitment to exploring the tragic tension between the American ideal and its diminished actuality.[7] Michael Sragow finds Peckinpah to be "the bravest, most gifted, and most troubling poet of the American screen."[8]

All of these assessments tend to gloss the underlying connection between Peckinpah and the turbulent era of the late 1960s and early 1970s. The years from 1968 to 1974 saw the production of his finest body of work, from *The Wild Bunch* through *Bring Me the Head of Alfredo Garcia* (1974), after which, beset by unconquerable personal demons, Peckinpah's artistic talents went into an irreversible decline. The films that followed *Alfredo Garcia* tend either to be embarrassments (*Convoy,* 1978) or to exhibit only fitful interludes of sharpness, clarity, and control. The coincidence of Peckinpah's best work with a sustained period of social ferment and turbulence should not be dismissed as merely fortuitous. It should, instead, be posed as one of the questions needing investigation. Why Peckinpah, and why then? By doubling the question, we begin to ask after some of the critical issues that have remained neglected by much Peckinpah scholarship. Asking "Why Peckinpah, and why then?" permits us to understand why his audacious brand of filmmaking could not have surfaced before 1969 and why it would have been less remarkable in 1979 or 1989.

Obviously, Peckinpah's work as a director begins well before 1969. On television, his directing work included episodes for twelve different Western series from 1956 to 1960, a show for *The Dick Powell Theater* in 1962, and the celebrated production of *Noon Wine* in 1966 that, in turn, helped give him another opportunity to direct features. On film, *The Deadly Companions* (1961), *Ride the High Country* (1962), and *Major Dundee* (1964) display Peckinpah's distinctive revisions of the Western genre, but their formal designs exhibit none of the audacious audiovisual montages, or the edgy, probing, in-your-face examinations of violence that would become central to his work during the spectacular burst of creativity that resulted in the release of seven films between 1969 and 1974.

Clear precursors of Peckinpah's mature style exist in the earlier work. However, the magisterial loveliness of *Ride the High Country* notwithstanding, had his talent not erupted within the American cinema and burst upon the pop cultural landscape with the ferocity of the post-*Dundee* work, he would not today be regarded as a seminal and legendary American director. His gentle films of this period—*The Ballad of Cable Hogue* (1970) and *Junior Bonner* (1972)—are well-crafted, heartfelt, sensitive works, but they are in a minor key. The chords they sound are part of the complete structure of his work, but if we only had these, plus *Ride the High Country,* Peckinpah would remain an interesting, accomplished, but minor director. *Cable Hogue* and *Junior Bonner* become arresting because of the sudden switch to the minor key and for the polyphonic voices they thereby add to Peckinpah's work. It is precisely because of their radical difference in tone, their easy, laid-back approach to image, narrative, and character, that they assume the especially striking proportions they do. Context is a determining factor, and it is the tragic despair and apocalyptic violence of the surrounding films that accentuate the playfulness of *Cable Hogue* and *Junior Bonner.*

Peckinpah, who liked to observe that "Things are always mixed,"[9] and that "There was no such thing as simple truth,"[10] did not have a single or simple attitude toward anything in his films. The electric tensions and uniquely provocative edge to his work are due to the impacted and contending moral and emotional perspectives entangled within the films. No other American filmmaker's work was or is so deeply fraught with polarized energies shimmering across antagonistic force fields, like the magnets on David Sumner's desk in *Straw Dogs.* This is why Peckinpah cannot simply be dismissed with a convenient label, such as fascist or misogynist, and why sympathetic critics err, too, when they try to minimize the place of violence in his films and to emphasize, instead, Peckinpah as "a generous, loving, vulnerable" director.[11] Peckinpah's work can exhibit these qualities, but its hard edge, its ruthless exploration of the physical horror and emotional pain of violence, demonstrates, rather, a tougher attitude toward both filmmaker and viewer. Peckinpah ruthlessly explored and displayed his own demons on screen (e.g., Pike Bishop's alcoholic despair that precedes the final shoot-out in *The Wild Bunch* or Benny's selfish betrayal of Elita's trust and love in *Alfredo Garcia*), and he granted the audience little quarter—and no safe vantage point—from which to observe the unfolding brutalities depicted in *The Wild Bunch, Straw Dogs,* and *Alfredo Garcia.* Peckinpah insisted that the cruelty and sadism depicted in his films, and exhibited toward their viewers, were meant to serve a cathartic and ennobling function. The didactic intentions of his work aimed to place violence in an instructional frame whereby the viewer might contemplate it and learn from it. We will have much to say about this attempt in subsequent chapters, because this project and its outcome are not easy to evaluate. Peckinpah meant to study violence through film, not to exploit it, even though he sometimes faltered and failed, and this study of violence was not meant to comfort or reassure viewers but to enlighten them.

I do not wish to imply that the treatment of violence is the only thing of importance to be found in his films. Indeed, a remarkable network of additional concerns runs through the films and gives them an unmistakable internal structure: the fading of the West and its eclipse by modernity, the betrayal of friendship, and the corrupting influence of money are obsessively, intensively brokered in the films, and they have been ably interpreted by other commentators. However, as I have previously noted, an apologetic orientation tends to characterize Peckinpah's most sympathetic critics (Seydor and Bliss), who acknowledge that the films are violent, but then quickly add that the films are about much more than this and are more sensitive and humane than his detractors grant—that they are, indeed, "suffused with a deep and expansive love."[12] It is easy to understand the imperative for this rhetorical emphasis. The labels "fascist" and "misogynist" have clung to Peckinpah's work with devastating effects and have diminished his critical reputation to the point of oblivion for the last fifteen years. But we needn't be especially gentle with Peckinpah's work to rehabilitate it. Let us meet its violence head-on, halfway, just like it always should have been studied, without exaggerating or minimizing its effects or moral orientation. Asking "Why Peckinpah and why then?" means asking about the violence in his films, asking when Peckinpah's voice erupted full blast within the American cinema, and asking why.

Directors such as Hitchcock, Josef von Sternberg, George Cukor, Vincente Minnelli, and Hawks developed unmistakable stylistic signatures which emerged and were elaborated across a large and diverse body of films. I do not wish to risk an old-fashioned auteurism by celebrating these, or any directors, as the only originating force behind a film's mise-en-scène and narrative, but in the case of these directors, clear and recurrent design features do exist in their work and contribute to our sense of what a Hitchcock or a Hawks film entails. Furthermore, one needn't tie these filmmakers to the peculiarities of a social era in order to understand those designs. By contrast, other directors can seem extraordinarily sensitive to the social zeitgeist in which they are working. These would include Frank Capra, Douglas Sirk, Robert Aldrich, Oliver Stone, and Sam Peckinpah. Michael Bliss asserts that Peckinpah's films succeed only when "their concern is with timeless problems associated with loyalty, trust, love, death, and betrayal."[13] Peckinpah's work certainly retains an ability to speak to contemporary viewers, but it also remains tied to the currents of the social era in which the films were produced. To remove them from that context by emphasizing timeless themes is to deny them their most resonant vitality and an important source of their internal design. Recognizing this does not diminish the stature or validity of the work, but it does enable us to sidestep the epistemological pitfalls of the old-fashioned auteurism which tended to treat a director as a transcendent motive force. Like everything else about Peckinpah's films, the connections between them and the era in which they were made are complex and multifaceted. To understand what made Peckinpah's work possible at the time it burst with full fury upon the pop cultural landscape, we need to emphasize three interlocking constituents: Peckinpah's internal dynamics, changes in the film industry that profoundly altered the creative possibilities for late sixties cinema, and resonant currents of sociopolitical change and thought at large in the culture during that time. Together, these factors help explain why Peckinpah's mature work emerged in the late 1960s and not ten or twenty years earlier or later.

The first area we need to examine—Peckinpah's internal dynamics—is the riskiest and the most uncertain, but it cannot be ignored. Films are the products of human agency. My aim here is not to reduce Peckinpah's films into a set of symptoms or to compose a psychobiography, but to show how their very possibility is founded on precarious, and short-lived, congruencies prevailing between artist, industry, and social period.

Peckinpah's own remarks and the recollections of those who knew him indicate that he was an extraordinarily volatile and mercurial personality who rebelled against the rigid moral authority he perceived in his family. He once said, "I'm the only Peckinpah in four generations who has not gone into law."[14] His father was a lawyer, his maternal grandfather, Denver, was a district attorney and superior court judge, and his brother, Denny, entered the law. Peckinpah told Garner Simmons that the family's dinner talk centered on law and the Bible and that, from these debates, he learned that truth was a relative thing.[15]

When he spoke of his father in interviews, Peckinpah invariably idealized him. ("My Father? He was a man. Completely . . . My father was a great trial lawyer, a great judge, a great man, and a great father."[16]) However, the parental atmosphere he encountered as a child was, according to Weddle's recent biography, one marked by chronic, repressed anger. Weddle argues that Peckinpah's ambivalence toward his childhood was rooted in his conflicting desires for the world of aesthetics and feminine sensitivity, embodied by his mother (whom he came to resent), and for the world of cowboying, hunting, and camping he enjoyed among the male company of David and Denver, who showed little tolerance and much animosity for young Peckinpah's enjoyment of reading. His sister-in-law recalled that Denver "used to take it out on Sam quite frequently because Sam liked to read. He always loved to read. Denver's attitude was, if you were a real boy you were outside riding horses, hiking, and doing things like that."[17] Like Hemingway, Peckinpah initially was extremely close to his mother, and he developed a strong feminine side that was at odds with his troubling conviction that aesthetic pursuits were somehow unmanly. Peckinpah's sister observed that he was "basically a woman, emotionally" but was embarrassed by it because of the strong masculine role models in the family.[18] Like Hemingway, Peckinpah would spend the rest of his life in a destructive macho posture defending against the feminine components in his psyche.

The especially deadly charge in the childhood home, as Weddle presents it, was the repressed animosity between his parents and the polite denial that anything was wrong, with his mother, Fern, resorting to manipulative tactics to get her way and his father, David, acquiescing to keep the peace. Peckinpah was physically disciplined by both parents but was forbidden by his father from showing any anger in the house. David's temper was fierce when it did erupt. He was capable of knocking his son to the floor and beating Peckinpah's sister so hard that she would be marked for days.[19] Camille Fielding, wife of Jerry (who scored several of Peckinpah's films), believes Peckinpah's rage stemmed from these insoluble emotional contradictions.

> Not like any childhood I knew. You fell down and wanted to cry and your dad wouldn't let you. Hit you if you cried. It's a nightmare thing, and I heard this coming out of him [Sam]. It hurts when you fall off a horse and nobody gets up to help you . . . A little kid. Not to be able to cry, to show pain. I think a lot of his rage stems from that.[20]

In later life, with the many severed friendships, burned personal and professional bridges, and failed marriages, Peckinpah would become horrendously well-acquainted with the price of this rage. He would remark that he considered himself a terminal outsider, desiring a stable home and marriage, but "I get into too many problems, I drink too much, and I get into too many fights."[21] Peckinpah recognized that, for him, "tenderness and violence sometimes go hand in hand,"[22] and that his chronic anger fueled his art. "Everything I do comes out of anger."[23] During the most productive years of his career, Peckinpah was able to control, contain, and channel this anger. Eventually, its dark impulses overwhelmed his career and life and destroyed his ability to work, but before this would occur, Peckinpah's internal fires helped lead him toward the conviction that violence is a primal human appetite and a compelling one for cinematic examination. That his inclination toward this examination was profound, and of long-standing duration, is evident in the harsh, hard-edged portrait of frontier life on his 1960 TV series *The Westerner,* especially its visual attention to the physical impact of bullets on the human body and on objects in the environment, and in the early effort to master slow-motion violence and squib work on *Major Dundee* (all of which was among the footage deleted by Columbia Pictures prior to its release).[24] But it was not until 1969, with *The Wild Bunch,* that Peckinpah radically and successfully transgressed the parameters governing the representation of screen violence. After several years without any film work, he was desperately hungry and eager to prove himself. Most crucially, his inclination to explore the impulses of human violence was now in synch with a changed film industry that afforded directors more creative freedom and that was institutionally renouncing old rules and taboos. In addition, the sociocultural revolution within American society was generating a complex empirical and ideological support system that would legitimize and nourish Peckinpah's personal and creative inclinations. We need to explore these institutional and sociocultural factors, because without them Peckinpah's inchoate sense of self and world would not have connected so profoundly or memorably with the language of cinema.

New Creative Freedoms in Hollywood Cinema

Between the release of *Major Dundee* in 1964 and the release of *The Wild Bunch* in 1969, the Hollywood industry, and American cinema culture generally, underwent major changes. Peckinpah did not pioneer any of these changes. Others explored the new thresholds of creative freedom in Amer-

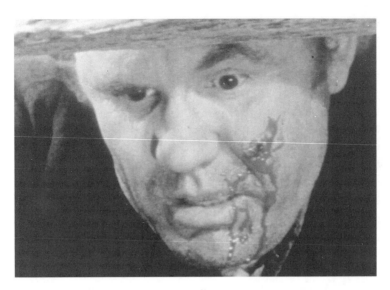

Peckinpah's interest in presenting honest depictions of violence on screen was deep and long-lasting and predates *The Wild Bunch*. In *Ride the High Country*, a quick zoom-in to the corpse of Joshua Knutson (R.G. Armstrong), shot in the face, presents a shocking image of gun violence. Frame enlargement.

ican cinema well before he did. But he certainly benefited from the new institutional arrangements in the industry and its fundamentally altered cultural relationship with the public. These upheavals in the industry and in its relationship to the audience were the essential preconditions for the emergent cynicism, irony, and brutality of Peckinpah's mature style.

The factors which would help produce a new cinema in Hollywood in the late 1960s are complex, but they coalesce around two watershed events: the revision in September 1966 of Hollywood's thirty-six-year-old Motion Picture Production Code and the creation two years later of the Code and Rating Administration (CARA) with its G-M-R-X classification scheme. The old Production Code had imposed a plethora of specific content restrictions on Hollywood film, and the major studios had agreed not to distribute any film that did not receive a seal of approval from the Production Code Administration. By the 1950s, this system of self-imposed censorship was crumbling. Unprecedentedly frank films like Otto Preminger's *The Moon Is Blue* (1953) and *The Man with the Golden Arm* (1955) went straight to theaters without a code seal. Moreover, by the 1950s, studios had lost control of their first-run theaters, government censor boards were under attack by the courts, and, in 1952, the Supreme Court finally granted films the same First Amendment protections that media like newspapers and magazines had long enjoyed. (Following a court decision in 1915, films had been excluded from this protection on the grounds that they were strictly a business.)

The MPAA's revision of the code in 1966, which effectively scrapped the lengthy list of content rules in the old code and substituted ten broadly phrased guiding principles (e.g., "Restraint shall be exercised in portraying the taking of life"), was a belated acknowledgment that social mores had fundamentally changed since the old rules had been formulated in 1930 and that distributors were now more willing to handle films that had no code seal of approval. The MPAA declared, "This revised code is designed to keep in closer harmony with the mores, the culture, the moral sense, and the expectations of our society."[25] By replacing the old code's specific prohibitions with vaguer and more general guidelines the MPAA intended to create "an expansion of creative freedom." Jack Valenti, who became president of the MPAA in 1966, noted that the revised code would significantly expand the creative license of filmmakers.

The most significant feature of the revision was the provision for designating certain films SMA (Suggested for Mature Audiences), thereby labeling frank films by designating their content as acceptable for only a portion of the general viewing audience. This was the beginning of the now-familiar practice of relaxing censorship via policies of niche marketing to target audiences. As the content barriers began to come down, stable cultural landmarks also began to change. New York's Radio City Music Hall, which had long served as a showcase for family entertainment, caused a stir when it agreed to play Stanley Donen's *Two for the Road* (1967) which carried an SMA tag. Music Hall president James Gould noted that because of changing times, the Radio City forum would no longer be an automatic guarantee of family-oriented shows. "You've got to be conscious of the subtle changes taking place and bend with them."[26]

The National Catholic Office of Motion Pictures responded with skepticism and some anxiety to the new SMA tag, and in the first ten months following the revisions NCOMP gave seventeen films a condemned rating, an all-time high that signaled an increasing friction between film producers and distributors and censorship organizations. Cornel Wilde's *Beach Red* (1967), condemned by NCOMP, carried an MPAA seal of approval.[27] At one time, the threat of a condemned rating from the Catholic Office could kill distribution of a picture, but no longer. Paramount and MGM reported no trouble booking nationwide *Blow-Up* (1966) and *Hurry Sundown* (1967), despite Catholic opposition. No theater circuit in the country would now back off from a film with a condemned rating if it showed clear profit potential.[28]

The MPAA pushed its revised code over the objections and concerns of theater owners and social watchdog groups about the rising tide of profanity, violence, and sex in new films. The MPAA argued that all films with seals had been made within "the creative boundaries of reason and good judgment"[29] and urged viewers to reorient themselves to the new style, aims, and functions of the modern, harder-edged picture (e.g., 1967's *Bonnie and Clyde, In Cold Blood,* and *Point Blank,* and 1968's *The Fox, The Detective,* and *Barbarella*). The "new revolutions" in taste and values in society required a new orientation by viewers to films that embodied those changes. Viewers who complained about profanity or violence in films "fail to realize that films have changed to reflect our changing culture," admonished the MPAA's community relations associate.[30]

By defending the role of film in the vanguard of social change, the MPAA helped spearhead and defend the new climate of creative freedom for filmmakers. President Valenti trumpeted the virtues and necessity of a new breed of nonconformist filmmakers. Testifying on December 19, 1968, before the National Commission on the Causes and Prevention of Violence, which had been convened in part because of the new levels of violence in film, Valenti proudly announced that

> There is a new breed of filmmaker. And mark you well this new filmmaker, because he's an extraordinary fellow. He's young. He's sensitive. He's dedicated. He's reaching out for new dimensions of expression. And he is not bound—not bound—by the conventions of a conformist past. I happen to think that's good.[31]

The impetus for this new climate of creative freedom was the gale winds of social protest and countercultural values that swept through American society after 1966 and, of more immediate economic and institutional importance, the emergence of a sizable youth audience for motion pictures and of a younger generation of studio executives who were willing to flout motion picture conventions. An MPAA audience survey, conducted by Daniel Yankelovitch and Associates, revealed that in 1968, 48 percent of box-office admissions were from the 16–24 age group.[32] The vice-president of advertising and publicity at Twentieth Century–Fox stressed the connection between the changing content of the new American cinema and this youth audience. "We are tied to the youthful market of the future, we have to keep up with the rhythm of young people. Films have already attained the pace of our times. They are treating outspokenly the main themes worrying [the] contemporary world."[33] *Bonnie and Clyde, The Graduate* (the biggest rental film of 1968), *2001: A Space Odyssey* (1968), *Rosemary's Baby* (1968), and *Easy Rider* (1969) were all smash hits with the young audience before broadening their appeal to older viewers.

With respect to *The Wild Bunch,* a studio analysis of 768 preview cards from viewers in Fresno and Kansas City found, overall, a 60 percent negative reaction to the picture. Only 20 percent of the viewers rated the picture as excellent or outstanding, and these tended to be viewers in the 17–25 age bracket. *Wild Bunch* producer Phil Feldman drew the appropriate conclusions from these data. He wrote to Peckinpah, "Therefore, there can be no doubt that that's the audience we are playing to and that's the audience that goes to the movies. . . . Rather than trying to get the whole 60 percent in our camp, which we could never in a million years do, let's get the 20 percent between 17 and 25, which I think we can do."[34]

Ken Hyman, Richard Zanuck, and Robert Evans, the young, top production executives at Warner Bros.–7 Arts, Twentieth Century–Fox, and Paramount, believed in making a new style of picture, in unleashing new creative forces in Hollywood, and in allowing directors more creative latitude on productions. Following Gulf and Western's takeover of Paramount in October 1966, of 48 directors on productions with definite starting dates, 28 (60 percent) had no directorial credits prior to 1963.[35] Of this new climate at Paramount, Evans noted, "The strongest period in Hollywood history was the '30s when most of the creative people were young. The trouble is that most of them are still around making movies, and we've neglected to develop new talent."[36] Director Jack Smight noted that the new production executives were greenlighting pictures "which never would have been made before," including Smight's own *The Illustrated Man* (1969).[37] Ken Hyman noted that during his tenure as production chief at Warner Bros.–7 Arts, he respected the director's creative authority. "I never took control of a picture away from any director. If I had an objection to his cutting, I fought for my view, but I was always the first to admit I was wrong."[38] Hyman was a key supporter of Peckinpah's creative authority on *The Wild Bunch* (a Warner Bros.–7 Arts film). When he left the studio following its acquisition by Kinney National Services in the first half of 1969, just as *The Wild Bunch* was going into release, he was replaced by

John Calley and Ted Ashley, the latter of whom instigated the cutting of the picture. If Peckinpah's film ultimately fell victim to events following a conglomerate buy-out, he was able to make it because of the industry's uniquely new, change-oriented, auteur-centered policies.

Always ready with a diagnosis of the latest pop-culture trends, in 1967 *Time* magazine referred to "the shock of freedom" in the new Hollywood films. Pictures like *Bonnie and Clyde, Reflections in a Golden Eye* (1967), *In the Heat of the Night* (1967), and *The Graduate* (1967) embodied a daring new freedom from convention and censorship. "U.S. movies are now treating once-shocking themes with a maturity and candor unthinkable even five years ago . . ."[39] Recalling the conditions that permitted him to marry slapstick comedy with unprecedentedly graphic violence in the gangster film *Bonnie and Clyde,* director Arthur Penn noted the special legitimacy that production executives might grant an iconoclastic director's style and vision. "What was happening at that time in Hollywood was that enormous power had devolved upon the directors because the studio system had kind of collapsed. We were really running it, so we could introduce this new perception of how to make another kind of movie."[40]

While the industry adjusted its production practices to accommodate "a new breed of filmmaker" for a new audience, and Jack Valenti's MPAA promoted, and defended, the new freedom of content in American cinema, these changes inevitably caused friction between filmmakers, viewers, and social watchdog groups, lending the cultural atmosphere surrounding cinema, as in so many other areas of American social life at the time, considerable volatility. The battles over movie content were primarily fought over three issues: profanity, sexuality, and violence. Of these three, the last is of crucial importance for us in relation to Peckinpah's films, not simply because of their graphic content, but because the gore he unleashed in *The Wild Bunch* was not a revolutionary accomplishment but rather was the culmination of several years of steadily escalating (and profitable) violence in American cinema. Whatever didactic purposes Peckinpah wanted his movie violence to have, he was permitted to portray and examine it so closely and so graphically because, by 1969, graphic movie violence was an already established fact of life and a very profitable one for the industry, and because such violence connected with the energies of destruction coursing through American society.

So much had changed so fast that, a mere three years before *The Wild Bunch,* the American cinema's representation of violence and the roughness of the West was a world removed from where it would be when Peckinpah's film premiered. In 1966, the National Catholic Film Office criticized the MPAA's revised Production Code when Richard Brooks' *The Professionals* (a film whose tame, tourist's vision of Mexico Peckinpah specifically intended *The Wild Bunch* to rebut) failed to receive an SMA advisory. The church group objected to the film's "brutality, erotic situations" and "coarse language."[41] Seen today, the picture seems very quaint, and its violence appears odd because it lacks the exploding squibs that became so dominant a year later. By 1967, the trend toward harder-edged and more graphic movie violence was unmistakable and powerful. United Artists acquired for U.S. distribution three Italian films that had already done impressive business in European markets. Intending to replicate the success of its James Bond series, UA set a staggered release schedule for Sergio Leone's "trilogy" and pitched its ads to accentuate the serial nature of the films. *A Fistful of Dollars* (promoted as "The first motion picture of its kind.

Sergio Leone's spaghetti Westerns, starring Clint Eastwood as an implacable bounty hunter, brought a new kind of violence to the Western. The successful distribution of Leone's "Dollars" trilogy in the U.S. in 1967 demonstrated the popular acceptance of this more cold-blooded style. The floodgates of film violence were beginning to open.

It won't be the last.") was set for a January release, followed by *For a Few Dollars More* in May ("The second motion picture of its kind. It won't be the last!"), and *The Good, the Bad and the Ugly* in December.

Leone's cynical, dirty, opportunistic West was unlike anything Hollywood filmmakers had produced. Box-office registers rang across the country, and post-Leone Hollywood Westerns would bear the unmistakable *Dollars* influence.[42] Leone's Westerns did not feature much spurting blood or squib-work, but they piled up a huge number of bodies on screen and cut Western violence lose from the moralizing that had always accompanied it in the pre-Leone Hollywood period. In Leone's West, violent death was quick, plentiful, and was viewed dispassionately, stripped of the ritualizing codes that had surrounded it in Hollywood Westerns. Leone's violence impressed audiences, and alarmed social watchdogs, not because it was graphic (it generally wasn't) but because it was so abundant and so incredibly cold-blooded. While others (Penn and Peckinpah) would popularize slow motion and bloody squibs, Leone's revolutionary impact lay in helping shear screen violence free of the reassuring moral context that had always governed it in past films. Critics alarmed at the popularity of the *Dollars* films condemned their brutality and objected that this new style of screen violence was responsible for the pictures' box-office success. Discussing *Fistful*'s phenomenal U.S. business, Robert Landry, writing in *Variety,* complains, "That 'Fistful of Dollars' is a blood-bath is no doubt part of the b.o. explanation. There is sadism from start to finish, unmitigated brutality, a piling up of bodies."[43]

The release of the second *Dollars* film in May, 1967, was quickly followed by the opening of two hyper-violent American pictures, Robert Aldrich's cynical portrait of World War II, *The Dirty Dozen,* in July and Penn's romantic celebration of gangster rebels, *Bonnie and Clyde,* in August. These two pictures, especially Penn's film, ignited a storm of controversy over the ugly turn movie violence had now taken, and battle lines were quickly drawn. Bosley Crowther devoted several pieces in *The New York Times* to trashing these two films and warning about the effects of such graphic violence. He writes, "By habituating the public to violence and brutality . . . films of excessive violence only deaden their sensitivities and make slaughter seem a meaningless cliché."[44] Crowther calls Aldrich's film "a studied indulgence of sadism that is morbid and disgusting beyond words."[45] At the time Crowther's pieces appeared, the terrible social violence of 1968 was still in the future, but the nationwide riots of 1967 led him to caution filmmakers to adopt policies of restraint during times of social upheaval, lest movie images inflame already raging passions. *Newsweek*'s reviewer, in the first of two pieces devoted to *Bonnie and Clyde,* condemned it for possessing "some of the most gruesome carnage since Verdun,"[46] but he reversed his opinion on the film's merits the following week while still maintaining that the picture's "gore goes too far" and that *The Dirty Dozen* was a "trash" film in which the characters "cry themselves a river of blood."[47] In September 1967, Sherrill Corwin, the president of the National Association of Theater Owners, stepped into the fray to caution filmmakers about "the ever increasing insertion of excessive violence and sadism" in current films.[48] Corwin warned the industry that the "undisciplined brutality" of the new pictures might raise the threat of outside censorship because of potential public backlash against the climate of creative freedom which seemed to many like unprincipled license. "The kind of sadism and viciousness that used to be considered 'shock value' is now being escalated to the extent that pressure is developing from community groups and national organizations in protest over the excess."[49]

The outrage stimulated by *The Dirty Dozen* and *Bonnie and Clyde* and the specter of outside censorship that had always terrified the industry were simply not powerful enough to counter the complex factors pushing American film toward ever greater frankness and brutality. The sociopolitical climate in the country during these years exerted a tremendous influence, one that was decisive for Peckinpah, and we will turn to this in a moment. For now, it must be stressed that the economic payoff could be tremendous for studios producing the new graphic violence. *The Dirty Dozen* was the top-grossing film of its year, and although *Bonnie and Clyde* earned only $2.5 million in rentals for 1967, by July 1968 it had earned $28 million in domestic and foreign rentals (on a $2.5 million production cost).[50] The film's box office life was extended to an extraordinary degree by the publicity and controversies that surrounded its violence, as well as by its ten Oscar nominations. So impressive was repeat business for the film in its second run that *Variety* placed it in an "impossible to project" category.[51] *Bonnie and Clyde*'s tenacious performance would land it twenty-two times on *Variety*'s weekly list of the top dozen box-office earners, a record topped at the time only by *Mary Poppins* (thirty-two times on the list in late 1964 and early 1965).[52]

The spectacular box-office performance of the new film sadism (beginning with Leone and extending through Penn) was a watershed event in the history of American cinema. It demonstrated the chasm between the letter of the existing restrictive film codes and the concerns of social

Robert Aldrich's hyper-violent *The Dirty Dozen* was condemned as trash by *The New York Times'* reviewer but was the top-grossing film of 1967. Screen violence was becoming big box office. Courtesy of MGM Television.

watchdogs, on the one hand, and, the movie-going public's appetite for bloody spectacle on the other. *Time* observed, accurately, that "in the wake of *Bonnie and Clyde,* there is an almost euphoric sense in Hollywood that more such movies can and will be made."[53] The industry would henceforth be much less cautious about pushing the envelope of acceptable screen content, and a climate was now getting established in which Peckinpah would be encouraged to explore bloody spectacle by studios hoping for another *Bonnie and Clyde.* Warner Bros.–7 Arts counted on *The Wild Bunch* to be a big-budget hit, and producer Phil Feldman would congratulate Peckinpah for filming violence so brutal that it aroused the ire of the MPAA prior to release.

The Wild Bunch is an epic Western dealing with the last days of a band of outlaws led by Pike Bishop (William Holden). The outlaws—consisting of Pike, Dutch (Ernest Borgnine), Angel (Jaime Sanchez), and the Gorch brothers (Ben Johnson, Warren Oates)—survive an ambush which destroys the rest of the gang and which was instigated by the railroad they intended to rob. They cross into Mexico where they steal guns for the corrupt General Mapache. Mapache seizes and tortures Angel, whereupon the Bunch confront and kill him. This precipitates a general slaughter during which the outlaws destroy Mapache's Aqua Verde headquarters and are themselves killed in the process.

Production of the *Wild Bunch* straddled the industry transformations outlined above. The MPAA's initial reaction to and evaluation of the script reflected the realities of the revised Production Code during the pre-CARA period when production of the film commenced. Given the existing parameters governing movie content, the MPAA deemed the proposed film, as scripted, to be largely unacceptable. "In its present form this story is so violent and bloody and filled with so many crudities of language that we would hesitate to say that a picture based on this material could be approved under the Production Code."[54] The MPAA added, however, that if the material was toned down, an SMA label might be possible.

The sensational box-office success of *Bonnie and Clyde* was widely regarded by the industry as the harbinger of a new kind of filmmaking. *Bonnie and Clyde*'s detailed slow-motion violence helped make Peckinpah's *The Wild Bunch* possible.

MPAA concerns centered on the script's abundant profanity and on several sequences where the bloodletting was considered excessive or unacceptably graphic. These included the action during the opening shootout in which a farm boy on a wagon fires a shotgun into the face of Buck (one of the outlaws), blinding him, after which another of the Bunch, Lyle Gorch, shoots and kills the boy. According to the MPAA, this action "will have to be handled with great care not to be visually sickening."[55] Other objectionable material cited by the MPAA included Pike's killing of the wounded Buck in the arroyo (deemed "excessively brutal"[56]), Mapache cutting Angel's throat (deemed "unacceptable"[57]), and the extensive crowd killings during the Agua Verde massacre (deemed "a blood bath").[58] Despite these MPAA concerns, principle photography on *The Wild Bunch* began on March 25, 1968, and concluded on June 27, 1968,[59] under the revised Production Code. However, by the time the picture was being edited the code was gone, and the new ratings system was in place. In the negotiations with the MPAA that followed principal photography, none of these episodes, or others to which the MPAA objected (Angel being dragged by the automobile, Lyle manning the machine gun, and Crazy Lee, another outlaw, being riddled with bullets), were deleted from the film, but they were rendered less graphic through careful editing. The SMA category was now history, and the CARA system gave Peckinpah and his producer enhanced freedom and flexibility in retaining and shaping their graphic screen violence. Of key importance for this film's remarkable production history, Peckinpah and his editors could cut the film to merit an R-rating rather than to satisfy a (revised) Production Code.

With respect to the boy in the wagon who is shot by Lyle, the MPAA objected to the bullet hit and the blood, so editor Lou Lombardo omitted these and caught the boy in mid-fall, well after he has been struck by Lyle's shot. (In a letter to Warner Bros. executive Ken Hyman, producer Phil Feldman outlined the necessity for this manner of editing the footage and discussed specific editing solutions to the MPAA's objections.[60]) The editing feels a little jagged here, and the action may even seem a bit confusing. Critics have sometimes contrasted the apparent optical confusions in the film's opening massacre with the clarity of perspective in the Agua Verde shoot-out and have interpreted this as a stylistic statement about the unity of purpose with which the outlaws are fighting at the end. By contrast, at the beginning of the film, they are a more fractious group. The most confusing imagery in the opening shoot-out is the action in which the boy in the wagon shoots Buck, and is shot, in turn, by Lyle, but this

The editing of Lye Gorch's shooting of the boy in the wagon omitted the bullet strike and caught the boy, as seen here, in mid-fall and at a somewhat confusing angle. MPAA objections necessitated the abrupt editing. Frame enlargement.

Pike's killing of Buck in the arroyo was edited to play mainly on Buck's back and with quick, oblique views of his bloodied face. Frame enlargement.

raggedness occurs for very pragmatic reasons rather than for ones of thematic symbolism. These ragged cuts were a function of having to pare back this very fast-moving material to satisfy the MPAA.

With respect to Buck's killing in the arroyo, this scene was edited to show mainly his back with very few, quick, flash glimpses of his bloody face. Angel's drag by the automobile was shortened, with fewer close-ups of his ragged body. The editing of Mapache slitting Angel's throat deleted a side view of this action and the blood that followed. (Peckinpah was now shooting *Cable Hogue,* and Feldman worked at the editing console with

Lou Lombardo to make this trim.) This alteration enabled producer Feldman to reassure the MPAA that "all that happens is that Mapache completes his stroke over Angel's throat. There is no spurt of blood, but merely a show."[61] This is the one revision that clearly dates the film's violence. By today's standards, the throat cutting seems somewhat anticlimactic because it is so abbreviated and so without evident bloodshed. But the film could not have been released (as an R-picture) without this change.

In discussing with his director the need to alter the film to minimize its bloodshed, producer Phil Feldman was keenly supportive of Peckinpah's desire to push the limits of what was acceptable, and he interpreted the MPAA's objections as proof that their intentions for the film would be successful. Prior to the onset of principal photography, Feldman sent Peckinpah a copy of the MPAA's script report and included this assessment: "I am sending you a copy of the MPAA report from Shurlock. I think you can disregard this on the whole. As a matter of fact, I am rather pleased, as I am sure you are, that he finds it objectionable."[62] At the same time, Feldman urged Peckinpah to carefully assess the extent of the picture's bloodshed in relation to other prominent and trend-setting films of the period. This would help Peckinpah gauge tolerance levels for violence in potential viewers of the film. Feldman specifically urged Peckinpah to look at Leone's *Dollars* films. "I think it might be good for you to have a comparative basis before you finally decide just how far other people have gone in the field of blood and gore and what the public is comparing us to."[63]

The editing of Mapache's slitting of Angel's throat deleted the side view of the action that showed the blood spurt. What survives in the film is a quick front view of the knife passing across Angel's throat followed immediately by cutaways to the horrified faces of the Bunch who witness this action. Frame enlargement.

The importance of Feldman's support for Peckinpah's audacity in designing the film's extreme violence has been overshadowed by subsequent events—chiefly, the film's Feldman-sanctioned recutting for distribution (and not for censorship). Feldman, however, was a fine producer, and, as his memos to Peckinpah demonstrate, he was exceptionally dedicated to helping make this an outstanding production and was closely involved with Peckinpah in shaping the film's artistic design. (Feldman, for example, suggested that Peckinpah treat the killing of the bounty hunters, who pursue the Bunch throughout most of the film, as an off-screen event. Peckinpah shot footage showing the deaths of the bounty hunters, but he decided to follow Feldman's advice. He praised Feldman as "absolutely correct."[64]) While, as we have seen, Peckinpah had his own personal reasons for gravitating toward depictions of violence on screen, he was singularly fortunate to have returned to filmmaking, after *Dundee,* at precisely the moment when he would have institutional support and encouragement from the industry and his producers in forging a transgressive cinema. He couldn't have had it any other way.

Well before the release of *The Wild Bunch,* the MPAA's Valenti was actively defending the new freedom of American filmmakers from the growing public outcry. In February, 1968, in a postscreening discussion following *In the Heat of the Night* at the University of Houston, Valenti stressed the importance of bringing "old movie standards out of the archaic and arcane and into current trends."[65] Valenti's line of defense against condemnations of film brutality entailed emphasizing how filmmakers were inevitably responding to, and reflecting, a revolution in social mores that was underway in the larger culture, a defense that implicitly acknowledged the economic incentives for filmmakers to mirror these changes on screen. Valenti also contextualized the new movie violence in relation to the ongoing Vietnam War, a brilliant rhetorical move that was effective because of the undeniable connections between the revolution in movie violence and the late-sixties crucible of sociopolitical violence. Valenti said, "For the first time in the history of this country, people are exposed to instant coverage of a war in progress. When so many movie critics complain about violence on film, I don't think they realize the impact of thirty minutes on the Huntley-Brinkley newscast—and that's real violence."[66] Arthur Penn claimed not to have anticipated the public outcry that followed the release of *Bonnie and Clyde* because the movie violence he stylized seemed so pale next to the real violence of the war and the cultural period of which the film was part: ". . . it didn't even occur to me, particularly, that it was a violent film. Not given the times in which we were living, because every night on the news we saw kids in Vietnam being lifted out in body bags, with blood all over the place. Why, suddenly, the cinema had to be immaculate, I'll never know."[67] As we will see, Peckinpah, too, measured the explicit bloodshed in his films against the real blood spilled in the war and concluded that moral outrage against the reality of the war was a more principled response than anger directed at fictional movie images. For Peckinpah, as for Valenti and Penn, the war validated the new violence in American cinema, which could be seen as a symbolic response to it.

The climate of social violence in America in 1968 and the public outcry over movie violence were rapidly forcing Valenti to do more than issue public statements about the importance of creative expression in cinema. The murder of Martin Luther King in April 1968 and of Robert Kennedy in June spurred Valenti to meet with studio executives and filmmakers to urge "upon them increased restraint and heightened responsibility in portraying violence" and the avoidance of "aimless cruelty and senseless brutality."[68] They pledged their cooperation in restraining movie violence that lacked aesthetic justification, but, as subsequent productions indicate, this cooperation was short-lived. Valenti assured Congress and President Johnson that a new proposed movie rating classification system would offer a "response" to public anger over perceived links between contemporary cinema violence and social violence.[69] (*Variety* reported that following the shooting of Robert Kennedy, Manhattan pedestrians were visibly shaken by a theater marquee advertising a Columbia Western, *A Time for Killing.* "How can they have a title like that?," one asked.[70]) On October 7, 1968, the MPAA announced its new Code and Rating Administration and the G-M-R-X system of classification that would cover all films released after November 1, 1968.

The brilliance of the CARA plan lay in its solution to the deepening crisis of movie violence and the growing schism among filmmakers, social watchdog groups, and moviegoers. The CARA plan simultaneously extended new restrictions (on the age of viewers permitted to see films in the R and X categories) and new freedoms (for filmmakers to be even more daring since children would be excluded from seeing the results). The adoption of the CARA system helped institutionalize, and thereby strengthen, the revolution in movie content that had begun following the code revision in 1966. *Bonnie and Clyde* was a pre-CARA film. *The Wild Bunch,* during the latter phases of its production, was post-CARA. Peckinpah clearly seized the initiative in this new, more liberal industry climate and pushed screen violence to unprecedented levels, darting through the open door the new system had just given him. Peckinpah did not single-handedly bring graphic violence to American screens. He was the beneficiary of a trend in this direction that was already established and well underway and was driven by powerful industry incentives.

Violence in Sixties Culture and Society

Peckinpah, though, was not simply taking maximum advantage of the new alignments within the industry regarding screen content. The exceptional brutality of *The Wild Bunch* cannot be separated from the social climate in which it was made because it is inextricably a part of that environment, as were Peckinpah's intentions in representing violence on screen. To insist on this point is to recover the history of the film and the social history of the era. The violence of *The Wild Bunch,* as a Western, is certainly conditioned by generic imperatives, and it speaks to audiences nearly three decades later with a scarcely-mellowed ferocity. It does transcend its time, yet to understand that film fully, we must view it synchronically as well as diachronically. The violence of that film, and of Peckinpah's work in general, fed off of the climate of violence endemic to the era and was a conscious response to it, not a mere reflection of it.

For those living through the era, the violence of the Vietnam War and the disintegration of U.S. society—emblemized by the political assassinations, urban riots, antiwar violence, and rising street crime—represented what Sartre would call the untranscendable horizon of lived experience. It was an inescapable crucible shaping thought and perception. It was what blinded Arthur Penn to the intensity of the carnage in *Bonnie and Clyde.* It shaped and stimulated Peckinpah's own movement toward a cinema of violence, melancholy, and cruelty, and it fired him with a messianic sense of purpose in bringing violence to the screens of America. The strife of the era roused him to new heights of creativity and made him a man with a mission by providing a historical framework within which his individual rage and artistic interests in violence might transcend their narrowly personal basis and resonate with broader currents of intellectual and cultural energy. The late sixties provided Peckinpah with the soapbox he needed from which to construct his cinematic explorations of violence and cruelty. We now need to examine how Peckinpah's views on human violence are symptomatic of the late 1960s and how they conform to the more general cultural dialogue on social violence underway during those years. Peckinpah was a keen observer of the cultural landscape. This fact has been minimized in most criticism and analysis of his films, which tend to treat Peckinpah's representation of violence in abstracted and generic terms. Weddle, by contrast, in his biography of Peckinpah, has noted the relevance of the period for Peckinpah's work, arguing that the director's "personal struggles were a microcosm of those tearing his country apart at the seams."[71]

By 1968, when Peckinpah had returned to feature filmmaking and was working on *The Wild Bunch,* the Vietnam War was at its height, with American troop levels at 460,000, with 13,000 dead, and with mass mobilization against the war producing crowds of 100,000 at demonstrations in New York and Washington, D.C. During the first nine months of 1967, urban riots erupted in 128 cities, with fires causing extensive damage in Detroit and Cincinnati. Nearly 14,000 people were arrested in just 22 of these cities.[72] The National Commission on the Causes and Prevention of Violence reported that from 1963–1968 more than two million persons participated in social protest. "Civil rights demonstrations mobilized 1.1 million, antiwar demonstrations 680,000, and ghetto riots an estimated 200,000. Nine thousand casualties resulted, including some 200 deaths."[73]

Coincident with such episodes of mass protest, the national rates of violent crime significantly increased during the decade. Steep increases in homicide, rape, aggravated assault, and robbery fed a sharp public fear of street crime and nourished the law-and-order platform of Richard Nixon during the 1968 and 1972 presidential campaigns. The National Commission on the Causes and Prevention of Violence noted that "Violent crime (particularly street crime) engenders fear—the deep-seeded fear of the hunted in the presence of the hunter. Today this fear is gnawing at the vitals of urban America."[74] Pollster Lou Harris found that 65 percent of his national sample in late 1968 believed that crime and violence were the country's most pressing problem, that 81 percent believed all law and order in the country had broken down, and that, because of fears of street crime, 51 percent said they would shoot an attacker if personally threatened.[75] In 1971, 21 percent of his respondents believed it was important to have a gun in the house to protect against intruders. Harris wrote that, because of these fears, "Life had been reduced to the raw and primitive proposition of physical survival right outside the house where one lived."[76] The narrative of *Straw Dogs,* about thugs who break into a house and menace the couple living there, and the anxieties the film dramatizes, are part of this climate, as are some of Peckinpah's more notorious declarations, such as his 1974 assertion that "I have a gun in my house and I'm prepared to use it. I don't feel like killing anybody, but if anyone breaks into my house they're going to be met with as much force as I can muster."[77]

The assassinations of Martin Luther King and Robert Kennedy had a staggering impact on American culture and seemed to confirm the general perception that an uncontrollable tide of violence was sweeping across the nation. Surveying this strife, the National Commission concluded that

> the decade of the 1960s was considerably more violent than the several decades preceding it and ranks among the most violent in our history. The United States is the clear leader among modern, stable democratic nations in its rates of homicide, assault, rape, and robbery, and it is at least among the highest in incidence of group violence and assassination.[78]

In his chronicle of the rise and fractious disintegration of the Students for a Democratic Society, Kirkpatrick Sale stresses the importance of grasping the pervasiveness of late sixties political violence which he terms "extraordinary" in its scope: "It took place on a larger scale—in terms of number of incidents, their geographical spread, and the damage caused—than anything seen before in this century."[79]

The events of the late sixties put violence upon the cultural agenda as a topic for commentary, fear, fascination, and for urgent commands that it be understood so that it could be controlled. Writing about student radicals, Kenneth Keniston famously notes that "the issue of violence is to this generation what the issue of sex was to the Victorian world."[80] He points out that crime, riots, and political assassinations have made American society into one obsessed with violence. "The fear of violence has led to a fascination with it that further surrounds us with its symptoms."[81] Former SDS member Todd Gitlin has diagnosed violence as "the siren song of the late Sixties"[82] and notes that violence became part of the fantasy life of the entire society,[83] an endless obsession fueling public discourse and cultural production. Sixties culture, he suggests, was fixated on a mythology of "death as the final refutation of plenitude," with sacrifices extending from JFK to Malcolm X, Martin Luther King, Bobby Kennedy, Jimi Hendrix, Jim Morrison, Janis Joplin, and the outlaw heroes of *Bonnie and Clyde* and *Easy Rider*.[84] Peckinpah's outlaw heroes in *The Wild Bunch* partake of this mythology of death, achieving transcendence and release from a corrupting social history through a violent martyrdom. As with these other cultural heroes, their passage to a house justified would need to be a violent one.

The social and political violence of these years, especially emblemized in the Vietnam War, led many intellectuals and public figures to conclude that American society was uniquely diseased with appetites for destruction. Peckinpah shared in this commentary. Keniston notes that, despite its claims to peacefulness, the U.S. "is in fact one of the most violent societies in the history of the world."[85] Susan Sontag in 1967 diagnosed the famed American energy as essentially "the energy of violence,"[86] and Martin Luther King, declaring in 1967 his opposition to the Vietnam War, called the U.S. "the greatest purveyor of violence in the world today" and decried the "tragic death wish" of American society.[87] As Robert Kennedy died, Arthur M. Schlesinger Jr. condemned the American "compulsion toward violence." He said, "We are a violent people with a violent history, and the instinct for violence has seeped into the bloodstream of our national life."[88]

Peckinpah agreed with this diagnosis of American society, and he noted that contemporary social violence was but a manifestation of the underlying nature of American culture. His views in this respect demonstrate not just his sensitivity to the ongoing social turmoil, but also his tendency to understand it historically and culturally. Like Schlesinger and Sontag, he contextualized the contemporary conflicts as the manifestation of a deeper principle of exploitation and destruction in American culture. Surveying the recent past from the vantage point of 1974, just after the hemorrhage of the sixties had subsided, he told a Canadian interviewer that the scandal of Watergate posed as grave a threat to democracy as did the social unrest the country had gone through. The violence that erupted during these years, Peckinpah said, pointed to more fundamental truths about America than people were comfortable admitting, truths that were incompatible with the institutions of democratic governance. In the wake of Watergate, politicians were attempting to reassure everyone that the country was still essentially democratic. But, he added, "We all know that behind our falsely reassuring democratic facades, violence has very deep roots. It has shaped our history, and the whole country knows very well that it has more often solved its problems through violence than through the official channels of democracy."[89] Peckinpah then spoke of the antidemocratic distribution of power in the country and its historic use against minority groups. "Look at what was done to the Blacks, the Indians, the homosexuals, and to all the minorities who would not conform to the norm or to the voice of the strongest. They were squashed."[90] He concluded by observing that the present turmoil was the result of past mistakes. "Those who have been too long oppressed by the violence of power are waking up, organizing, and fighting for their rights. Inevitably, the conflict can only resolve itself in violence. We are paying the price, today, of our past mistakes and weaknesses."[91] In a 1972 interview, Peckinpah more succinctly put forth his views. He said, "The whole underside of our society has always been violent and still is. It's a reflection of the society itself."[92]

Peckinpah shared the temper of the times in his contextualization of violence in American society. His voice joined those of Schlesinger, King, and Sontag. Like them, he was moved by a sense of urgency in responding to the contemporary unrest. As a symptom of this urgency and sense of crisis, Peckinpah and other commentators sometimes resorted to metaphysical categories to describe social phenomena, and they stressed the need for society to confront its own violence and, by confronting it, learn to control it through self-knowledge. Schlesinger had urged Americans to "recognize that the evil is in us" and that it was "a primal curse" fixed on the nation.[93] Peckinpah, too, was tempted to generalize the problem of violence and to relate it to primal human impulses. "We're violent by nature," he insisted in 1972.[94] "When you see the degree of violence in men, you realize that we are still just a few steps up from the apes in the evolutionary scale."[95] In this remark about evolution, and in others that he made, Peckinpah exhibited a tendency to make reactionary-sounding pronouncements (influenced by the work of anthropologist Robert Ardrey), declarations that have led some critics to regard him as a primitivist, as a director who celebrated brutality and made a cult of violence.

As we will see in the next chapters, though, Peckinpah's work is very far from celebrating these attributes, despite his own tendency at times to sound like a right-wing primitivist (as when he asserted that human behavior is driven by "purely animal instincts"[96]). Peckinpah may have been confused at times about what he thought (these confusions give his best films their edginess and their electric charge), but he was very consistent in his descriptions of what he intended his representation of screen violence to accomplish. Like Schlesinger, who, distraught by the decade's traumatic violence, urged Americans to "uncover the roots of hatred and violence and, through self-knowledge, move toward self-control,"[97] Peckinpah wanted his screen violence to lead viewers toward greater self-knowledge and control of their own darker appetites. In his statements on violence and his approach to it in cinema, he always emphasized his intention to use it in a constructive and enlightening way. "I attempt to portray violence for what it is. We are a violent people and have been since the beginning. We should understand the nature of our affliction and channel it—not close our eyes and hope that it will go away. Because it won't—not ever."[98] He told Barbara Walters in 1974 that "I don't put violence on the screen so that people can enjoy it. I want them to understand what it is," and added that unfortunately most people come to see it because it excites them.[99] He emphasized his belief that human survival depends on confronting and controlling violent behavior: "If we don't recognize that we're violent people, we're dead . . . I would like to understand the nature of violence. Is there a way to channel it, to use it positively?"[100]; and "Violence is a part of life, and I don't think we can bury our heads in the sand and ignore it. It's important to understand it and the reason people seem to need violence vicariously."[101]

Peckinpah consistently stressed that his goal was not to make violence attractive but to show its horror, not to celebrate it, but to confront the viewer with its essential ugliness. In one statement on violence, composed in connection with *The Wild Bunch,* he maintained that screen violence, used properly, should repel people, upset them, and make them sick. (Implicit in Peckinpah's perspective is an alternate conceptualization of the idea of pleasure as it relates to movie entertainment. We will pursue this briefly later in this chapter and more fully in Chapter Five.) "When the truth of violence is shown on the screen," he maintained, "it is frightening—disgusting—it makes people sick. It should make them sick."[102] Violence, he said in 1969, is "ugly, brutalizing and bloody fucking awful. It's not fun and games and cowboys and Indians, it's a terrible, ugly thing," adding that he hoped people would be sickened and dismayed by the killing in *The Wild Bunch.*[103]

Nineteen sixty-eight was the most violent and turbulent year of the decade, and Peckinpah shared the national revulsion over the ongoing social violence. Responding as a sensitive artist, he felt compelled to describe its significance, and its aesthetic stylization in the production of this film, in terms that stressed his own moral and humane response to the destructive energies consuming American society. His insistence upon the ugliness of violence, in formal statements, in interviews, and via the aesthetic structure of his films, establishes a clear link between him, his films, and the shocked, grieving America of 1968. At that time, he could not have seriously discussed, or presented publicly, violence in any other context but as a scourge and a horror. The evidence for this perspective on the appalling nature of violence is very clear in the films, as we will see. Violence was a horror in America after 1968, and it is a horror in Peckinpah's films. Interestingly, the National Catholic Office of Motion Pictures perceived *The Wild Bunch* as a film that demythologized violence in a salutary way. NCOMP saw it as an essentially helpful film in a time of social violence

Peckinpah aimed to use graphic screen violence to provoke and upset his viewers. His approach, though, was not free of its own contradictions.

and rated it as morally unobjectionable for adults, with reservations. NCOMP felt the film "could help thoughtful viewers to understand who we are and where we have come from in a way that, considering the history of the Western genre, is singularly healthy."[104]

The sadness expressed toward violence within the narratives and mise-en-scène of his films demonstrates that Peckinpah shared in his nation's reaction to the brutal events that consumed the late 1960s. "I tried to emphasize the sense of horror and agony that violence provides,"[105] he said about his objectives in *The Wild Bunch*. He noted that the bloody events of 1968 and the raging debates about the social effects of movie violence were discussed during production of *The Wild Bunch* in relation to its violent sequences, but that they went ahead with the film as originally planned because "we thought we had a point to make about violence, that it's awful, this kind of violence."[106]

Peckinpah's revulsion was the revulsion of America. Like other Americans, he acknowledged "the horror of President Kennedy's assassination and his brother's death."[107] He shared the nation's shock and outrage over such savageries as the My Lai massacre, when American troops slaughtered civilians in the South Vietnamese village of My Lai, and the slaughter of Leno and Rosemary LaBianca, Sharon Tate, and others by the Charles Manson gang. Following these killings, in a gesture of compassionate support, on August 27, 1969, he wrote to Roman Polanski (Tate's husband), "I don't know what to say, except I hope you continue to work. You must. Maybe someday, someone will find a path of reason through the insanity that surrounds us."[108]

The wording in this kind letter is most significant and informative. For Peckinpah, the violence consuming America constituted a kind of social insanity. He understood that it was dangerous and destabilizing to the republic, while, on the personal level, leaving an awful legacy of human wreckage and tragedy. The Tate-LaBianca killings were especially vicious and irrational and left Peckinpah, like so many others, shaken and disturbed. Yet, despite the evident madness of the perpetrators, these killings seemed to resonate with the times, and Peckinpah was sensitive to this resonance and its importance for his work. He argued that his violent images had to be assessed within a social context that contained real brutality and actual death, worse than anything he might dream up for the screen. For Peckinpah, *The Wild Bunch* held a mirror up to contemporary America, and he repeatedly contextualized this film and others with reference to what he considered to be the organized brutality of the war and the national hypocrisy surrounding its prosecution. When asked in 1969 why he didn't make a film about Vietnam, if he wanted to make a statement against war and violence, he offered this oft-quoted reply: "The Western is a universal frame within which it is possible to comment on today."[109]

Of all the events that were part of the war, the My Lai incident particularly disturbed him. He felt a special fury and disgust not just over the shooting of civilians by American soldiers, but also for the Army's cover-up of the affair and its attempt to block the investigation. Among the possessions that Peckinpah kept, and which is now among his collected papers, is a prepublication excerpt from journalist Seymour Hersh's book, *My Lai 4: A Report on the Massacre and Its Aftermath,* which was published in 1970 and contains the accounts of American soldiers who participated in the massacre.

On March 16, 1968, the U.S. Army's Charlie Company killed 347 unarmed Vietnamese men, women, and children in an attack on a South Vietnamese hamlet. The incident and its cover-up emblemized for Peckinpah the brutality and corruption of the Vietnam War and of the society that was waging it. Peckinpah rejected appeals to patriotism as a defense against a full inquiry into My Lai, and he considered such efforts to use patriotism as a means of deflecting truth to be a modern kind of fascism. He recoiled at the possibility that Lt. William Calley, commander of one of the platoons participating in the massacre, might go free, and he believed that any failure to prosecute Calley would demonstrate that the country was sick—that it tolerated murder disguised as patriotism. Were this to happen, Peckinpah felt Americans would stand before each other and before the world, stripped of honor. On April 4, 1971, while in England working on *Straw Dogs*, Peckinpah sent a telegram to President Nixon urging him to press for a full investigation of the My Lai incident. He was afraid that, though Calley was on trial for his part in the incident, the full scope of the responsibility for the killings would not be uncovered and those involved would escape prosecution.

> Dear Mr. President, I am working outside of the country but I am not an expatriot. I am an American and ex-Marine and as such I must beg you to follow through and press even further in answer to the question who is responsible for the massacre in My Lai. Freeing Calley even for a short time may be politically advantageous but morally it only serves to indicate the sickness within our country. It is not really the question of what he felt he should do. The fact is what he did and there is no form of patriotism to justify the wanton killing of women and children outside of Nazi Germany. I must beg you once again to consider the moral issues involved and not the political implications. Your country and mine needs a strong and direct line to truth. Otherwise we are without honor of ourselves and with the world.[110]

Peckinpah's outrage over My Lai, and the war itself, influenced his reactions to the public outcry over the violence in his films. Peckinpah was struck that some viewers seemed to care more about make-believe movie violence than about what was happening in Southeast Asia. In this respect, the war demonstrated a kind of moral schizophrenia in America. "They were ragging me about all the violence in *The Wild Bunch*. And then, four months later, they sprang My Lai on us,"[111] he said. As late as 1974, three years after Calley's trial and his own telegram to Nixon, Peckinpah was still upset about the war, and he used it as a moral point of reference when corresponding with viewers who were critical of the violence in his films. He received a flurry of letters from adults and schoolchildren angered by the scene in *Pat Garrett and Billy the Kid* (1973) in which Billy and his gang shoot the heads off live chickens. An animal rights advocate had organized a letter-writing campaign to protest the film, and Peckinpah replied to his attackers, sometimes patiently, sometimes caustically, and he rebutted complaints that his work exhibited cruelty to animals. The logic of his argument was strikingly consistent throughout the replies he sent to his critics. He pointed out that the chickens were obtained from a slaughterhouse, given a few extra days of life, and then, after they were killed, were eaten by hungry villagers who lived on the location where the scene was shot. He then asked his correspondents whether they only cared about the welfare of animals and, if not, whether they had done anything to stop the Vietnam War and its violence against human beings. "What were your efforts against defoliation in Viet Nam?" he queried one correspondent.

> The fire bombs that scarred children on both sides in a stupid God-damned tragedy and stupid God-damned War?! As far as I'm concerned, your own self-pitying form of Watergate that permits the slaughter of human beings while crying 'wolf' for things that don't exist is a great waste.[112]

To another, he wrote,

> What is your opinion on My Lai and Lt. Calley shooting a 2 1/2 year old girl in the back, while she was running away? Was he hungry? Perhaps it might be a good idea and far more appropriate for you to write to the dead girl's mother. But maybe not. I understand she was shot too. . . . Obviously, you must have voted for Richard Nixon whose valued [sic] judgments seem consistent with yours. Unfortunately, he is dealing with the lives of human beings.[113]

Peckinpah replied more gently to the schoolchildren who wrote him, but his argument remained consistent. To one, he wrote,

> I am delighted to hear from young people who have a conscience because there is a lot in life to be concerned about. I suggest you ask your teacher to tell you about My Lai and what Lt. Calley did to a 2 1/2 year old child in Vietnam. Explain to her that, although this man committed one of the most terrible crimes, he is coming out on probation after only a few years in jail.[114]

Peckinpah summarized his attitude toward the protests against this scene in *Pat Garrett* in a letter to another schoolchild. "It's a sad world if one only receives letters about man's eating habits instead of man's cruelty to man."[115] The My Lai incident, and the war that lay behind it, proved to be an enduring outrage for Peckinpah. As late as 1976, he remarked, "Nixon's pardoning Calley was so distasteful to me that it makes me really want to puke."[116]

Beyond the Vietnam War, Peckinpah's social perspectives and his outlook on America resonated with the generational critique of American society offered by the student radicals and by their intellectual mentors. These include C. Wright Mills, who analyzed and condemned the American "power elite," and Herbert Marcuse, whose *One-Dimensional Man,* a key text influencing the terms of late sixties radical political analysis, describes the repressive tolerance of modern America, where the system absorbs protest and nullifies it through a widespread distribution of consumer goods, thereby ensuring a public dependent for its pleasures on the existing arrangements of power. The generational critique of liberalism by student radicals opposed to the Vietnam War, and "the system" that underlay it, appealed to Peckinpah, and he declared his support for their protests.[117] We should first examine the terms of this generational critique of American society and then explore how Peckinpah's work was consistent with that critique.

In a famous speech delivered at the March on Washington in November 1965, Students for a Democratic Society (SDS) President Carl Oglesby noted with irony that the Vietnam War was not being waged by evil monsters but by good liberals, asserting that Assistant Secretary of State William Bundy, Secretary of Defense Robert S. McNamara, and President Lyndon Johnson "are not moral monsters. They are all honorable men. They are all liberals."[118] The institutional system of modern America, which Oglesby terms "corporate liberalism," that is, liberal thought in service to the corporate state, overwhelms the individual's moral conscience by turning otherwise good people into instruments of the system. Oglesby's analysis of corporate liberalism had a large impact on subsequent radical thought.[119] Declaring his opposition to the Vietnam War, Martin Luther King decried the spiritual bankruptcy of a "thing-oriented" American culture in which instrumental calculations replaced conscience and morality.

> We must rapidly begin the shift from a 'thing-oriented' society to a 'person-oriented' society. When machines and computers, profit motives and property rights are considered more important than people, the giant triplets of racism, materialism and militarism are incapable of being conquered.[120]

In *One-Dimensional Man,* Marcuse argues that the culture of modern capitalism sustains itself by immobilizing the psyches of its subjects via the pleasures of a widely-distributed system of consumer goods and leisure. "Today this private space has been invaded and whittled down by technological reality," he wrote. "Mass production and mass distribution claim the entire individual. "[121] For late-sixties radical thought, "the system" was laying waste to Southeast Asia in order to sustain American corporate power and a consumer culture that was deforming the spiritual and moral possibilities of the American people. According to Susan Sontag, "the quality of American life is an insult to the possibilities of human growth; and the pollution of American space, with gadgetry and cars and TV and box architecture, brutalizes the senses, making grey neurotics of most of us."[122]

Peckinpah participated in this generational critique. The political system, he believed, that was pursuing war in Southeast Asia was corrupted by an unprincipled exercise of power, and its representatives, albeit well-dressed, personified the savagery of the system. "Look at who the people are voting for—Nixon, Wallace—killer apes right out of the caves, all dressed up in suits and talking and walking around with death in their eyes," he said in 1972.[123] Like the radical opponents of American corporate society and its foreign policy, Peckinpah felt a special antipathy for Nixon, whom he called a "cocksucker" out to "ruin the country"[124] and whom he pictured in memorably depraved surroundings in *Bring Me the Head of Alfredo Garcia.* In that film, he put Nixon's face on a phony dollar bill on the wall behind the bar where Benny plays piano, and Nixon's face also adorns the cover of *Time* magazine, read by an amoral executive getting a pedicure by two whores.

Less obviously, in *The Wild Bunch* Peckinpah sounded contemporary notes of antigovernment opposition by having Pike Bishop declare, "We share very few sentiments with our government." In another scene, Harrigan, the venal railroad baron who presides over a massacre in San Rafael that he has incited in an effort to get the Bunch, tyrannically asserts, "We represent the law." In 1969, these lines had an unmistakable resonance. Discussing the character of Harrigan, Peckinpah drew a parallel with the repressive brutality of Mayor Richard Daley's Chicago police force in its clash with antiwar demonstrators during the 1968 Democratic National Convention. Referring to the sequence in the film where Harrigan instigates the massacre, Peckinpah said, "This was shot before the Chicago incidents, but I think they more or less prove the point I was trying to make, that power corrupts just as much as lawlessness."[125]

The killers in suits employed by wealthy executives in Peckinpah's modern-day films, *The Getaway* (1972), *Alfredo Garcia,* and *The Killer Elite*

Like New Left social critics, Peckinpah viewed institutional authority in America as being often corrupt and exploitive. Harrigan in *The Wild Bunch* personifies the ruthless economic forces of a modernizing West. Armed with a private police force of gutter-trash killers, he instigates the film's opening massacre. © 1969, Warner Bros.–Seven Arts, Inc.

(1975), visualize Peckinpah's conviction of the lethal nature of corporate America, with its interlocking economic and political interests. Peckinpah viewed modern America as a society where the highest levels of power are wielded by businessmen and politicians with blood on their hands. He described Cap Collins, the villainous intelligence agency executive in *The Killer Elite,* as "prototype Haldeman" and Maxwell Danforth, CIA head in *The Osterman Weekend* (1983), as an Alexander Haig figure.[126]

The executives in suits who populate his contemporary-life films are manifestations of this corruption and of a society in which materialism and barbarism exhibit a Janus face. His views of American history, dramatized through the narratives of *The Killer Elite* and *The Osterman Weekend,* are inflected by paranoia and see conspiracies at work in the mainte-

The killers in suits who populate Peckinpah's contemporary-life films are emblems of the political and social corruption and barbarism that he believed characterized twentieth-century America. Robert Webber and Gig Young are the remorseless assassins in *Bring Me the Head of Alfredo Garcia.* © 1974, United Artists Corp.

nance of power. In this, he was like many Americans whose views of their society and history were irreparably altered by the assassination of President Kennedy and the lingering, unanswered questions about what really happened in Dealey Plaza. He said that he refused to film any of *The Getaway* in Dallas because it was the site of JFK's death, and his vision in *Pat Garrett and Billy the Kid, The Killer Elite,* and *The Osterman Weekend* presents an America dominated by power elites who ruthlessly assassinate any who get in their path. Though the historical evidence is by no means so clear, Peckinpah was convinced that Garrett's murder was an early example of corporate state–sponsored assassination: "You see, the same people who had hired Garrett to kill Billy years later had him assassinated, because as a police officer he was getting too close to their operation. . . so he was assassinated. And it still happens today."[127]

The man who defended Garrett's assassins, according to Peckinpah, "later became United States Secretary for Interior, which may be some comment on today's government."[128] In an alternate ending for *Pat Garrett and Billy the Kid,* Peckinpah added a similar observation on a printed title at the film's conclusion.[129] This paranoid vision of American history was a legacy of the JFK killing, and it was consistent with the radical generational critique of America that soon followed as the society fissured in the late sixties. In his moments of darkest pessimism, he ruled out any grounds for hope or progressive social change. He considered the society spiritually dead and the system capable of killing again to prevent change. If George McGovern really challenged the war, Peckinpah felt, the Democratic senator from South Dakota would be a likely target for assassination. Speaking before McGovern secured his party's nomination to run for president in the 1972 election, Peckinpah said, "I doubt whether he's tough enough to cut it. If he turns out to be, they'd better throw a metal shield around the poor bastard and keep it there. The rifle shot that rang out in Dallas in 1963 was a very big and ugly noise."[130]

Peckinpah dismissed the possibilities for progressive social change because, like Marcuse, he considered Americans to be brainwashed by the media and lulled into a spiritual torpor by an abundant but deadening consumer culture. These attitudes, like Sontag's condemnation of the plasticness of America (and represented by Mr. Maguire's famous advice to Benjamin Braddock in *The Graduate*), were part of the generational rejection of the "thing-oriented" establishment culture that characterized sixties radicalism. Peckinpah noted that he considered it essential to his art that he not get anesthetized by the abundant consumer comforts of American society. "I want to get rid of this creature-comfort thing. . . . [I]f I get sucked into this consumer-oriented society, then I can't make the pictures about it that I want to make."[131] Like Sontag and Marcuse, he warned about the tendency for the media, especially television, to supplant real, lived experience and to produce a deadened, conformist society. He said,

> The country has no attention span. We're television oriented now. We'd better all wake-up to the fact that Big Brother is here. . . . Most people come home at night after work, have a couple of knocks before dinner and settle down in

their living death rooms. The way our society is evolving, doctor, has been very carefully thought out. It's not accidental, we're all being programmed, and I bitterly resent it.[132]

The Osterman Weekend, with its world of internecine espionage, assassination, and pervasive electronic surveillance, conveys Peckinpah's nightmare about the authoritarian technologies and repressive nature of modern America. At the end of the film, all of the people are gone, and only the TV monitors remain, the glowing eyes of the modern state. For Peckinpah, "You turn on that box; you're programmed. . . . 1984 isn't here—it's passed."[133] He retained this Marcusean suspicion of the repressive potential of technology even after the sixties and its generational critique of materialism had subsided. Discussing the social effects of television in 1977, he remarked, "We're dealing with a brainwashed country."[134] He told a BBC radio interviewer in 1982, "Technology ran over Hogue [referring to the scene in *The Ballad of Cable Hogue* where Cable is run over and killed by an automobile], technology ran over England in the Industrial Revolution, and technology is running over the world today."[135]

When Pike Bishop rejects the principles of his government, when Junior Bonner stares with disgust at the TVs and plastic homes of desert suburbia, when television talk-show host John Tanner in *The Osterman Weekend* warns viewers to turn off their televisions, when Mac in *The Killer Elite* warns Mike Locken that "there's not one power system that really cares about its civilians," when Steiner in *Cross of Iron* confesses his hatred of all military officers and uniforms, and, more positively, when Cable Hogue finds his paradise in the desert of butterfly mornings and wildflower afternoons, Peckinpah's films give articulate shape to the myriad forms of late sixties radical thought and antiestablishment sentiment. His films mirror the national precoccupation with violence that shaped those years and the extent to which violence had infused the inner fantasy life of the culture. The era's romantic yearning for the apocalypse, coupled with a lack of faith in modern American society, led to visions of transcendence achieved through death, as demonstrated in the cults surrounding Hendrix, Joplin, Morrison, and the fates of the heroes in *Easy Rider* and *Bonnie and Clyde.* The defeats of Peckinpah's heroes, outlaws on the run from bourgeois America, and their occasional apotheosis in death represent a grand fulfillment of this tragic-romantic zeitgeist.

Peckinpah was not an explicit spokesman for late-sixties ideologies. He was too ambivalent and anti-intellectual in his own thought for that and was too much of a free spirit to be allied to any form of organized social activity or protest. But his personal rage and feeling of estrangement from the present circumstances of life in modern America (best represented in his nostalgia for the Denver Church ranch of his youth and his deep sorrow over its loss) helped produce an important resonance between his personal situation and the America of post-1968. As Peckinpah remarked, in terms that clearly apply to his own work, "Great works [of art] emerge out of passion . . . and of a very great degree of coincidence between the artist and the society in which he lives."[136] Peckinpah's "coincidence" with the social era illuminated a direction in which he felt compelled to take his art, as well as a dilemma he was never able to resolve. Robin Wood expresses this problem better than anyone: "Peckinpah's work to date witnesses the predicament of the artist who is vociferously anti-Establishment yet lacks any defined ideological alternative: it has the strengths and limitations which such a description suggests."[137] If the cynicism and bitterness of the later films sometimes seem so overwhelming, that is because this predicament remained intractable. Its intensely felt nature helped give the films their edge, and if Peckinpah was unable to find in his work a way out of the traps history had set for modern America, his inquiries in this direction remain of lasting interest, as the next chapters aim to demonstrate.

If we return to our earlier question—Why Peckinpah and why then?—we can see that the period of the late sixties provided an essential framework in which he could work out his contradictory feelings about violence, explain and express his alienation and bitterness about Establishment America, and give full vent to his ironic sense of life. The era provided Peckinpah with a supportive social envelope for cinematic explorations of all these conditions. Peckinpah was a man who prized the ambiguities of human behavior and morality, and the defining event of the era, the Vietnam War, exposed the terrifying ambiguities of American principle, character, policy, and behavior. As one historian has stressed,

> It was a liberal war fought in an age of high liberal expectations, and yet to its critics it signaled the persistence of imperialism, racism, and arrogance among leaders who were otherwise enlightened people. It combined the rational efficiency of bureaucracy, technology, and intellect, yet put it to use in a war that was rationally indefensible.[138]

The traumatic consequences of the war for America (and for Southeast Asia), their protracted, violent impact upon the ideals of democratic culture, their corrosive effects upon the republic, these would nurture, nourish, and confirm Peckinpah's ironic, jaundiced view of life and of American identity. And the whirlwind of violence and destructiveness that the war unleashed abroad and at home provided an external validation for his inner tumult and desires to understand and explore the effects and place of violence in human life.

Peckinpah, then, seized the violence theme partly because it had already been placed on the national agenda, and no doubt because it was a fashionable and sexy topic. But his exploration of this issue, I believe, was totally serious and generally nonexploitative even if he was at times a coconspirator in the media's construction of him as "Bloody Sam," prophet of violence. The late sixties gave Peckinpah the climate of artistic freedom—and the romantic veneration for the outlaw sensibility—necessary for his formal experimentation in film, as well as providing the relaxation of moral standards and industry rules of content requisite for his cinematic displays of graphic brutality. Even more, because it was profitable, the industry encouraged filmmakers to move in this direction. Finally, the era gave Peckinpah the social validation, the external confirmation, and the supportive sociopolitical justification for his visions of chaos, tragedy, and destruction by confirming through social turbulence his sense of their essential validity. Peckinpah's radical gesture was to disengage his cinematic exploration of violence and brutality, and the ironies and ambiguities of the American character, from the immediate social context that made them possible, a context that gets only oblique reference in the films.

In *Straw Dogs,* for example, campus protests against the war are indirectly implied when Professor David Sumner's wife, Amy, tells him that he left America and the university because he did not want to take a stand. In the finished film, David simply asks, "Commit to what? I was involved with my work," but his original reply contained explicit references to political radicals blowing up banks and social dissent on the university campuses. These were cut after Peckinpah conferred with producer Daniel Melnick and ABC Pictures head Martin Baum.[139] The replacement lines heard in the film—"You want something out of me that it's not right to deliver. That's not what I was there for"—were looped in postproduction. With his characteristically oblique approach to character and drama, Peckinpah disengaged violence from the era which foregrounded it. This has helped his films to retain an ever-contemporary voice, but it has also beclouded the conditions that made his work possible and has encouraged a critical tendency to see him as a kind of timeless auteur. Yet Peckinpah could not have made his films at any other time. In the late 1950s, the Production Code had not yet been overturned. By the late 1970s, 1980s, and 1990s, his didacticism regarding violence (his belief that it is inherent in human affairs and therefore has to be understood so it can be controlled) had lost its punch because it no longer bespoke the felt urgencies of a social period and because the blood in his films had been overwhelmed by the newer and more flamboyant gore spectacles of Scorsese, Tarantino, Verhoeven, and others.

If the sixties impelled Peckinpah on his cinematic journey to explore violence in human affairs, we need now to examine the precise nature of this exploration and portrayal. As we will see, he was no primitivist glorifying violence, yet a simple characterization of his work as antiviolent is misleading and reductive, because many paradoxes abound in it and in the issues surrounding the representation and viewing of screen violence. Peckinpah's was a dialectical representation of violence, not a simplistic one, produced by the superimposition within the films of shifting frames of perspective. The deployment of these multiple frames, and not the flashy montage editing of his films, is his true cinematic accomplishment and constitutes the lasting richness of his work. We now turn to an exploration of these multiple frames of perspective.

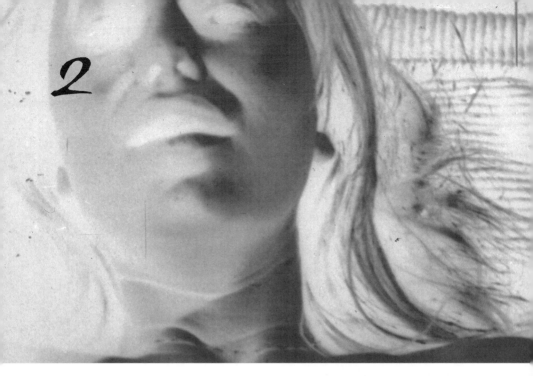

Aestheticizing Violence

OF ALL THE FILMMAKERS at work in the American cinema during the late sixties and early seventies, Peckinpah was the most sensitive to the national currents of sociopolitical violence. As his remarks about the killing of JFK, the Chicago incidents, Vietnam, and the My Lai massacre demonstrate, Peckinpah clearly recognized the dark strain of violence within the heart of 1960s America, and he conceptualized his work in cinema as a response to this. Only Arthur Penn comes close to Peckinpah in his sensitivity to the strains of sixties violence. Penn can talk most eloquently about his work, while Peckinpah rarely would or could. Oftentimes, when speaking about the meaning of his films, Peckinpah would deliberately strike the most outrageous poses. At the height of his own controversial reputation as a poet/exploiter of screen violence, Peckinpah described *Alfredo Garcia* as a film about "somebody [who] gets pissed off with all this bull, and takes a gun and shoots a lot of people and gets killed."[1] Such remarks were calculated to play to Peckinpah's detractors by making him seem especially right-wing or nihilistic. (As I have discussed in the Introduction, however, this belligerent self-presentation is a problematic and untrustworthy guide to the films.) By contrast, the clarity and acuity with which

Arthur Penn has discussed his work makes him seem by far the more insightful artist-poet of American screen violence.

Peckinpah, though, embraced the theme of violence in his work far more thoroughly than did Penn, and, with montage editing and slow motion, he explored its stylistics more extensively. Peckinpah did this because he felt the issues more intensely, and engaged them more passionately, than did Penn. Penn's very precision and control as a filmmaker give his work a cooler, more distant tone than is characteristic of Peckinpah. (The only Penn film whose violence comes close to the heated grotesquerie of Peckinpah's work is *The Chase*, 1966.) The violence issue burned with a powerful intensity for Peckinpah. Whether he looked inside, at his own seething rages, or outside, at the blood running in the streets of America and being spilled in the jungles of Southeast Asia, his conviction that violence was a central component of human experience was strengthened. This intensely felt relationship to the problem of violence, in both his personal life and in his perception of the tragedy of American history, was conjoined with Peckinpah's ironic orientation toward life and near-schizophrenic sense of the admixture of opposites. The resulting combination helped produce films that are unruly, contrary, off-kilter—in a word, messy —so unlike the disciplined design of Penn's work. But this very unruliness is also the sign of an audacious social vision and of a daring filmmaker.

At this point, we need to grasp the radical thrust of Peckinpah's work, radical in its critique of American society in a time of crisis, and radical in its efforts to undermine and reorient the viewer's conventional relationship with screen violence. Peckinpah understood the consequences of his assault on the usually safe vantage point from which viewers watch movie violence. Most films do not hold viewers accountable for, or implicate them in, the violent spectacles they witness. Peckinpah's films do, and this is one reason for their controversial nature. Peckinpah said that people want to walk out on his films, "but they can't. They can't turn their faces away. They watch, and that makes them mad."[2] The ambivalent responses that his films create in viewers are the complex result of Peckinpah's careful audiovisual designs, melancholic presentation of narrative and characters, and self-conscious attempts to deconstruct the violent spectacles. These are the three principal frameworks whose interplay constitutes the dialectics of death operative in his films. The first framework, Peckinpah's audiovisual design of screen violence, examined in this chapter, raises complex issues of spectacle, montage aesthetics, self-reflexivity, and catharsis that simultaneously open onto issues of film history and theory and the social effects of media violence. I will try to disentangle these as they are relevant for understanding Peckinpah's work and screen violence in general.

First, we need to consider what he did to aestheticize violence and why, and then we can evaluate some of its consequences for film and society and assess the success of his endeavors when measured against their intentions. Peckinpah used a montage-based aesthetic, characterized by multicamera filming at varying speeds and rapid cutting, to break with realism in order to substitute a *stylized* rendition of violence. This point is most important, given the common critical (and wrong-headed) view that Peckinpah's signal contribution in the late sixties was to bring to American cinema a more realistic depiction of violence whereby the bloodless deaths portrayed in previous decades of film gave way to a more forthright, and truer, presentation of gore. This view has tended to obscure the important point that Peckinpah aimed to stylize his materials and that this stylization proceeded from his conviction that it was the only way to wake people up to violence in a culture whose brutality had anesthetized them to bloody death. Peckinpah believed people had become inured to violence through the medium of television, which domesticated the violence of the Vietnam War and, by sandwiching it between commercials, insinuated it into the daily routines of consumer life. In a culture and during a period so heavily saturated with killing, people had become oddly desensitized, Peckinpah believed, and he felt that by heightening violence through the artifice of style he could break the cycle of consumption in which the era's disturbing social violence was embedded. His remarks on this point reveal a filmmaker with a didactic social agenda and an awareness of how camera style might serve that agenda:

> We watch our wars and see men die, really die, every day on television, but it doesn't seem real. We don't believe those are real people dying on that screen. We've been anesthetized by the media. What I do is show people what it's really like—not by showing it as it is so much as by heightening it, stylizing it. . . . The only way I can do that is by not letting them gloss over the looks of it, as if it were the seven o'clock news from the DMZ. When people complain about the way I handle violence, what they're really saying is, 'Please don't show me; I don't want to know; and get me another beer out of the icebox.'[3]

The montage aesthetic served Peckinpah's didactic intentions precisely because the elaborate stylizations it permitted were so decisively a rupture with previous screen traditions of representing violence and with the unremarkable visual presence of daily TV violence. Peckinpah was very insistent that his visual approach was a reaction against the existing movie traditions which he considered to be misleading and grossly out of step with the times. He believed that "violence in motion pictures is usually treated like fun and games."[4] In a letter to Paul Staniford, a lawyer and friend of the Peckinpah family (and whose name Peckinpah gave to a character in *Ride the High Country*), Peckinpah declared, "I personally feel it's time Hollywood quit glamorizing violence and let people see how brutalizing and horrible it really is. This is what I tried to do [in *The Wild Bunch*]."[5] By breaking the established representational conventions, Peckinpah hoped to convey the horror of violence to viewers he believed had been rendered complacent by decades of painless, bloodless movie killings. In late-sixties America, the traumatic impact of real social violence was misaligned with the tradition of bloodless movie violence. The violence of the Vietnam War was quite real. Yet to Peckinpah, conventional movie violence, and television news, seemed to be performing a narcotizing function, insulating people from the events around them. As we saw in the last chapter, Peckinpah's belief in this narcotizing function was consistent with the radical critique of popular culture in that period (as represented in the writings of Sontag and Marcuse). By using graphic imagery of bloodletting and the montage aesthetic, Peckinpah aimed to bring the era's violence inside the movie theater, which would no longer function as a place of refuge by shielding viewers from horrific images. Peckinpah's work aimed to place the filmic representation of screen violence into proper synchronicity with the era whose convulsions engulfed the sensibilities of filmmaker and audience alike. His object in doing this was to create a socially beneficial effect. "To negate violence it must be shown for what it is," he argued, "a horrifying, brutalizing, destructive, ingrained part of humanity."[6] If the narcotizing functions of the media were broken, Peckinpah believed, people would see violence for what it is and thereby stand a chance of gaining more control over it and its destructive effects upon a nation in turmoil. After receiving a letter from a viewer critical of *The Wild Bunch*, Peckinpah wrote back and asked that the viewer consider that the graphic screen carnage had these larger objectives. "I am sorry you did not enjoy *The Wild Bunch*. Perhaps some of its vulgarity and violence will remain with the people who will see it and they will understand better the nature of this continuing plague that infects our country."[7]

With this description of Peckinpah's objectives in mind, we need to examine the distinctive structure of the montage editing in his films, its operation and effects, because we will want to measure the presence of this aesthetic framework against the other two frameworks examined in the next chapters and to evaluate his objectives in relation to this style. A convenient place to begin is by situating Peckinpah's montages in relation to the cinema traditions and filmmakers that have influenced his work. I then examine three distinct categories of montage editing found in his work and their characteristic manipulations of time and space. Finally, questions about the cathartic effects of screen violence need to be considered, initially in this chapter, and then more fully in the next, because Peckinpah fervently believed in catharsis as the psychological end toward which his montage spectacles were directed. If he was wrong about the cathartic effects of screen violence, where does that leave all the bloodshed in his films? Does it leave his work, as many have charged, without any redeeming foundation?

Antecedents of Peckinpah's Montage Style

Despite its visual audacity, Peckinpah's montage aesthetic does not represent an original or unique application of stylistic principles in the way of the long take–long shot formula in the films of Miklós Jancsó or Jacques Tati or the low camera positions and compositional frontality in the films of Yasujiro Ozu. Jancsó, Tati, and Ozu's films represent original and unmistakable, uniquely defining permutations of cinema style. Most filmmakers do not work in such an iconoclastic manner, and certainly Peckinpah did not. The essential influences on his montage aesthetic are easily identified. The most important influence is the work of Akira Kurosawa. More distantly and generally, there is the montage editing of Sergei Eisenstein, and most immediately (in relation to *The Wild Bunch*) is Penn's demonstration of slow-motion and multicamera filming in *Bonnie and Clyde*. (Other precedents, more prosaic, perhaps, were also important. While working in the early 1950s as a stagehand at KLAC-TV in Los Angeles, Peckinpah watched an experimental film made by another station employee. It included a slow-motion shot of a falling lightbulb that intrigued Peckinpah. Also, prior to cutting *The Wild Bunch,* Lou Lombardo showed Peckinpah an episode of the TV show "Felony Squad" that he had edited that included some slow-motion work during a gunfight.[8])

Kurosawa, whose *Rashomon* (1950) Peckinpah always cited as a favorite film, doubtless because its theme of the relativity of truth deeply appealed to his sense of irony, exerted a decisive stylistic influence upon Peckinpah's work in several ways. Beginning with *Seven Samurai* (1954), Kuro-

Kurosawa's use of multicamera filming, montage editing, and slow motion in *Seven Samurai* was a key influence on Peckinpah's use of these stylistic devices.

sawa customarily used from three to five cameras running simultaneously to film his scenes. This approach gave him much better coverage of that film's complexly choreographed fight scenes and also helped to elicit better performances from the actors by extending the length of each take. Peckinpah obviously appreciated the strategic advantages that multicamera filming afforded the shooting of action scenes. For the scene in *Bring Me the Head of Alfredo Garcia* where the professional killers Quill and Sappensly massacre a Mexican family, Peckinpah used five cameras, two of which were running at high speed to produce slow motion.[9] On *Junior Bonner,* for the critical sequence in which the bulldozers wreck Ace's house, Peckinpah employed four cameras: two high-speed cameras with zoom lenses at opposite angles on the house, an Arriflex wide angle for a long shot on the front of the house, and an Arriflex telephoto for a low angle on the right of the house.[10] Covering the action simultaneously from so many angles and with different camera speeds amplifies the material available for montage editing, an obvious strategic advantage given Peckinpah's desires to transform the normative conventions of American cinema.

Kurosawa's multicameras, though, describe a fixed and unique geometry of space. They are often set at right angles to one another so that the cuts shift the viewer's axis of vision by 90 degrees. While space in Kurosawa's cinema is extremely angular, the disjunctiveness of his cutting is softened somewhat by the recurrent regularities of these 90-degree perspective realignments. The angularity of Peckinpah's cutting exhibits none of the rectilinear "normality" of Kurosawa's 90-degree-angle shifts. Peckinpah's angularity is totally acute or oblique, always off-center, and, as a result, it imposes a much higher degree of fragmentation upon the space that it carves up. Peckinpah learned from Kurosawa's disjunctive editing of space and carried its implications much further, as the cutting throughout *Straw Dogs* clearly demonstrates.

Kurosawa's cinema also taught Peckinpah about the perspective-distorting effects of telephoto lenses, a signature Kurosawa element that became a signature Peckinpah element, because the telephoto lens works extremely well in conjunction with multicamera filming. By equipping multicameras with long-focal-length lenses, the cameras can be positioned more easily about the periphery of the set. Since the focal length of the lenses will produce a narrow field of view that can be used to prevent the cameras from seeing each other, telephoto lenses facilitate the blocking of multicamera positions. Peckinpah quickly grasped the implications of this advantage. *Ride the High Country,* a nonmontage-based film, does not conspicuously utilize telephoto lenses, while *The Wild Bunch,* a montage and multicamera film, clearly does, as do many of his later films.

In addition to the multicamera filming, disjunctively angular cutting, and reliance upon telephoto lenses that Peckinpah found in Kurosawa's work, the most explicit area of influence from Kurosawa to Peckinpah is, of course, Kurosawa's exploration of slow motion within scenes of violent death. (Kurosawa's use of slow motion was also an important influence on Walon Green in his thinking about the script for *The Wild Bunch,* though he did not write out these ideas. He told an interviewer, "The violence in slow motion is very expressly in the script. I put the slow motion in because when I wrote it, I had just seen *The Seven Samurai,* which had the first use of slow motion in an action scene that I'd ever seen." Peckinpah scholar Paul Seydor points out that Green told him this claim was an error: that he did not, in fact, write slow motion into the script, but was thinking about it while working on the script because of the Kurosawa film, which had tremendously impressed him.[11]) This interest appeared as early as Kurosawa's first film, *Sanshiro Sugata* (1943), but it was *Seven Samurai* (1954), widely seen and admired in the West, with its all-male band of heroes, adventure narrative, and martial values, that explicitly demonstrated the stylistic patterning that the intercutting of footage shot at different camera speeds could bring to the dramatic and temporal rhythms of a scene. Kurosawa's work occasioned Peckinpah's famous remark, following completion of *Ride the High Country,* "I'd like to be able to make a Western like Kurosawa makes Westerns."[12] Weddle's biography claims that Kurosawa's use of slow motion was primitive compared to the complexities introduced by Peckinpah. "Editorially it was static. The weaving of slow motion into the very fabric of a sequence . . . had still to be achieved."[13] While it is true that Peckinpah used slow motion far more extensively than Kurosawa (and that he began using it well before *The Wild Bunch,* as Weddle and Seydor have pointed out), who seemed to have only an occasional interest in the device, the essentials of Peckinpah's usage are clearly already contained in *Seven Samurai.*

Contrary to Weddle's claims, Kurosawa does cut in and out of the slow-motion footage in a dynamic manner. During the scene where the leader of the samurai, Kambei (Takashi Shimura), rescues a kidnapped child from a crazed thief and kills the thief with a short sword, Kurosawa dynamically intercuts footage filmed at normal speed with slow-motion footage so that the rhythms of the scene oscillate between these two different temporal modes. The mortally wounded thief crashes through the hut's doorway to the village square outside where amazed onlookers witness his dying. Kurosawa intercuts three slow-motion shots of the thief crashing through the door, running a few steps forward, and rising up on tiptoe with three normal-speed shots of the onlookers' reactions. Since movement also occurs in these shots, the scene builds an internal tension between these differing rhythms. After these six shots, Kurosawa shows the thief fall to the ground in slow motion but without the sound of an impact. This sound has been withdrawn from the scene, setting up a dynamic visual-acoustic conflict that accompanies the temporal conflicts.

But the visual-acoustic conflicts in the film are more subtle still and hold yet greater relevance for Peckinpah's work. During the scene's slow-motion shots, Kurosawa includes amplified sound effects—the baby's cry, the mother's scream, howling wind—which involve no temporal distortion. Amplified, but temporally unmodified, sound accompanies the slow-motion images, and this disjunction emphasizes the heightened artifice of these images, their uniquely expressive power. What we have yet to appreciate is not only how fundamentally Kurosawa's brief exploration of slow-motion effects influenced Peckinpah's work, but also how Kurosawa had already made the essential discovery that temporal nonsynchrony between image and sound accentuates the contrast of footage shot at differing camera speeds. The normal-speed sound emphasizes the otherness of the slow-motion image. This visual-acoustic principle is basic to the expressive power of such sequences.

Kurosawa's disjunctive editing and audiovisual combinations are indebted to the montage tradition exemplified by Eisenstein and so, too, is Peckinpah's work. Care needs to be exercised in extending these comparisons, however. Eisenstein's montage principles belong to a rich and specific ideological and social context that informed his filmmaking, a context that does not translate to either Kurosawa or Peckinpah, who both employed a much more limited use of montage. Despite this, Peckinpah's montages in *The Wild Bunch* have been compared to Eisenstein's as if in a direct line of descent. Weddle calls Peckinpah's editing the most creative and revolutionary montages since Eisenstein's *Potemkin* (1925). As David Bordwell notes, however, the montage editing in Hollywood films, music videos, and TV commercials "lies far from Eisenstein's sophisticated conceptions of montage. At best, the 'montage' in such media artifacts is metric and rhythmic, seldom tonal or overtonal, and it makes no attempt to achieve the large-scale motivic density that is central to Eisenstein's practice."[14] The Odessa Steps massacre in *Potemkin,* for example, features a complex orchestration of graphic, volumetric, kinetic, and temporal elements in a design whose intricacy surpasses the narrower range of manipulations Peckinpah carried out in his montages. This is why Eisenstein looms as a more distant and general example for Peckinpah's cinema rather than as a direct and immediate influence. While it is true, as Bordwell points out, that Eisenstein expanded his ideas about dialectics and visual conflict to such a general level that they sometimes lose useful specificity, Eisenstein's insights into the disjunctive audiovisual relationships that montage makes possible nevertheless have lasting value. Furthermore, in his theoretical writings and sound filmmaking, Eisenstein grasped the importance of sound as an additional montage element, rather than as a mere prop for the images, and he noted the principle that we have just specified in relation to Kurosawa's work: namely, that "slowing down or speeding up the projected sound produces a phenomenon that is not analogous to accelerating or retarding the visual picture. The spoken words are not pronounced slower or faster; they become higher or lower in pitch."[15]

In keeping with this principle and following Kurosawa, Peckinpah also re-articulates sound during the slow-motion shots by amplifying selected effects. The cries of the baby and mother and the howling wind are selectively amplified during the slow-motion shots in *Seven Samurai* to accentuate the temporal mismatch between the audiovisual tracks. In the opening shoot-out in *The Wild Bunch,* when an outlaw crashes his horse through a glass window in slow motion, the sound of shattering glass heard at normal tempo is mixed above the general battle sounds to accentuate the temporal mismatches, and when Dutch (Ernest Borgnine) falls off his horse into a wooden structure in slow motion, the amplified crunch of wood is the dominant sound. In Peckinpah's work, the slow-motion image is carefully contrasted with amplified sound effects to create an intermodal, cross-sensory montage, and, as we have established, the expressive power of these combinations had been explicitly demonstrated by Kurosawa in *Seven Samurai* (and in *Sanshiro Sugata* before that, although it is virtually certain Peckinpah never saw this film, because it did not receive international distribution).

In public interviews, where he tended to strike a contentious pose, Peckinpah could be singularly ungracious about acknowledging his cinematic debts, except for the case of John Huston's *The Treasure of the Sierra Madre* (1948) which he freely conceded was a powerful influence on *The Wild Bunch.* (Interestingly, so explicit was the Huston influence on the film's design that Edmond O'Brien wrote to Peckinpah to say that, in playing Freddie Sykes, he didn't want to do a Walter Brennan, "and I don't want to think of it as a Walter Huston–treasure of love jazz either." Walter Huston, father of John, played the old prospector in *The Treasure of the Sierra Madre.*) When told that the editing in *The Wild Bunch* was in a class with Kurosawa's editing in *Seven Samurai,* Peckinpah replied "Better" and, elsewhere, remarked snidely ". . . the only movies I want to like are my movies. I don't want any other son-of-a-bitch making good movies."[16] Despite this public posturing, the Kurosawa influence was an important one for the design of Peckinpah's work.

Interestingly, in light of this, Peckinpah's archived papers contain an exchange of letters with Toshiro Mifune, Kurosawa's favorite lead actor who became an international star by virtue of his frequent appearances in Kurosawa's films. This exchange is brief but it implicitly acknowledges the intersection of these two lines of cinema. Writing in 1968, Mifune wished Peckinpah the best of luck with his new picture, *The Wild Bunch,* which had not yet been released, and Peckinpah replied, in June, 1969, just before the film went into national release, with the "hope that you enjoy my picture *The Wild Bunch*."[17] Fittingly, years later, Kurosawa personally requested that Peckinpah come to Japan for the Tokyo premiere of *Kagemusha* (1980), an invitation that Peckinpah formally accepted.[18] Furthermore, despite the caveat that we have noted in comparing Peckinpah's work with that of Kurosawa and Eisenstein, these relationships achieved some degree of self-consciousness during the production of Peckinpah's films. On *Cross of Iron,* production designer Ted Haworth told Peckinpah that a particular effect would be "Kurosawa Peckinpah at his best."[19] Discussing with Peckinpah the story structure as scripted for *The Wild Bunch,* producer Phil Feldman noted that an improperly placed scene with the bounty hunters "would interrupt your Eisenstein structure."[20]

Assuming his contentious public persona, Peckinpah claimed to have seen *Bonnie and Clyde* only after finishing *The Wild Bunch* and retrospectively laid claim to Penn's slow-motion work, remarking "they did all my

Selective amplification of key sound effects emphasizes the temporal mismatch of sound and image as a member of the Wild Bunch crashes in slow motion through a glass window. © 1969, Warner Bros.–Seven Arts.

shtick."[21] Despite this claim, wardrobe supervisor Gordon Dawson recollected that Peckinpah wanted to surpass *Bonnie and Clyde*'s violence and stylistics while in production on *The Wild Bunch*. Furthermore, in a letter of March 19, 1968, Warner Bros. confirmed with the film's production manager that a print of *Bonnie and Clyde* would be shipped to Peckinpah's Mexico location for a screening the next weekend (March 23–24). This was immediately prior to the start of principal photography on the 25th. Peckinpah was studying Penn's film and wanted to see it before commencing work on his own. He knew exactly what he was doing on *The Wild Bunch* and how it related to Penn's achievements in *Bonnie and Clyde*.[22] Peckinpah's occasional lack of grace when assessing the relationships between his own filmmaking and the achievements of others has perhaps influenced scholars and critics who point to the Kurosawa connection but then emphasize that Peckinpah transcended and surpassed it by becoming the filmmaker who most fully demonstrated the expressive power of intercutting slow motion with normal-speed footage. While Peckinpah certainly did more with slow motion than Kurosawa, he did not discover any aesthetic principles that were not already contained in Kurosawa's work. In this respect, Kurosawa was the stylistic mentor, Peckinpah the disciple. Penn was far more gracious in acknowledging Kurosawa's importance for the multispeed montage that caps *Bonnie and Clyde*. Discussing his conceptualization of that scene, he remarked, "Having seen enough Kurosawa by that point, I knew how to do it."[23]

If Peckinpah did not discover anything new about intercutting slow-motion shots into a montage sequence, he undeniably extended and built upon the principles informing Kurosawa's editing of multicamera footage. Like Penn's use of slow motion within the bloody montage that concludes *Bonnie and Clyde*, which Penn said conveyed "both the spastic and the balletic" qualities of the gangsters' death agonies,[24] Peckinpah's editing emphasized the brutality of physical violence while also giving it a graceful beauty. This contradiction between the aesthetic beauty of the visual spectacle and the emotional and physical pain that Peckinpah also dramatized as part of his screen violence is a complex and important one, and we will return to it later in the chapter. For now, an instructive comparison with Penn's films can help illuminate why the slow-motion inserts in Peckinpah's films are more striking and achieve a more heightened stylistic intensity than do Penn's.

Penn began to explore slow motion in *The Left-Handed Gun* (1958), about the legend of Billy the Kid, during the scene where Billy (Paul Newman) kills Deputy Ollinger (Denver Pyle), a scene that Peckinpah closely re-creates in *Pat Garrett and Billy the Kid.* It is important to note here that Penn's film contains numerous images and bits of business that Peckinpah borrowed for his own film, including the Christ pose Billy adopts when Garrett arrests him following the Stinking Springs shoot-out. Both films also reference the fascinated reaction of children to violent death, a major Peckinpah preoccupation. In Penn's film, a little girl runs out and laughs at the dead Ollinger, who has been blown out of his boot, while Peckinpah's film shows kids playing and laughing on the gallows that has been erected for Billy. And, again, much of this can be traced back to Kurosawa, who in *Seven Samurai* had shown children playing and climbing on the fortress walls built to protect the village from the bandits and across which much killing would occur.

When Billy shoots Ollinger, Penn cuts from a slow-motion shot of Ollinger waving his arms and starting to fall backwards to a fast-motion shot of his body hitting the ground. The transition from slow to fast motion is abrupt, and as a stylistic design it is clearly an experimental effort. "I was just playing with the medium," says Penn.[25] The experimentation doesn't work very well because the action rendered in slow motion—Ollinger flailing his arms—is not effectively suited for the temporal manipulation. It is neither balletic nor spastic. By contrast, in *Bonnie and Clyde,* Penn more shrewdly incorporates slow motion by intercutting it at multiple points with the jerky convulsing of the gangsters as they are riddled with bullets. By alternating between slow and apparently accelerated tempos (the apparent acceleration produced at normal film speed by virtue of the Texas Rangers' fast rate of fire), Penn successfully brings out the balletic and spastic qualities of the scene. Furthermore, Penn switches to slow motion at a more judicious moment than in *The Left-Handed Gun.* After a quick series of glances between Bonnie and Clyde that conveys their awareness of what is about to happen, Clyde runs toward Bonnie at which point they are raked with machine gun fire. As Clyde starts to fall, Penn switches to slow motion for the first time so that the arc of Clyde's dying fall is poetically extended.

The imagery is extremely vivid, and it discloses a fundamental principle that Peckinpah would observe in his own films: slow motion is especially powerful when it correlates with a character's loss of physical volition. Clyde's dying arc; the trajectories of falling, dying men shot from the rooftops of San Rafael or the army personnel blasted off the flatcars of the train in *The Wild Bunch;* the Gorch brothers dead on their feet but kept up con-

Before perfecting slow motion in *Bonnie and Clyde,* Arthur Penn began to explore its potential for stylizing action in *The Left-Handed Gun* during the scene where Billy the Kid (Paul Newman) shoots Deputy Ollinger. Inspired by Penn's visualization, Peckinpah re-created this scene in *Pat Garrett and Billy the Kid,* but with a more successful use of slow motion.

vulsively by the impact of bullets fired by Mapache's men; Holly's mortal fall, blasted backward across the saloon by the force of Pat Garrett's shot; Lt. Triebig's grotesque writhing under Steiner's machine gun fire in *Cross of Iron*—all of these slow-motion images derive their poetic force from the metaphysical paradox of the body's continued animate reactions during a moment of diminished or extinguished consciousness. Slow motion intensifies this paradox by prolonging it. It is not just the moment of violent death which is extended, but the mysteries inherent in that twilit zone between consciousness and autonomic impulse, that awful moment when a personality ceases to inhabit a body that is still in motion. Peckinpah, and Penn, intensified the trauma of violent death by visualizing this loss of human volition in a tangle of rioting flesh and nerve. To achieve maximum intensity on this point, it was necessary to employ extremely fast camera speeds, for only by slowing down the action could the metaphysical poetry of these scenes be elicited. This is why the slow-motion insert in *The Left-Handed Gun* does not work very well. The slow speed is not slow enough, and Ollinger has not yet lost control of his body.

As we can now see, ample precedent existed in the films of Kurosawa and Penn for the stylistic inflections that Peckinpah would explore. However, with characteristic solipsism, Peckinpah claimed to have gained insight into the cinematic usage of slow motion through personal experience. He got into the habit of telling interviewers that during his military service in China in 1945 he realized how slow motion might apply to such scenes after seeing a Chinese passenger shot while riding on a train. Peckinpah called it one of the longest split seconds of his life.[26] On other occasions when he told the story of learning about slow motion, it was he who had been shot: "I was shot once and I remembered falling down and it was so long . . . I noticed that time slowed down and so I started making pictures where I slowed down time, because that's the way it is."[27] We should be very skeptical of these claims, because they sound like retrospective attempts to justify a stylistic inflection in the face of hostile critical reception (criticism that Peckinpah's slow motion was self-indulgent) by attributing to the style an empirical and phenomenological foundation in personal experience.

If, as he claims, Peckinpah's slow motion has its basis in real perceptual experience, then—and this is the implied message to his critics—he is no exploiter and glorifier of screen violence but merely an observer of the psychological reality of living through a violent experience. But, phenomenologically, there seems no necessity for equating the vividness of a brief traumatic episode with a subjective sense of extended duration. This may occur, and perhaps it did for Peckinpah, but it does not seem to be a necessity. It seems more likely that Peckinpah was struck by the stylistic manipulations of Kurosawa and Penn, began trying them himself, and subsequently projected his World War II memory onto the results. Through their montage structures, Peckinpah's films effect a formal transformation of violence, not an imitation of its psychological contours. These montages may incorporate psychological dimensions of meaning, as we shall see, but they function as aesthetic translations of the idea of violence, not as mimetic constructions that seek to imitate faithfully the contours of an experience. The complexity of these formal transformations constitutes one of Peckinpah's claims to being a great filmmaker, not his dubious assertions about the psychological basis of his slow-motion editing.

Slow-Motion Inserts

Peckinpah's aesthetic transformation of violence through montage led him toward three principal types of montage construction: the relatively simple, slow-motion insert crosscut into the body of a normal-tempo sequence; the synthetic superimposition of multiple lines of action with radical time-space distortions in a montage set-piece; and montages approaching Eisenstein's notion of intellectual editing, wherein the viewer is moved to cognitively grasp psychological or social truths. Let us now examine each of these modes in turn, beginning with the first and simplest.

Slow-motion inserts crosscut into the body of a normal-tempo sequence may be found in all of Peckinpah's post-*Dundee* films. Even *The Ballad of Cable Hogue,* distinguished by its use of fast-motion footage and general absence of montage-based violence, opens with a Mexican beaded lizard (subbing for an iguana) exploding from gunfire in a slow-motion shot (followed by a three-frame "subliminal" flash) that is inserted (but not crosscut) into the body of an otherwise normal-tempo sequence. It is easy enough to locate similar moments in the other films. As previously noted, Holly's backward lurch in *Pat Garrett and Billy the Kid,* after Garrett shoots him, describes a beautiful, slow-motion arc across the saloon floor and is cut into this scene, which is otherwise free of such temporal distortions. *The Wild Bunch's* train heist is edited, for the most part, without temporal distortions, but when Pike throws the engineer and a crewman off the locomotive, the editing crosscuts their falling bodies, in slow motion, with the dying falls of the two soldiers Lyle Gorch shoots off the front of the train. In *Straw Dogs,* when the thuggish Tom Hedden (Peter Vaughan) blasts Major Scott (T.P. McKenna) with his shotgun, three shots crosscut with other action in the scene show Scott's misshapen body flying backwards with slow-motion grace. In *The Killer Elite,* when professional killer George Hansen (Robert Duvall) executes Vorodny (Helmut Dantine), three slow-motion close-ups of Dantine falling onto the couch are crosscut with normal-tempo close-ups of Hansen watching this action. In the next scene, when Hansen cripples his friend Mike Locken (James Caan) by shooting him in the elbow and knee, Locken convulses in normal time but rolls off the stool onto the floor in slow motion.

We could continue to multiply examples, but the essential point should be clear. One of Peckinpah's basic montage structures involves the sudden intrusion of one or more slow-motion details inserted or crosscut into the body of a sequence whose temporal rhythms are otherwise normal. The perceptual shock of such intrusions comes from the sudden disruption of ordinary time through the influx of an alternate mode of time. In most cases, when squib work is involved, the explosion of blood is not the main focus of the slow-motion insert. While the detonating squibs (electrical firing devices used to simulate bullet hits) were certainly shocking for audiences in 1969 when Peckinpah unleashed them, the bulk of the visual attention in the slow-motion inserts is devoted, as previously noted, to the body's loss of volitional control over its actions. The exploding squib behind Vorodny's head when Hansen shoots him is one of Peckinpah's most elaborate and graphically bloody, but it is only a few frames long, so that it appears as a flash cut despite occurring in slow motion. The aftereffects—Vorodny's slow fall onto the couch—take up much more screen time. Paul Seydor points out that Peckinpah purposely kept his slow-motion shots brief: "It is the build-up and the release that he wanted to capture, because perception and feeling, violence as psychological effect, are what chiefly interested him."[28]

While this is certainly true for such scenes as Vorodny's killing or, more remarkably, Garrett's killing of the Kid, the presence of extended, violent set-pieces in *The Wild Bunch, Straw Dogs, Bring Me the Head of Alfredo Garcia, Cross of Iron, The Killer Elite,* and *The Osterman Weekend* demonstrate that the act of violence, in itself, exerted tremendous fascination for Peckinpah. While I will argue in the next chapters that Peckinpah's work is distinguished by the emotional and self-reflective frameworks it builds around the violence that it depicts, Peckinpah was also obsessive about this concern for violence and enthralled by the possibilities that cinema offers for visualizing it. His interests included the build-up and release of tension, the psychological effects of violent action, as well as the action and act of killing itself, only part of which is visualized in the squib work.

The simplest of these cinematic possibilities lies in the momentary disruption of time by the brief, slow-motion insert placed to accentuate the lyrical appearance of the human body acted upon by violent physical forces that have extinguished its ability to respond in an intentional manner. It seems most probable that Peckinpah kept his slow-motion imagery brief not because he was interested exclusively in the psychological effects of violence, but rather because it worked best that way from a visual standpoint. Brevity accentuates the poetic effects of slow motion. Too much slow motion, or for too extended a period, would rob the scenes of their kinetic charge and their physical edge by making the action seem like it is occurring underwater or in a strange condition of weightlessness. By quickly (i.e., briefly) puncturing normal time and space with the slow-motion imagery, Peckinpah could stress the balletic beauty that, as a film-maker, he discovered he could create within a maelstrom of death, and he could retain the sharp edge of physicality that was essential to his didactic intention.

This physicality is communicated by the normal-tempo images, not the slow-motion inserts, and by the sound effects that sensuously detail the thud of bullets into flesh, the violent exhalation of breath, shattering pottery, or crashing glass. When one of the outlaws is shot from his horse in the opening massacre of *The Wild Bunch,* we see rider and horse fall in beautiful slow motion. Because the pair's falls are so extended and the rate at which man and animal strike the ground is so gradual, the spill, as an image, lacks physical dimension. But on the soundtrack, as the horse goes down we hear a loud cracking sound like a bone breaking, and this gives the image a concreteness that the slow motion has removed from it. Peckinpah used the expressive poetry of slow motion to elicit balletic effects and to visualize that moment when death or grievous wounding robs or threatens to rob the body of its spirit or personality. He was striking a delicate balance between the slow-motion inserts and the normal-tempo continuum of the sequence proper. Too much slow motion would become ludicrous because it would bog down the violent outburst and remove all sense of its physical consequences. Slow motion, therefore, had to exist in a state of tension with the normal-tempo soundtrack and body proper of the sequence. Extended slow-motion imagery would not create this requisite tension. Slow motion had to constitute a brief interlude, disrupting the texture of the scene to offer a privileged glimpse at the metaphysical mysteries of violent death. Too long a glimpse and its effects would be vitiated.

Peckinpah rarely employed extended slow-motion imagery. In the climax of *Straw Dogs* when David Sumner (Dustin Hoffman) grapples with Charlie Venner following the shooting of Norman Scutt (both Venner and Scutt are members of the gang that has invaded the Sumners' house), Peckinpah presented their struggle in a lengthy series of slow-motion shots. It is an interesting usage, but it softens the hard edge the film's violence has heretofore had. The viewer feels that little harm can come to either David or Charlie while they slog slowly around as if underwater. Significantly, when David brings the mantrap down on Charlie's head, the film reverts to normal speed. Furthermore, because the slow-motion shots have lasted an uncommonly long time, the transition back out, to normal tempo, feels abrupt and harsh. The paradoxical thing about the brief slow-motion inserts that typify Peckinpah's work is that they mesh so well with the ordinary temporal continuum. When the insert is brief, the editor can slip into and out of the decelerated moment in a highly fluid manner. Despite the temporal disruption, strong continuity prevails, unlike the just-described scene from *Straw Dogs* where the return to normal time occasions a perceptible loss of continuity.

Slow-motion images are not of themselves dynamic. Their tendency is toward inertia, a deceleration not only of represented time but of the internal rhythms and pacing of the sequence in which they appear. They become dynamic with reference to their surrounding context—the normal-tempo actions against which they play as stylistic opposites. By maximizing this opposition, Peckinpah and his editors could give the slow-motion inserts a dynamism which they do not in themselves possess. Intercutting slow motion with normal speed became an essential and highly effective way of achieving this. When two thugs in *Bring Me the Head of Alfredo Garcia* lose control of their station wagon, it skids off the road, churning up a huge spray of dirt. This is rendered in two slow-motion shots that are crosscut with the startled reactions of passengers on a passing bus. The decelerated action of the skid is slowed down so much that the resulting images seem robbed of nearly all movement, which heightens the dynamic contrast with the normal-tempo imagery. The viewer experiences a perceptual shock because of this radical misalignment between the alternate tempos. Intercutting the two accentuates the misalignment and the dynamic contrast and works against the tendency for slow motion to create inertia and a brake on the action.

Later in that film, when the protagonist, Bennie (Warren Oates), ambushes these thugs and shoots them, Peckinpah had his editors crosscut three slow-motion shots of one thug's dying fall with normal-tempo images of Bennie exchanging fire with the other. Peckinpah's most effective uses of slow motion almost always occured with this kind of intercutting. As we have noted, when Weddle discusses Peckinpah's editing, he refers generally to his "weaving of slow motion into the very fabric of a sequence."[29] Though Weddle does not discuss how this occurs, we can now see that it occurs through a brief but sustained contrasting or crosscut series of shots that accentuate different modes of time. The dynamic qualities of the technique lie in the accentuation of these differences. To achieve this accentuation, it is imperative that the represented actions—a skidding car, a shooting victim flung backwards—be ones that explicitly occur with, and denote, speed or force. This, in conjunction with the cross-cutting, sets up two types of opposition within the editing. The slow motion is set into a relation of striking opposition with the normal tempo of the surrounding imagery, and, internally, the slow-motion shots by themselves contradict the viewer's narrative understanding of the speed at which these events are actually occurring.

When Peckinpah's slow-motion inserts fail to observe either of these principles, and when there is an insufficient narrative context supporting the device, the dynamic force of the technique is diminished. Near the end of *Alfredo Garcia,* when Bennie guns down a pair of corrupt executives and their hired guns in the El Camino Real hotel suite, he steps in front of a mirror (more on mirrors in Chapter 4) to drill his last opponent. Peckinpah showed this man flung backwards against a table and chair and crashing to the floor in a single, rather extended slow-motion shot. Because this action is not crosscut with normal-tempo shots of Bennie's reactions or any other ongoing activity, and because it lasts too long, the deceleration of time here becomes what it rarely ever does in Peckinpah's films—a simple slowing down. It is nondynamic because it has minimal structural relationship with the surrounding material. A much better set of isolated slow-motion inserts occurs in *Straw Dogs* when Major Scott is shotgunned by Tom Hedden. The inserts acquire considerable force by virtue of the narrative context. Scott is the narrative's chief authority figure, and with him dead, the viewer knows that all hell is about to break loose as the gang of thugs converges on the Sumners' house.

Peckinpah incorporated the brief slow-motion interlude into his more complex montage sequences because the dynamic oscillation between normal and decelerated time demands a continuing perceptual reorientation from viewers. He apparently hoped the stylistic artifice would alternately immerse viewers in the spectacle on screen and then realign their perspective through the nonrealistic slow-motion insertions. These perceptual realignments he hoped would re-establish a new, less complacent and passive relationship between viewers and the screen spectacle, would, as he put it, wake viewers up to what violence is really all about.

This functional intent was in addition to the other uses to which he put slow motion, which we have just reviewed: to create a temporal dialectic across the body of a scene; to interrupt the concrete physicality of violence with more abstract contemplations of its balletic and metaphysical aspects; and to shuttle between these concrete and abstract dimensions in a way that would superimpose them on top of each other. Before evaluating the extent to which his montage editing of different film speeds successfully establishes a new viewing position for film spectators, we need to explore how Peckinpah incorporated slow motion into more elaborate montages that work as extended violent set-pieces. These extended spectacles of death and destruction appear, of course, in *The Wild Bunch* and *Straw Dogs* and, to a lesser extent, in *Alfredo Garcia, The Killer Elite, Cross of Iron,* and *The Osterman Weekend.*

Extended Montage Set-Pieces

As we have seen, the editing of the opening and closing battles in *The Wild Bunch* has been compared to the Odessa Steps scene in Eisenstein's *Potemkin.*[30] Yet despite their more exhilarating quality, they lack the enormous structural variety and richness that characterize the Eisenstein sequence. Like that sequence, however, these scenes in *The Wild Bunch* take what exists in the narrative as linear, separate lines of action (e.g., each member of the Bunch separately trying to escape the ambush, the bounty hunters picking their targets, and the panicked reactions of the pedestrians caught in the cross fire) and integrate them as a synthesized collage of activity. The film's editor, Lou Lombardo, remarked that, following Peckinpah's advice, he

> intercut all the separate lines of action. I might start with this guy being hit, then cut to that guy being hit, cut to this guy falling, that guy still falling, then cut to somebody else over there getting hit, to a horse spinning over there, somebody going through a window there, and then back to the first guy just landing on the ground. I meshed it. I took every piece of action and intercut it with another.[31]

Indeed, the shot lists that survive among Peckinpah's papers, corresponding to the opening and closing shoot-outs in San Rafael and Agua Verde, present a linear and chronological list of images.

25. Three soldiers shooting from arches and are killed by Tector's rifle fire from small room.
26. Close on Eppers roll off into barrels.
27. Soldiers charge through door and dining area and are driven back by machine gun fire.
28. POV of buzzard.

29. Close on three soldiers being killed in open door over explosion area by Tector's rifle fire. They are replaced by six soldiers that are killed by machine gun fire.

30. Close on six soldiers charging across roof in front of small wall. They are killed by machine gun fire.

31. Close cuts of soldiers shooting from various positions killing Pike and Dutch.

32. High fall with dummy.

33. Simulated high fall with arri on shock cord into Gorch.

34. Close on machine gun fire crossing wall and into roof of kiosk.[32]

As Lombardo's description indicates, and as a careful viewing of the film demonstrates, the basic device used to mesh the lines of action is crosscutting. However, instead of a simple cutting back and forth, the lines of action are interrupted for extended periods by cutaways to other things before they resume. In its elaborate patterns of crosscutting, Peckinpah's editing performs four distinct functions. It slows down, interrupts, parallels, and returns to ongoing lines of action. These functions collectively establish the collagelike structure of the montage set-pieces, and they are clearly illustrated by a scene within the San Rafael massacre that opens *The Wild Bunch,* one that Lombardo alludes to in his description of how he meshed the lines of action. The Bunch have just robbed the depot and are being fired upon by the rooftop snipers. They return fire, hitting two victims on the rooftop. An early, written visualization of this scene differs substantially from the final montage and describes mainly a linear progression of images with little intercutting.

23. Bounty hunter Shannon rises up to fire and is hit and wounded, starts to pitch forward over the parapit [sic].

24. Another bounty hunter (who?) grabs for him, exposes himself and is hit and killed, slumps back releasing Shannon who rolls down the roof and pitches to the street.

25. Burt sees the body fall beside him and jumps on his horse racing out firing steadily until he is caught in the bounty hunter fire, causing both he [sic] and his horse to plunge through the window of the dress shop.

26. Wild Bunch:—Pike stays in the street with Dutch as the others die or mount and ride out.

Two rooftop victims, two different film speeds, and the simultaneous resolution of these lines of action. The editing in *The Wild Bunch* reconfigures space and time. Frame enlargements.

27. Then following, Frank who has been wounded while mounting, is shot while riding out and goes into a drag still clutching the bags of silver from the pay station.

28. As Frank is dragged down the street, the horse is shot down.[33]

The editing in the finished film parallels the falls of both rooftop victims by crosscutting between them, but it also interrupts these lines of action by cutting away to other, ongoing lines of action before returning to the two victims. As victim one ("Shannon" in the early shot continuity) topples forward, off the roof, the first cutaway occurs to a shot of Pike running out of the depot office. The next shot returns to a continuation of the previous action as victim one falls below the bottom of the frame line. The next three shots are all cutaways. Angel, another of the Bunch, dashes out of the depot office, returning fire as he runs. A low-angle long shot of the rooftop snipers is followed by a high-angle long shot of several of the Bunch shooting towards the snipers from inside the depot. After these three cutaways, the montage returns to victim one, and slow motion is introduced to retard the rate of his fall. The composition is very dramatic. The victim arcs against the blue sky, the slow motion suspending him weightlessly in space.

The next three shots are more cutaways, but they also introduce the fate of the second rooftop victim. In the first cutaway, a medium shot shows the Bunch firing from inside the depot. Then, in the next shot, the second rooftop victim is struck and falls forward, towards the camera. Next, a medium shot shows Angel running from the depot, firing, continuing an action introduced six shots previously. The next shot, in slow motion, returns to the first victim, continuing his lethargic descent to earth. Next, the montage cuts to the second victim still toppling forward, but not off the roof. His fall will be broken by the rooftop ledge. A medium close-up shows Deke Thorton firing from the roof. Then, in the next two shots, both victims land simultaneously, in a matched cut, victim one in the street and victim two on the rooftop ledge.

The editing reconfigures, stylistically transforms, the deaths of the two rooftop victims. The action cuts away from victim one's fall four times, initially for one shot, then for three shots, again for three shots, and finally for two shots. Two cutaways interrupt the fall of the second victim, for two shots each time. The cutaways and the use of slow motion impose a marked distortion upon the time and space of the represented action. The editing creates a false parallel between the two victims. Victim one falls off the roof in slow motion, and victim two, hit later in the sequence, falls at normal speed, yet they strike ledge and street at precisely the same moment, as the matched cut that closes off these events indicates. The editing imposes a false parallel between normal time and decelerated time. The simultaneous impact of the two victims represents an impossible time-space relationship within the sequence, yet Peckinpah and Lombardo convincingly intercut normal speed and slow motion to extend this discontinuity. This is certainly what Peckinpah meant when he rejected allegations that his work represented a greater realism, stressing instead that it stylized violence, heightened it through artistic transformation.

The elaborate montages of *The Wild Bunch* effect such an artistic transformation of space, time, and perception by rendering space and time as totally plastic and unstable entities. Time slows, stretches, folds around on itself and becomes the fourth dimension of a spatial field in which the ordinary laws of physics do not apply. When the outlaw trying to flee the rooftop sniper ("Burt" in the early visualization) crashes his horse through a storefront window, three slow-motion shots of this action are intercut with three normal-speed shots of another rider crashing to the street after his horse is shot out from under him. The cutting creates a false spatial parallel. The amount of space traversed by each rider who takes a spill is roughly the same—from saddle to ground—but the different rates of time also constitute differing spaces, since time and space alike are part of a four-dimensional continuum. By intercutting the falls of these riders in slow motion and normal speed, Peckinpah and Lombardo reconfigured space as well as time. The slow motion implies an alternate spatial field in which the reconstituted dynamics play out.

Peckinpah and Lombardo also employed the pattern of interrupting on-going lines of action with cutaways to other events in a way that is analogous with their use of slow motion—to extend the duration of the represented events and retard their completion. In the concluding shoot-out at Mapache's headquarters, the film's crowning montage set-piece, Pike bursts into a room where a woman stands, shoots into a mirrored door to kill a soldier hiding there, and is then shot by the woman on whom he had turned his back. This simple series of events is broken up and extended with a very long set of cutaways. After Pike shoots the soldier, the action cuts away from him for seventeen shots, which show, primarily, Dutch using a woman as a shield as he exchanges gunfire with Mapache's men. Then, returning to Pike, a single close-up shows him glancing outside the woman's room. A second lengthy cutaway, twenty-eight shots long, shows Lyle Gorch behind the machine gun, howling like a demon. Then the action returns to Pike, still in the room, at which point he is shot. The elaborate cutaways extend the duration of the action and thereby expand time.

As this description indicates, Peckinpah and Lombardo did not employ slow motion in any simple capacity. The slow-motion inserts are placed within a complex montage that crosscuts multiple lines of action so that the slow motion functions in concert with the extended cutaways to reconfigure time. Furthermore, the temporal manipulations include not just deceleration but also parallelism, disruption, and resumption. The resulting stylistic transcends a naturalistic presentation of violence, and it is notable that critics have discussed Peckinpah's work as if its use of bloody squibs and slow motion were more realistic than previous generations of Hollywood gunfights. It certainly is bloodier, but Peckinpah's is far from a realist's aesthetic. Peckinpah's montage set-pieces in *The Wild Bunch* work primarily on the level of form rather than by their representational content. They work as exquisitely crafted artifacts that emphasize physical spectacle. Their design foregrounds the hyperkinetic spectacle so that it becomes a detachable part of the film. Although, within the narrative, complex issues of character and theme lead up to and into the slaughter at Mapache's headquarters, in terms of its montage design this scene is complete, self-contained, and utterly sufficient unto itself. For the filmmakers involved, the scene must have been a lot of fun to craft and edit. Herein lies a significant problem for the didactic uses to which Peckinpah wanted to put his screen violence. We will explore this after considering the third category of Peckinpah's montage construction, explicitly denotative or intellectual montage.

Poetic and Psychological Montages

The first two categories that we have examined do not distort the proper chronology of narrative events. They remain faithful to the chronological sequencing of events that is customary in commercial cinema. They differ from one another mainly in their degree of structural complexity, the extended montage set-pieces employing the same kind of crosscutting between different temporal modes that is found in the simpler cases whereby slow motion is briefly inserted into the body of a nonmontage sequence. By contrast, in the third category of montage, Peckinpah and his editors moved beyond strict considerations of narrative chronology and towards more poetic and psychologically expressive effects. The psychological material that organizes these montages is remarkably consistent from film to film, demonstrating that these poetic montages are not just a recurring feature of Peckinpah's style but that their use correlates with a specific representational content. We will first survey the appearance of this third montage category throughout his work, and then we will consider the connection between these montages and the violent montage set-pieces.

This third category of montage first appears in full maturity in *Straw Dogs*, but the flashback scenes in *The Wild Bunch* are embryonic signs of Peckinpah's interest in using editing to poetically transcend narrative chronology. Peckinpah dropped those flashbacks in highly strategic places in the film to suggest that, for Pike and Deke, the past interpenetrates the present, that its scars and shame are a continuing, lived reality. Deke (Robert Ryan) was an old comrade of Pike's who was captured by Pinkerton agents hired by the railroad Pike and Deke had been robbing. While partying in a bordello, Deke, sensing danger, asks Pike whether they shouldn't be more cautious and wonders how Pike can be so sure the railroad won't come after them. Pike grandly replies "Being sure is my business," at which point the Pinkertons break in. Pike escapes, but Deke is captured and imprisoned. Harrigan frees Deke on condition that he lead the bounty hunters after Pike and the Bunch.

After the massacre in San Rafael that Harrigan engineers in his ruthless effort to capture or kill the Bunch, Deke and the bounty hunters set off in pursuit. That first night, the Bunch and their pursuers are encamped at separate locations, and the film intercuts scenes that convey the thoughts of Pike and Deke. Beside separate campfires, each man reflects on the night of Deke's capture in the bordello and Pike's escape. They share the same flashback (it is intercut with shots of each man's face), and Pike's pompous assertion, "Being sure is my business," reverberates through each man's memory. By giving each man the same flashback, and having them share it at the same instant, Peckinpah asserted that the laws of consciousness, of the mind and subjectivity, transcend time and space.

This insight, and his continuing interest in it, would lead Peckinpah towards sequences of sustained cinematic brilliance in the later films, but in *The Wild Bunch* he had not yet worked out all of the implications for rendering it cinematically. Pike and Deke's shared flashback, for example, is inserted quite conventionally into the fabric of the scene, with no violations of narrative chronology. The psychological material, which the flashback discloses, has not yet begun to overwhelm and resequence narrative

Peckinpah's developing interest in poetic montages that illuminate a character's subjectivity is apparent in *The Wild Bunch*. Pike Bishop and Deke Thornton share the same flashback. Peckinpah would explore the implications of this scene throughout his later work. Frame enlargement.

as it does in the later films. Simmons reports that Peckinpah and Lombardo originally went into the flashback with straight cuts, rather than with the studio-mandated dissolves that now appear. Lombardo referred to their original cut of the flashbacks, sans dissolves, as "subliminal,"[34] and it demonstrates that Peckinpah was already thinking of moving fluidly between psychological space and the outward, physical spaces of the narrative proper. This interest, therefore, appears in incipient form in *The Wild Bunch,* where it has not yet been conjoined with the kind of poetic montage editing it would require for its fruition. The film that followed, *The Ballad of Cable Hogue,* about the seriocomic adventures of a grizzled prospector who finds water in the desert and builds a thriving business around the water hole, largely abandons the rapid, dense montage editing of *The Wild Bunch* in favor of split-screen effects and the more traditional, lap-dissolve-based montages of classic Hollywood films.

In Peckinpah's next film, *Straw Dogs,* he returned to the fluid intercutting of physical and psychological spaces that had begun to interest him in *The Wild Bunch.* The cutting throughout the film gives its scenes a nervous, edgy charge. Many compositions are de-centered, and the angular changes in camera position across succeeding shots are often disorientingly oblique. Peckinpah's editing carved space up into fragments, and these fragmentary visual spaces correlate with the charged emotional tensions among the characters. Space in the film—psychic, physical, visual—is fraught with conflict, subject to attack from without, and requiring vigilant defense.

The narrative deals with the growing animosity between an American professor, David Sumner, and a gang of rowdy workmen in a Cornish village. David has come to Cornwall with his wife, Amy (Susan George), who is native to the village. The Sumners' presence incites an escalating climate of hatred and violence that climaxes when the gang violently attacks the couple in their house. Prior to this, however, two members of the gang, Venner and Scutt, assault and rape Amy after luring David away from the house under the pretext of taking him on a hunting trip. Up until the point where Charlie Venner (and then Norman Scutt) attacks and rapes Amy, the camera remains trained on the outer world of behavior and physical action and brilliantly captures the hostile expressions and emotional dynamics among David, Amy, and the village thugs. At the point of Amy's rape, however, the film begins to explore suggestive and poetic visualizations of an individual's inner suffering in response to physical pain or violence.

As Charlie forces Amy to lie back on the sofa and begins to remove his

Peckinpah's compositional spaces in *Straw Dogs* brilliantly define the tensions among the central characters. During an argument, Amy and David Sumner are isolated from one another by the village thugs who, in the composition as in the narrative, come between them. The camera's low angle and the ceiling on the set add to the oppressiveness of the physical space. Frame enlargement.

shirt, the editing intercuts shots of Charlie with images of David, Amy's husband, and this intercutting establishes a psychological association between the two characters from Amy's point of view. This association does not exist in the scene as written in the script. There, it plays as a more distanced, third-person perspective. In the script, the rape scene is interrupted with descriptions of David on the moor where Charlie and Norman have abandoned him after he accompanies them on a bogus hunting trip.[35] The alternation in the script between these two scenes suggests that the crosscutting of this material in the finished film had already been anticipated in preproduction. However, the complex flash intercutting of the subjective montage (unscripted) that we will examine here is crucial in determining point of view in the scene and in understanding its inner psychological dynamics. During filming, Peckinpah's choices of lenses and camera angles established the action from an interior point of view (Amy's terrified response to what is occurring). During editing, he used the poetic, associative intercutting of Charlie and David to clarify the similarities in

treatment of Amy and to capture her emotional grasp of
Peckinpah's instructions to his editors stressed the need
e associative connection between Charlie and David: "Re-
vid in bed in between flash cuts of Venner and Amy. Add at
wo cuts of David in bed with Amy before cutting to him
ningle the shots of David in bed and David outside with the
dition, Peckinpah instructed his editors, "As Venner kisses
Amy, go to shot of David, as Venner pulls away. Then go back to Venner
straightening up, hold longer. Then back to David for longer cut, then
back to c/u of Amy."[37]

A close inspection of the shot series within the rape sequence where
this associative intercutting occurs reveals several interesting features of
design. A rapid series of shots conveys Amy's welling terror and her rushing thoughts as she makes the connections between David and Charlie.
The series is composed of twenty-seven shots which run just under eleven
seconds. The shot breakdown is as follows:

1. Charlie removes his sweater. A low-angle view representing Amy's
   perspective as she lies beneath him. 25 frames.
2. David removes his undershirt. A low-angle view representing Amy's
   perspective in an earlier scene as she lies beneath him before they
   make love. 20 frames.
3. Close-up of Charlie's face as his sweater comes off. Low angle. 23
   frames.
4. High-angle view of Amy's breasts, representing Charlie's perspective.
   7 frames.
5. Medium long shot of David sitting on a rock. The image derives from
   David's present location in the narrative while the rape occurs. Charlie and Norman have lured David away from the house by taking
   him on a bogus hunting trip, then abandoning him. 9 frames.

(facing page, and continued on page 78)

The rape scene in *Straw Dogs* is presented as a subjective montage from Amy's anguished perspective during which she associates her husband with the rapist. These
frame enlargements represent shots 23–27 as described in the text.

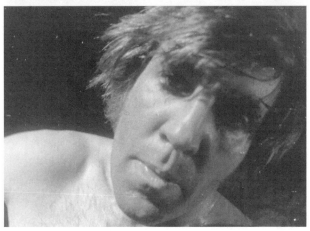

6. Low-angle close-up of Charlie's face as his arm comes down. 15 frames.

7. High-angle view of Amy's breasts. 6 frames.

8. Low-angle view of David after he has removed his undershirt. 13 frames.

9. Low-angle close-up of Charlie's face. 15 frames.

10. Close-up of Charlie unfastening his belt. 11 frames.

11. Extreme close-up of Amy's face, terrorized. 6 frames.

12. Close-up of Charlie unfastening his belt. 11 frames.

13. Low-angle close-up of Charlie's face. 15 frames.

14. Extreme close-up, Amy's face, terrorized. 7 frames.

15. Medium long shot of David sitting on a rock. 14 frames.
16. Close-up Charlie's hand on his zipper. 4 frames.
17. Extreme close-up, low angle, Charlie's face, distorted via a wide angle lens. 4 frames.
18. Extreme close-up, Amy's face, terrorized. 4 frames.
19. Low-angle view of David after he has removed his undershirt. 6 frames.
20. Extreme close-up, low angle, Charlie's face, distorted via a wide angle lens. 4 frames.
21. Extreme close-up, Amy's face, terrorized. 4 frames.
22. Medium shot of David on rock. 10 frames.
23. Close-up Amy gasping under Charlie. 16 frames.
24. Extreme close-up, low angle, Charlie's face, distorted via wide angle lens. 4 frames.
25. Extreme close-up, Amy's face, terrorized. 4 frames.
26. Low-angle view of David without undershirt. 3 frames.
27. Extreme close-up, low angle, Charlie's face, distorted via wide angle lens. 3 frames.

All of the low-angle shots in this series represent Amy's physical perspective on the action, and Peckinpah used the optical design of the shots to convey the interior components of her perspective. The most explicit depiction of Amy's horrified response to Venner is conveyed in a series of four low-angle close-ups in which Venner leans into the camera, accentuating the wide-angle distortions of his face. In this case, the angular distortion becomes a metaphoric embodiment of Amy's frenzied perceptions, of the fear and revulsion that possess her and through which she sees Venner.

Amy's escalating fears are also captured in the rapid pace of the editing. What would be an otherwise ordinary pattern of crosscutting between Charlie and Amy opens out, instead, into an associational montage by virtue of the seven images of David which are interposed in the body of the sequence. The association of David and Charlie is especially explicit in shots 1–2, 8–9, and 26–27, where matching compositional elements create a strong link between the images. The extended series 17–22 accentuates and reinforces the association by virtue of its duration across six shots. Note also the extremely rapid pace of the editing. Most of the shots in this series 17–22 are one-sixth of a second in duration.

In this respect, shots 24–27 are especially striking. The four shots together last just over one-half second, and the last two are only three frames long (one-eighth second each). The rate of cutting here, especially shots 26–27, is below the minimum duration a viewer needs to recognize the image on screen. Peckinpah and his editors had to know that a three-frame shot was much too brief to permit a viewer to clearly see the pictured image. It is, therefore, tempting to speculate that their edits here were intended to be subliminal. It is precisely the association between David and Charlie, conveyed in shots 26–27, three frames each, that operates at this "subliminal" level. A viewer watching the scene cannot see these images, not in a way that permits recognition of their content. Throughout the series until this point, Peckinpah showed Amy's perception of the link between David and Charlie. Each man treats Amy with emotional and physical brutality, and she "sees" her husband in the moment when Charlie undresses before raping her. By virtue of their extraordinarily brief duration, shots 26–27 seem designed to make the association between the men in the viewer's mind's eye, as well. These shots are no longer just visualizing Amy's psychological perspective but are also working now on the viewer, subliminally extending Amy's perceptions of that David-Charlie link to the viewer. In point of fact, there is little experimental evidence that demonstrates the effectiveness of subliminal editing. But the design of the sequence does suggest that a concept of subliminal editing guided some of the cutting, specifically the concluding association of David and Charlie. Peckinpah would refer to such images as "flash cuts."

After her rape, Amy attends the church social with David and keeps reliving the rape when she sees Charlie and Norman, her attackers, at the function. The intercutting here, scenes of the church social alternating with Amy's subjective perceptions of the rape, counterpoints the outer world with Amy's traumatized inner self. The nausea and horror that she feels, conveyed in the reprised rape imagery, erupts onto the sights and sounds of the church social, which themselves become ever more raucous and disturbing as symptoms of Amy's anxieties. Internal psychological material explodes onto the outer social stage as the intermixing of the outer and inner frames of perception achieves a density and complexity beyond even the earlier associations conveyed during the rape montage and well beyond the flashback material in *The Wild Bunch*. The subjective design of the church social scene was not scripted. The film's shooting script does not visualize Amy's distress in the manner that assumes such striking proportions in the finished film.[38]

In the script, the visual and emotional perspective is entirely third person. In shooting the scene, however, and especially in editing it, Peckinpah devoted considerable attention to Amy's anguish and gradually intensified the subjective components of the scene until her anxieties, visualized in the crosscutting between Charlie and Norman as they appear in the church hall and as they appeared to her during the rape, become the emotional center of the scene. The design emphasizes Amy's pain and terror at meeting her attackers again and in such proximity. As such, the scene takes the point of view of the distraught victim of violence rather than the perpetrators. This is a significant point that bears on a frequent criticism of the film—namely, that it treats Amy in a harsh and misogynistic way. (We will take up this issue in the next chapter.) Peckinpah's instructions to his editors demonstrate how this design was elaborated in the editing and how important he considered the visualization of her distress to be. "Use two flash cuts of Amy and then go back to Janice. 'You've never worked a day in your life Tom,' group laughs, then insert two more flash cuts of Amy."[39]

The cutting is extremely quick throughout the scene, with many shots less than one second in duration. Some of the briefest images, as we will see, qualify as subliminal edits because they are far too quick for the viewer to consciously apprehend. The sights and sounds of the church social are organized around Amy's anguished state of mind, and their increasingly noisy and disturbing qualities are subjectivized externalizations of her fear and despair. The editing makes her suffering palpable through the image juxtapositions and through the rate and rhythm of the cutting. As the dominant focus organizing the scene's visual design, Amy's subjective point of view is foregrounded from the moment she enters the hall. As she walks in with David, she sees her attackers, Charlie and Norman, among the crowd through which she has to pass. Peckinpah used his multicamera approach to shoot the scene, and when Amy passes by Norman, Peckinpah cut to an extreme telephoto perspective in which Norman's back, as the foreground element, obscures the frame except for a small area on the left in which Amy is visible. The focal length of the lens creates a composition of domination and entrapment. Peckinpah then switched away from this extreme telephoto perspective as Amy walks by Charlie and Norman. An image from the rape appears, Charlie slapping her, in a twelve-frame (one-half second) superimposition alongside her face as she passes by them. Their proximity to her in the church hall is a torture, and it reintensifies the violence that they had inflicted upon her.

Amy seats herself with David as the noise in the hall, principally from children with toy noisemakers, becomes thoroughly abrasive. The first series of flash inserts occurs as Amy turns to look behind her and sees Norman and Charlie lounging against the wall. The series of shots is composed of:

1. Norman thrusting brutally into her from behind during the rape. 7 frames.
2. A boy in the church hall with noisemaker. 4 frames.
3. Charlie holding Amy down as Norman rapes her. 10 frames.
4. The boy with the noisemaker. 8 frames.
5. Charlie holding Amy down. 6 frames.

After this series which Amy "sees" when she looks back at Norman and Charlie, she turns away from them and faces forward in her seat. The images demonstrate that Amy's anxieties are being aroused not just from the memory of the rape but by her present surroundings. The children's noisemakers—rolled paper tubes they blow into and which become elongated and erect when making noise—assume an increasingly phallic quality. Amy makes this association, as the intercutting of the boy with the noisemaker and her rape images indicates. Furthermore, the association for her is a subliminal one, not one that she consciously notices but one that produces anxiety, nevertheless. The four-frame shot of the boy is a subliminal edit that viewers do not consciously notice because the flash is too quick. In this way, Peckinpah showed Amy's distress as displaced onto her surroundings, and he aligned the viewer's experience of the images with hers.

The next overtly subjective montage occurs when Amy turns again to look behind her and sees Norman surrounded by Riddaway, another member of the gang, and Charlie. Norman now has a phallic-appearing noisemaker, with fringe dangling from its tube and a balloon on the end. The montage, more elaborate, is composed of these shots:

(facing page)

After the rape, Amy's trauma and anxieties erupt during the church social as the editing again replicates her anguished perspective. These frame enlargements represent shots 2–4 as discussed in the text.

1. Norman unbuckling his belt during the rape. 9 frames.
2. Two children with noisemakers jutting toward the camera. 13 frames.
3. Norman in the church hall blowing into his noisemaker and inflating its balloon. 17 frames.
4. Amy's anguished face, in the church hall. 7 frames.
5. Norman unfastening his pants during the rape. 5 frames.
6. Amy's terrorized face, in extreme close-up, as Norman enters her from behind. 15 frames.
7. Norman with the noisemaker. 11 frames.
8. Children at a table in the church hall. 11 frames.

After this series, as before, Amy turns to face forward. Note that only three of these eight shots are from the rape itself, but the others contain the phallic noisemakers that have become generalized signs of Amy's trauma and help reawaken it. Thus, though most of the shots in the series are not of the rape itself, Amy's sexual terror is a component of the entire series. The feelings the rape has generated within her wash across the entire set of images in the montage. The entire series thus becomes an index of her subjectivity, as Peckinpah used editing to probe the psychic consequences of this sexual violence for its victim. To accomplish this, he called for a re-sequencing of certain shots to better emphasize those figures, like Norman Scutt, who hold a special salience for Amy. "Use the cut of Scutt standing in the crowd before you use the cut of Riddaway and Scutt together in the crowd, i.e., switch these two shots around, and intercut with David and Amy with the boys running past them."[40] As the noise of the gathering continues and Amy's agitation increases, she finally stands as if to leave. She sees, again, Charlie and Norman by the exit where she will have to pass, and pauses. Here Peckinpah intercut a twelve-frame insert from the rape showing Amy screaming in pain as Charlie holds her down so Norman can rape her.

The flash inserts from the rape are placed in three more places in the scene as additional signs of Amy's fear and sickness. The first occurs as Janice Hedden walks away from David, with whom she has tried to flirt, despite the fact that Amy is next to him. The Rev. Barney Hood, on stage, has just finished his newspaper trick in which he tears the paper in half only to make it reappear intact at the end of the act. As he tells the audience, "I think you'll find it hasn't been torn at all," his reference to tearing unleashes Amy's re-experience of the rape. His remark accompanies—

is heard "inside"—the image of Venner on top of Amy (13 frames). The scene then cuts to a shot of Amy's contorted face as she sits in the church hall (16 frames), followed by another shot of the rape (9 frames), then a cut to Barney on stage (13 frames), then to Amy's face (24 frames), then to a shot of Janice walking toward Henry Niles (16 frames), then back to Amy (19 frames), then to a musician in the church band (19 frames), then back to Amy (32 frames).

This extended series of shots creates a rush of disparate images that embodies the flood of memory and panic that engulfs Amy. Note that the rape images only correspond to two out of these ten shots. The others show that her anguish is generalizing well beyond the rape to include also the villagers assembled in the hall. The rape has altered Amy's relationship to her native village and its denizens whose presence for her is now unwelcome, oppressive, and fraught with tension. Previously at ease with the people of her village, Amy now feels estranged from them. Furthermore, the longest shot lengths in this series correspond to the close-ups of Amy's face and her desperate unhappiness. Peckinpah used the rhythm and duration of his shots to accentuate, and enable the viewer to understand, the nature and the dimensions of Amy's distress.

The next set of flash inserts occurs when Barney begins his glass trick during which the empty glass is magically filled with milk. Chris Cawsey, one of the gang, asks if it would work better with whiskey, precipitating Barney's exchange with Tom Hedden (the gang's patriarch) that Peckinpah referenced in the notes to his editor. Tom says he works better with whiskey, to which Barney replies, "You've never worked a day in your life, Tom." As the audience laughs at Tom, the scene cuts to this series:

1. Medium close-up of Amy's face, tense and tormented, as she sits in the church hall. 42 frames.
2. Flash image of the rape. 10 frames.
3. Amy's face, tormented. 14 frames.
4. Flash image of the rape. 9 frames.
5. Amy's face, tormented. 35 frames.

Once again, the longest shots are those which attend to her facial expressions as she tries to contain her feelings. As the trick is concluded moments later, Barney displays the glass now full of milk and says "If I convert you to this, Tom, that would be a miracle." The series of shots that follows includes the last of the subliminal rape imagery used in this scene. A shot of Tom laughing is followed by:

1. Amy's tormented face as she sits in the church hall. 13 frames.
2. Venner climaxing inside her during the rape. 10 frames.
3. Amy's tormented face. 21 frames.
4. Barney on stage, saying "Thank you very much," words that resonate ironically with her re-experience of the rape. 14 frames.
5. Flash image of the rape. 6 frames.
6. Amy's tormented face. 11 frames.
7. Barney on stage, saying "Thank you." 12 frames.
8. Amy's tormented face. 86 frames.

Peckinpah creates here a kind of Kuleshovian montage that invites the viewer to contextualize Amy's facial expression in terms of the surrounding material. As before, her expression receives an extended emphasis, especially in the extraordinarily long, eighty-six-frame shot that concludes the series. (All of the close-ups of her face used in these last three subjective series correspond to footage taken with the same camera position as Amy faces the stage, and Peckinpah and his editors even "cheated" by using this footage for the seven-frame shot of Amy in the earlier series where she was supposed to be looking behind her at Norman with his balloon noisemaker.) In this last shot series that has alternated between Barney Hood on the stage and Amy in the audience, note that the intercutting plays her anguish against Barney as well as the rape itself. The Rev. Hood is pastor of the village, keeper of its moral life, and as such his presence looming on the stage above Amy inevitably calls to her mind the defilement she has experienced. Amy's alienation is now profound and multidimensional. She is estranged not only from David and, of course, from her attackers, but also from the village and its spiritual life, which has come to seem sinister and perverted. These latter perceptions are visualized and externalized in the Black Mass imagery that predominates as the church social continues. Barney is robed in black, surrounded by dark, candle-bearing acolytes, and lit from below so that the shadows that define the contours of his face are unnaturally reversed.

Through the associative editing of these scenes, Peckinpah devoted sustained attention to Amy's suffering as a consequence of the violence and cruelty that are visited upon her. This careful attention helps make the film a work about her brutalization by the men in her life rather than, as Peckinpah's critics have maintained, an expression and endorsement of that brutalization.[41] In this respect, given the popular accounts of Peckinpah's antipathy during the production toward the character Amy and the actress who played her (Susan George),[42] the film's regard for Amy's suffering and emotional pain demonstrates that either he was being disingenuous in his comments to the press or he wound up making a different film than the one he thought he was making. In any case, *Straw Dogs* marks a dramatic leap forward, beyond *The Wild Bunch,* in its use of montage to collapse first- and third-person perspectives.

In *Junior Bonner,* Peckinpah's next film, he again extended and explored the unrealized promise of the subjective, associative editing employed in *The Wild Bunch.* The cutting follows a psychologically poetic logic, informed by what Freud termed "the omnipotence of thought," the inclination of the mind to reject the onerous conditions of reality by refashioning them into more acceptable forms. In the associative montages, Peckinpah employed the expressive powers of editing to transcend chronological time and sequential space, and tied these to his characters' needs to escape or deny the bitter, oppressive conditions of their lives. Junior Bonner (Steve McQueen) is an aging rodeo cowboy whose years and lack of income are eroding his ability to stay on the rodeo circuit. He lives as what his brother Curley contemptuously calls "a motel cowboy." The film studies the strained relations among the Bonner family during one July weekend when Junior returns for the hometown rodeo. Junior's father, Ace, used to be a minor rodeo star but has frittered away his money and talents on drink and is now too old to compete against the younger riders. The world, and the rodeo, has passed Ace by, as it will Junior. An early sequence in the film visualizes the displacement of Ace (and Junior), two aging cowboys, in a modernizing world. When Junior returns to his hometown, he attempts to visit his father, but arrives just in time to see Ace's house demolished by earthmovers to make way for a tacky suburban housing project engineered by Junior's brother, Curley. As the Denver Church ranch symbolized for Peckinpah a lost part of his youth, Ace Bonner's house represents a part of Junior that is now gone forever, a tie to his father and to the old-time rodeoing to which both have dedicated their wandering lives. The loss of the house is a powerful event for Junior, and the editing of the sequence visualizes the physical and psychological effects of this destruction.[43]

After the family ranch has been demolished, Junior Bonner (Steve McQueen) looks back and sees, in his mind's eye, the bulldozing of the ranch and then the house standing inviolate. Frame enlargements.

The montage is constructed so that Junior never directly witnesses the destruction of Ace's house. He sees the earthmovers converging, but his attention is distracted by another bulldozer, closer at hand, which blocks the path through the gravel pit down which he needs to drive. As he faces this construction vehicle, the cutting shows the viewer what Junior does not see: the demolition of Ace's house, rendered as a series of brief, slow-motion inserts into the body of the sequence. When Junior at last looks back at Ace's house, it is already gone, like the Denver Church ranch was for Peckinpah. "It's all gone,"[44] Peckinpah would say mournfully about that loss. Peckinpah did not anticipate the fate of this property, which he assumed would remain within the family, and when he learned that his mother had sold it, he was quite shocked.[45] Notably, in light of this, and in resonance with it, Junior, his attention deflected, does not see what happens to Ace's house. When he does see what has occurred, it is already too late. As Junior glances at the rubble, the editing reprises the bulldozing of the house, as the reprised images illuminate a psychological condition. The film cuts from a shot of Junior glancing sadly at the flattened property to slow-motion shots of the bulldozer plowing through the resurrected dwelling. These decelerated images are intercut with new material: a shot of an old photograph kept in the house of Ace on the rodeo circuit, two shots of the house intact (as it was), two shots of Ace on horseback in a rodeo, and one shot of the mailbox ("Ace Bonner" printed on it) being flattened by a bulldozer. This reprise shows Junior's obsessive psychological replaying of the loss of the house, and it is loaded with emotionally significant images of Ace that demonstrate the multiple levels on which this event resonates for Junior. Unlike the montage sequences in *The Wild Bunch,* the reprise presents screen images of Ace and the house's destruction that are nonsynchronous with narrative chronology. They represent the omnipotence of thought as it reasserts the primacy of memory and desire over the circumstances in life that have eroded the past and produced an alienated present.

The montage showing Junior's reimagining of the destruction of Ace's house asserts a defiance of narrative chronology and, therefore, of the history that will doom both Junior and his father. They will be cast aside as irrelevancies by the valueless businessmen, like Curley Bonner, who are bringing tract housing to the desert. The montage of subjectively associated images counters the narrative that ushers in a future of alienation and dispossession for Junior by reimposing, briefly, an alternate subjectivity, a nonalienated one that sees the house intact and Ace riding tall. Like the *Straw Dogs* imagery representing Amy's agonized perceptions, the reprised images, too, issue from trauma but go well beyond the associative properties of Amy's psychological imagery to construct a more elaborate visual structure based on the antinomies of desire, narrative, and history. Amy cannot emotionally deny the brute facts of her rape. By contrast, Junior's fantasy conjures the house anew, substitutes, briefly, for the narrative in which his father's home is destroyed, and supplants the historical processes that lie behind the narrative and are bringing an end to Junior's—and Peckinpah's—West.

In *The Getaway*, his next film, Peckinpah incorporates subjective imagery into a montage during the opening credit sequence that details Doc McCoy's frustrations with the daily routines of prison life. Doc (Steve McQueen) is a professional thief who is incarcerated when the film begins but who will be paroled early in exchange for pulling another heist. This job goes sour, precipitating an extended chase as Doc tries to elude the police and the corrupt businessmen who hired him for the heist and who now want him dead. At the beginning of the film, Peckinpah intercut images showing Doc's regimented life in prison with several flash inserts of Doc and his wife, Carol, in bed, caressing each other. The inserts represent Doc's memories and a denial of his present constraints. Later in the film, when Doc is released from prison and is rejoined by his wife, he stands next to a river and "sees" himself and Carol, in slow motion, diving into the water and cavorting there. The slow-motion imagery of Doc and Carol playing in the water is intercut with shots of Doc standing on the bank so that he seems to be watching, imagining, himself and Carol frolicking in the river. The scene ends with a shot of Doc, on the bank, running toward the water and then dissolves to a shot of him and Carol, soaking wet, walking into her apartment. The event itself—Doc and Carol in the water—is displaced by the editing so that it exists primarily as a subjective vision, held by Doc as he contemplates the present web of circumstance which has ensnared him (i.e., his promise to pull a bank job in return for early release) and the possibilities of real freedom which seem just beyond his grasp. Doc's desires, visualized in the slow-motion imagery, displace the narrative proper by intruding upon the chain of events and substituting for them. While it is implied that Doc and Carol actually jumped in the river, the viewer never sees this. It is omitted by the montage. Substituted for it is Doc's fantasy of doing so.

Peckinpah next employed this subjective design in *Cross of Iron*. The narrative generally deals with German soldiers fighting inside Russia dur-

As the editing presents it, Doc and Carol's swim in *The Getaway* exists in Doc's imagination as he stands on a riverbank gazing at the water.

ing World War II and specifically with the efforts of Sergeant Steiner (James Coburn) to protect the squad of men under his command amid the fighting that surrounds them. During the German retreat before the advancing Russian army, Steiner is wounded by a battlefield explosion. Significantly, Peckinpah conveyed the trauma of Steiner's wounding with a poetic montage. As Steiner is hit by the concussion of an exploding shell, the poetic montage disrupts the clear sequencing of narrative events. The montage intercuts past, present, and future actions in a suggestive approximation of the breakdown of Steiner's consciousness by the damage his body has suffered. The montage intercuts images of Steiner recoiling and collapsing on the battlefield with shots of him conferring with his men in their barracks and catching a harmonica a Russian prisoner (a boy) throws to him just before the boy is killed. These are images reprised from earlier in the narrative. They are intercut with shots of the nurse who will attend Steiner as she enters the hospital room where he lies (he is present in the montage both on the battlefield and in the hospital) and then shines a light into his face. A line of future narrative events is intercut into the montage as well. In a panic, his physical but not his psychological wounds healing, Steiner tries to escape from the hospital, runs down to a river, and jumps in. The dead Russian boy then reappears and again tosses the harmonica at him. Subsequently, the nurse rushes into the river after Steiner.

By intercutting the battlefield and hospital imagery with the images of Steiner from prior incidents, the montage disassembles the time-space relationships of the narrative, blurring the distinctions between past, present, and future and implying that all of these coexist within the mind and through its ability to recollect the past and project a future. Steiner's pain and disorientation render these events and experiences co-present for him as Peckinpah once again employed complex montage techniques to show the interior correlates of physical violence and to convey trauma through the disruption of the temporal and spatial boundaries established by narrative. As the film progresses, Steiner and his nurse attend a banquet honoring the hospital's wounded. Seated in a wheelchair, he believes he sees one of the men from his squad dancing on the balcony. Steiner gets up from the wheelchair, walks over to this man, and finds that he is a stranger. Steiner turns away, confused, and looks off-frame right. In the cut to his point-of-view shot, Steiner sees himself still seated in the wheelchair, and as he walks back to the chair, the editing switches between shots that show Steiner alternately alone on an empty balcony and surrounded by a festive crowd. Steiner sees himself removed from his body and sees the dancehall alternately crowded with the maimed bodies of dead comrades and empty of people. Steiner lingers in a psychological twilight zone, and the dissociated imagery of himself and others that he sees while recovering from his wounds represents an effort by his shattered psyche to painfully reassemble itself in a way that negates the brutalities that have been inflicted upon it by narrative and by history.

Like the subjective imagery incorporated into montage scenes in *Straw Dogs, Junior Bonner,* and *The Getaway,* these images in *Cross of Iron* study the response of the alienated self to conditions of trauma. Unlike the other two categories of montage studied earlier in this chapter, these involve psychic pain but not violent death, and, therefore, they indicate that montage for Peckinpah was not exclusively an instrument for stylizing external, physical carnage. While it may primarily have worked for him in those terms, we can now see that he was also drawn to its resources for envisioning alternate states of consciousness that exist in defiance of a character's material circumstances. The narratives of his films tend to be about char-

Steiner's battlefield wounding in *Cross of Iron* precipitates an extended subjective montage during which, while he recuperates in a hospital, he has several out-of-body experiences as signs of his psychological alienation.

acters waging a losing gambit against events that are extinguishing the conditions of their lives, and they dramatize processes of diminishment, disillusion, compromise, and defeat. Peckinpah often found solace in the bloody, violent resistance of these characters to their defeat, and he allowed them a subjective defiance as well in the eruptions of desire and denial that transform the narratives through the poetic montages of resistant subjectivity. I do not wish to overwork a comparison with Eisenstein, for the reasons enumerated earlier. However, in a way that is loosely analogous with the Russian director's category of intellectual montage, the unexpected and resonant image juxtapositions of these montages move the viewer to search for the principle connecting Amy's association of David with Charlie or Junior's vision of Ace on horseback amid the destruction of his house. The juxtapositions do not have the programmatic ideological content of the intellectual montages in Eisenstein's films, which is probably for the best. They have a real poetic vitality rather than a textbook stiffness. They prod the viewer to search for the expressive connection that links the disparate sets of images. As we have seen, in almost every case, this connection is a psychological one issuing from the emotional pain of trauma and estrangement.

Peckinpah is not generally considered to have been a modernist director like Jean-Luc Godard or Alain Resnais. Certainly his narratives are far from the radical experimentation of their work, but his interest in using cinema to reveal fluid states of consciousness, to capture a kind of free-association of images in the minds of his characters, and his concern in using the language of cinema to dissolve the rigid boundaries between inner and outer experience—all of these are as-yet under-appreciated aspects of his work that link it with the modernist approach to filmmaking. (I will explore Peckinpah's status as a modernist more fully in Chapter 5.) Peckinpah's poetic montages of displaced subjectivity disassemble narrative, consciousness, and temporality in much the same way Resnais had done, more systematically and extensively, in *Hiroshima mon Amour* (1959). Peckinpah was clearly working within the poetic tradition exemplified by that film and other modernist works that disassemble classical narrative.

In *Pat Garrett and Billy the Kid,* Peckinpah extended the expressive, antinarrative effects of his montages beyond the strictly psychological realm to encompass social and historical ironies. The film's opening and closing scenes show the killing of Garrett as an old man, in 1909, by (it is implied) the same people who had hired him to kill Billy. The body of the film takes place in 1881 and deals with Garrett's hunt for the Kid. The film begins with a montage sequence that intercuts Garrett's murder with his meeting with Billy at Old Fort Sumner in 1881, during which he warns Billy that he will be coming for him unless Billy leaves the territory. The intercutting of these scenes is one of Peckinpah's most brilliant montages and a complex repudiation of strict narrative chronology. In 1881, when Garrett finds Billy at Fort Sumner, Billy and his gang are idly shooting the heads off chickens. The intercutting of the two time periods makes it seem like the Billy of 1881 and his gang are killing Garrett in 1909. As Garrett is led into the ambush in the 1909 frame and his assassins aim their weapons, the editing switches to the 1881 frame before a shot is fired. The shot in which Billy cocks his pistol and aims at the chickens is followed by an image of one of Garrett's assassins aiming his rifle without firing. Only when Billy, from the past, fires (at the chickens) is Garrett shown, in the present (1909), being hit by a bullet. Then one of the 1909 assassins fires, and the cut shows not Garrett but one of the chickens from 1881 with its head exploding. The editing establishes a continuity that is nonchronological, crossing time periods to follow not a sequential but a historical dynamic.

The next images continue to associate Garrett with the chickens: the shot in which he is struck by one of his assassin's bullets is followed by a shot of a chicken exploding. The audio information then begins to bridge the historical periods. Billy aims his pistol. Over an image of Garrett falling from his buggy, one member of Billy's gang can be heard remarking, "Goddamn near perfect." Within the proper narrative chronology, the remark references the chickens, but within the associations established by the montage it connects with Garrett's shooting. The next image is of Billy firing, followed by a cut to Garrett writhing in slow motion on the ground while the laughter of Billy's gang from the earlier time period is heard. In context, they are laughing at Garrett's agony. Billy then tells one of his gang, Eno, to try his luck with the chickens, and the subsequent intercutting establishes a continuity across shots that shows Garrett being hit by both his assassins and by Eno from the past. In the concluding action of the montage, in the 1881 frame Garrett rides into Fort Sumner and joins in the chicken shooting. He stands behind Billy and fires, as if he were shooting at Billy (the ironies here are multifunctional and point in several directions). Billy's men dive for cover as Garrett shoots the chickens. As Billy laughs, Garrett fires from off-screen, followed by an image of the 1909 Garrett, on the ground, writhing. Garrett's shot from the past hits him in the present. Like Steiner's out-of-body visions in *Cross of Iron* and Amy's collapsing of the identities of the two men who have most brutalized her, the imagery of Garrett firing at himself is among Peckinpah's most poetic portraits of psychological alienation. The ultimate cost of that psychological alienation for Garrett is his own death, and the narrative proper of the film details the painful process whereby Garrett becomes progressively more estranged from self and friends.

The cutting freely intermixes the two time frames to develop the historical irony of Garrett's past actions, undertaken so he could change with the country, leading to his demise in later life. The poetic associations between the two time periods, though, are not primarily psychological. Instead, the montage visualizes the historical dialectic that Peckinpah saw at work in the story of Garrett and the Kid. It was a conspiratorial view of history, influenced by the killing of JFK and the Watergate saga, that sees the machinations of those in power as labyrinthine and tending toward the use and sacrifice of pawns like Garrett. (Peckinpah pursued this conspiratorial view with greater intensity in *The Killer Elite* and *The Osterman Weekend*. The production of these films no longer coincided with the countercultural era that nourished Peckinpah's best work, but they demonstrate that he was never able to disentangle himself from the late-sixties early seventies lessons of institutional corruption and abuse at the heart of the republic.) In actuality, the circumstances surrounding Garrett's murder remain unclear, particularly its connection to the Santa Fe Ring of politicians and businessmen who may have helped engineer Garrett's hunt for the Kid.[46] But Peckinpah clearly believed that Garrett was sacrificed on the altar of progress by the men who hired him to get the Kid, and this wonderfully evocative montage sequence represents his most sustained refusal of linear narrative time, a rejection whose purpose is not primarily to explore psychological estrangement but rather to represent the inner logic of history, albeit a history that is conceived with cynical and bitter irony.

In this third category of montage, the cutting highlights the subjective experiences of trauma, psychological pain, and emotional alienation, and, in the next chapter, we will see that Peckinpah expressly associated these qualities with violence—as its human cost. The poetic montages are not primarily given to representations of violent death. It is important to recognize that Peckinpah's use of montage was multifaceted. Indeed, it is possible that he was first drawn to montage as a means of stylizing violence, of giving it a kinetic and visceral charge, and subsequently began to appreciate its abilities to manipulate the viewer's response in less kinetic, more cognitively inflected directions. This recognition is apparent in embryonic form in *The Wild Bunch,* and it develops into sequences of great and controlled skill in the later films. Here Peckinpah's poetic uses of montage enabled him to cancel, briefly, the narrative trajectories of the films that move the protagonists toward an inevitable declension and defeat. By privileging the eruption of a displaced and tormented subjectivity, Peckinpah's poetic montages briefly retard the narrative movement toward the spiritual and/or physical extinction of the protagonists. The dynamic structure of these montages, with their flux of colliding, free-associating images, is symptomatic of their antinarrative status. Their energies spread out across different modes of space and time and move simultaneously in different directions, as, for example, Doc McCoy is pulled further into the despair and regimentation of prison life and back toward an idealized past with Carol. As expressions of the characters' renegade subjectivity, the fluid, kaleidoscopic structure of these montages simulates the process of thought itself in its visually based, nonlinear, nonlinguistic components. These montages are brilliant formal embodiments of the resistant subjectivities of Peckinpah's dispossessed characters.

Herein lies the connection across the classes of montage that typify his films. The violent montages stylize and kineticize the spectacle of bloody death. They visualize the loss of volition and control over the body, its transformation into a dehumanized object, and the extinction of humanity which inheres in every violent death. Peckinpah was both fascinated and disturbed by this, and he obsessively drew closer to watch it with his telephoto lenses and decelerated it to protract the crossing of that mysterious threshold between life and death. In his poetic and cognitively inclined montages, he explored the defiant assertion of human identity, of subjectivity and desire in the face of physical and spiritual pain, the very things that can be so successful in crushing the self, destroying the psyche. The violent montages visualize the torment of physical pain and death. The poetic montages illuminate the mind's ability to stave off the excoriations of flesh and spirit by denying temporality and exigent circumstance, albeit briefly. The violent montages are externally oriented, focused on bursting flesh and convulsing bodies, which imply, in turn, the extinction of the spirits and psyches that animated those bodies. The poetic montages are internally oriented, focused on the tenacity of memory and defiant desire, which imply, in turn, the brute and alienating external world that threatens the psyche with annihilation. Peckinpah's montages dialectically oppose the inner, atemporal frame of subjective desire with the outer frame of temporal causality and physical death, illuminating the former as the antithesis of the latter, but with a tragic recognition of how inescapable is deformation of the spirit and of death as the ultimate adversary of the psyche.

Limitations of the Montage Style

Despite the stylistic brilliance of his technique, how adequately does Peckinpah's montage style meet his didactic intentions? To evaluate this question and to help illuminate what I shall later emphasize as a significant evolution of style and moral content in Peckinpah's filmmaking, we should return the focus of this discussion to *The Wild Bunch*. As we have seen, Peckinpah always insisted that he aimed "to emphasize the horror and agony that violence provides."[47] Speaking of *The Wild Bunch,* he professed to hope that viewers would be "a little sickened by it, at least I hope so, or a little dismayed, at least dismayed—which is the effect that I'm trying for."[48] I think we should believe Peckinpah here and not assume that he was being disingenuous. (I will argue this point more fully in the next chapter.) Assuming, then, that these were his genuine intentions, how successfully does a montage aesthetic convey them? Is there a contradiction between Peckinpah's stated aims and the montage-based structure of his violence? Peckinpah himself noted that audience reactions were at variance with the responses he intended viewers to have. Writing to Paul Staniford, who had condemned the brutality of *The Wild Bunch,* Peckinpah observed that "better than 50% of the people who saw the picture felt as you did. However, better than 30% of the people thought it was an outstanding and much needed statement against violence."[49] Elsewhere, he admitted, "unfortunately most people come to see it [violence]—because they dig it, which is a study of human nature, and which makes me a little sick . . ."[50] He remarked on the disturbing response of an audience of Nigerian soldiers who saw *The Wild Bunch* and began firing their guns at the screen and professing their wish to die in battle like the Bunch. Peckinpah said, "I heard that story and I vomited, to think that I had made that film."[51]

As Peckinpah recognized, viewer reactions to *The Wild Bunch* included outrage and shock over the scale and explicitness of the violence but also excitement and exhilaration. Peckinpah's montages make violence pleasurable and beautiful by aestheticizing it and turning it into stylized spectacle. The very stylization that Peckinpah thought would wake people up to the horror of violence instead excited and gratified many. This pleasure is an inevitable result of the aestheticizing functions of Peckinpah's montage editing and its balletic incorporation of slow motion. The director occasionally acknowledged his own culpability in eliciting this dualistic response. "In *The Wild Bunch* I wanted to show that violence could be at the same time repulsive and fascinating."[52]

Many critics noted these contradictions in 1969 when *The Wild Bunch* was released. The reviewer for *The Nation* confessed his own complicity in sharing the audience's gleeful reaction to all the carnage. "At all this the audience laughed (and so did I), not with merriment, exactly, but in tribute to such virtuosity of gore."[53] The reviewer for *The Christian Century* noted that "even while gasping at Peckinpah's bloodbath, the people seated near me in the theater continued to cram their mouths with popcorn."[54]

Several perceptive reviewers pointed to this contradiction between Peckinpah's stated aims and his montage style: the style is so ritualistically elaborated in the opening and closing scenes of *The Wild Bunch* that it turns violence into a pleasurable spectacle. Furthermore, the excessive elaboration of these montages indicates that the filmmaker took an overwhelming interest and delight in the mechanics of crafting such set-pieces. Arthur Knight in *Saturday Review* pointed out that the stylistics of the film tend to displace the intended moral commentary. "But when the movies attempt to show violent killing in detail, the mind turns against the fact of death and toward the mechanics that produced it. And, curiously, one comes away convinced that the director was also more concerned with the mechanics than with the fact."[55] Joseph Morgenstern in *Newsweek* stressed the apparent falsity of Peckinpah's premise that the repetition of stylized violence could become an artistic device commenting on itself.[56] These reviewers are wrong in their dismissal of Peckinpah's moral involvement with his material and in their objections that the film is without ethical content. But they are dead right in arguing that the tendency of Peckinpah's montage set-pieces in *The Wild Bunch* is to spectacularize violence in ways that will incite the aggressive fantasies of many viewers. Recalling his first encounter with *The Wild Bunch* when he was a teenager, screenwriter Charles Higson stressed that the film's violence stimulated an "orgiastic" release of energy in him. "Once the film was over, I was exhausted and in a state of high nervous excitement. I wanted to go out in a blaze of glory. I wanted a Gatling gun. I wanted to be pierced by a hundred bullets."[57]

Peckinpah did not overtly intend to elicit this kind of reaction in his viewers, any more than Martin Scorsese wanted to arouse vigilante responses in viewers of his bloody *Taxi Driver* (1976), but both filmmakers crafted sequences that have done so. If we ask why, the answer lies in the way that Peckinpah, and Scorsese, too, was seduced by the artistic excitement of putting those violent montages together, of manipulating time and space with images of bodies flying this way and that. The sheer pleasure of crafting these montage scenes would have been exhilarating for Peckinpah. That pleasure is plainly evident in the flamboyant Agua Verde shoot-out and the San Rafael massacre. Through their dynamic energies, these montages convey the excitement and thrill of a filmmaker no longer in moral control of his material to the viewer, who reacts accordingly. Discussing *Taxi Driver*, which climaxes with an astoundingly bloody shoot-out, Scorsese exhibits confusion about his intellectual intent and the seductive excitement he derives from crafting screen violence. The audience, he says, was

> reacting very strongly to the shoot-out sequence in *Taxi Driver*. And I was disturbed by that. It wasn't done with that intent. You can't stop people from taking it that way. What can you do? And you can't stop people from getting an exhilaration from violence, because that's human, very much the same way as you get an exhilaration from the violence in *The Wild Bunch*. But the exhilaration of the violence at the end of *The Wild Bunch* and the violence that's in *Taxi Driver*—because it's shot a certain way, and I know how it's shot, because I shot it and I designed it—is also in the creation of that scene in the editing, in the camera moves, in the use of music, and the use of sound effects, and in the movement within the frame of the characters . . . And that's where the exhilaration comes in.[58]

As did Peckinpah, Scorsese wants to disassociate himself from the aggressive reactions of his viewers, but, like Peckinpah, he is keenly responsive to the physical and artistic pleasures of crafting screen violence. This contradiction accounts for the filmmakers' dismay at the responses of viewers to the scenes that they have so lovingly crafted and choreographed. Neither Scorsese nor Peckinpah wished to evoke violent fantasies in their viewers. When asked if that was their intention, both passionately denied it. But they could not disengage themselves, as artists, from the sensuous gratifications of assembling spectacularized violence. While one should not doubt the sincerity of their belief in their own stated intentions, one may still be amazed at their blindness to their own artistic complicity in stimulating the aggressive reactions of their viewers.

Recognizing this contradiction between Peckinpah's laudable moral intention of shocking his viewers into confronting the horror of violence and his own fascination with the montage spectacle in *The Wild Bunch* brings us to an important point. If the montage-based representation of violence were Peckinpah's only artistic contribution to late-sixties cinema and to the dilemmas of social violence wracking American society in those years, he should be condemned as an aesthete of violence, an inciter to aggression, a director whose films reinforced and added to the violence of those years. If the montage aesthetic were the only frame of analysis deployed on the issue of violence in Peckinpah's films, then he would be everything his detractors have claimed him to be: a glamorizer and glorifier of violence. Despite the structural brilliance of these montages, which we have traced in this chapter, kinetic montage editing, by itself, is a grossly insufficient means for analyzing Peckinpah's great theme of human violence. It is insufficient because it winds up glamorizing the spectacle and inciting the viewer to share in the aggressive fantasy. But montage was not the only frame of analysis deployed in the films. By superimposing two additional frames onto the montage aesthetic, Peckinpah's films reclaim the moral orientation that their use of the montage spectacle had threatened to forfeit, and they become part of the enduring humanistic inquiry into the phenomenon of human brutality. We turn now to an examination of these other two frameworks.

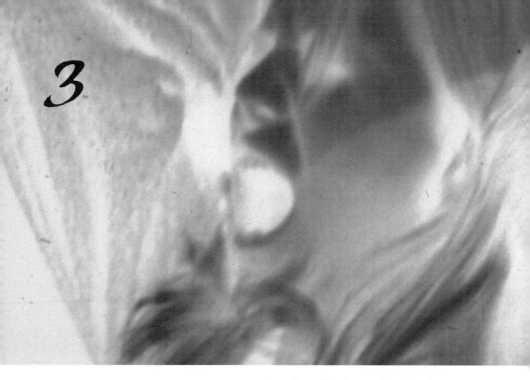

3

Melancholy and Mortality

PECKINPAH'S ATTITUDES toward the violence he depicted on film were
not always clear or coherent. They were sometimes marked by an ambivalent attraction for what he set out to criticize. The tendency for his montages to aestheticize violence, to turn it into an exciting visual spectacle,
worked at cross-purposes with his didactic intentions to drive home for
viewers the horrifying and ugly nature of violent death. The extended
montage sequences in *The Wild Bunch, Cross of Iron, The Killer Elite,* and
The Osterman Weekend emphasize the balletic, choreographic qualities of
the depicted violence. Peckinpah's brilliance as an editor threatened to un-
dermine his laudable intent to desanitize screen violence.

His cinema is, therefore, caught in a contradiction between the aesthetic excitement it offers viewers through its montage editing and the
moral revulsion toward violence which the narratives, characters, and dramatic situations often convey. This tension underlies the tendency of
Peckinpah's films to disturb viewers, who want to turn away from the carnage on screen but find that they cannot do so. The artistic cost of pursuing his didactic goals via a montage aesthetic was significant. It entailed an
occasional loss of coherence within the films in terms of their ability to

construct a solid perspective on the violence they depict, and it also threatened an inversion of Peckinpah's radical critique of violence whereby that critque might seem to become its opposite—namely, a celebration of violence and primitive impulse.

For many of the director's critics, Peckinpah's reputation is, indeed, that of an artist whose work celebrates violence. We now need to meet these criticisms head on. As noted previously, Joan Mellen calls Peckinpah's work "neofascist" and argues that his films were "hymns to male violence."[1] Peckinpah's intellectual influences exerted a disastrous impact upon his critical reputation, as did his own contentious descriptions of his films. For instance, discussing *Straw Dogs,* Peckinpah seemed to trumpet the animalistic nature of human behavior and to endorse the use of violence as an appropriate response to emotional conflict. Describing David Sumner, the protagonist who begins as a pacifist and ends up a killer, Peckinpah observed,

> He didn't know who he was and what he was all about. We all intellectualize about why we should do things, but it's our purely animal instincts that are driving us to do them all the time. David found out he had all those instincts and it made him sick, sick unto death, and at the same time he had guts enough and sense enough to stand up and do what he had to do.[2]

Peckinpah added that the film is about "what can happen when you deny your basic instincts and drives . . . ,"[3] and he professed to believe that "it's wrong—and dangerous—to refuse to acknowledge the animal nature of man."[4]

In elaborating this position, Peckinpah praised the work of anthropologist Robert Ardrey, whom he called a "prophet."[5] (Ardrey, in turn, writing to Peckinpah, expressed keen interest in meeting him.[6]) Peckinpah's affinity for Ardrey was surely wrong-headed, and he discussed Ardrey's work in connection with the release of *Straw Dogs,* thereby encouraging many to interpret the film as a kind of thesis picture designed to dramatize Ardrey's ideas of the territorial imperative, that is, of territorial incursions as instigators of aggression. David's defense of his and Amy's house against the thugs who would break in has come to be seen as a transparent reworking of Ardrey's ideas. We need to examine Ardrey's perspectives on human violence so that they may be disentangled from Peckinpah's own inchoate point of view.

Examining the Ardrey influence on Peckinpah will also enable us to explore the issue of catharsis in relation to Peckinpah's cinema. The radical thrust of Peckinpah's experiment with graphic screen violence takes the concept of catharsis as its impetus and justification. We need to assess Peckinpah's understanding of this concept, and the urgency which it possessed for him, because it furnishes a vital connection between his graphic depictions of screen violence and the social period through which he worked. If we can understand Peckinpah's efforts to move viewers of screen violence toward a cathartic experience, then perhaps we can find a way to resolve the problems posed by his use of montage to turn violence into a spectacle. On the other hand, if the concept of catharsis, applied to screen violence, turns out to be a fugitive, fictitious entity, with little real applicability, the damage to Peckinpah's screen project could be considerable.

Ardrey's Imperative and Aristotle's Theory of Catharsis

Robert Ardrey was a distinctive figure on the 1960s popular culture landscape because of a trio of books he penned that argue that much human behavior is based on instinctual responses that are of fundamental animal origin. *African Genesis* (1961), *The Territorial Imperative* (1966), and *The Social Contract* (1970) stress the primitive components of human identity and behavior. These works argue that it is the evolutionary past that exerts the decisive influences over behavior, not culture or its symbolic mediations: "We act as we do for reasons of our evolutionary past, not our cultural present, and our behavior is as much a mark of our species as is the shape of a human thighbone or the configuration of nerves in a corner of the human brain."[7] Ardrey believed that a propensity for aggression and violence is a property of all animal species, an unavoidable fact of life: "Aggressiveness is a quality innate in all living beings";[8] and ". . . the propensity for violence . . . exists like a layer of buried molten magma underlying all human topography, seeking unceasingly some unimportant fissure to become the most important of volcanoes."[9] Like Peckinpah, Ardrey argued the folly of denying the inevitability of violence in all human groups: ". . . we were born of risen apes, not fallen angels, and the apes were armed killers besides."[10] Convinced of the animal origins of human behavior, Ardrey came to view culture and civilization as sublimations of the killer instinct. (Ardrey thought highly of Freud, particularly Freud's work on the death instinct in *Civilization and Its Discontents*.) For Ardrey, civilization was a compact issuing from the species' need to regulate its instinctual propensity for violence: "I regard it as anything but a coincidence that the rate of civilization's rise has corresponded so closely with man's ascendant capacity to kill. Civilization is a compensatory consequence of our killing imperative; the one could not exist without the other."[11]

Ardrey's writing is colorful, tends to eschew subtlety or complexity, and, as we will see in a moment, it offers an extremely reductionist perspective on the phenomenon of human aggression. His influence on Peckinpah was an unfortunate one, measured in terms of the ensuing damage to Peckinpah's reputation and the ease with which his detractors could use his Ardrey-based comments to portray him as brutish and reactionary. Peckinpah certainly gave them plenty of ammunition. He would insist, with single-minded certitude, "Churches, laws—everybody seems to think that man is a noble savage. But he's only an animal, a meat-eating, talking animal. Recognize it."[12] In such polemical remarks, Peckinpah seemed eager to reduce the complexities of human behavior to a few simple, biologically-driven formulae. But we may question his apparent conviction of the adequacy of these formulae for explaining human behavior. His own skills as a dramatist sensitive to the nuances of human feeling and reaction would bend him away from such reductive prescriptions, and, in Chapter 5, we shall see that a belief in and a commitment to rationalism in thought and conduct form an essential, if surprising, foundation for his work.

Despite these important acknowledgments, we cannot simply dismiss the Ardrey influence as being superficial or unimportant. Ardrey's work offered Peckinpah the attractive mantle of scholarly repute in which he could cloak his polemics on human violence. In the wake of *The Wild Bunch* and *Straw Dogs,* journalists eagerly seized on these polemics, and encouraged them, because they made good copy. But there was a danger here for Peckinpah, and not just the obvious one of reinforcing people's prejudices about his work. It was the danger of actually becoming a celebrant of the dark, destabilizing forces that he sought to condemn, of passing from a radical, utopian use of screen violence to simple, unenlightened depictions of brutality, small in spirit and socially constricting. These two positions are probably never far apart, and an artist seeking to use violence constructively needs to exercise extreme care in controlling the crafted spectacles. The grossly uncontrolled violences in cinema today demonstrate what happens when this care is lacking. Peckinpah could not or would not be entirely thoroughgoing in his position on violence. Violence assumes powerful metaphoric dimensions in *The Wild Bunch* where it functions as a register of social corruption and as a harbinger of the apocalyptic dimensions of modern warfare—of a narrative world poised fatefully on the eve of World War I and the new tide of slaughter that it would inaugurate. Yet, as we have seen, the film's violence unleashes emotions in viewers that its formal design cannot control or recuperate. Furthermore, the slow motion, montage editing, and exploding squib effects in *The Getaway, The Killer Elite,* and *The Osterman Weekend* are without a radical edge or a controlled interrogation of their own nature as a screen construction.

Peckinpah's use of screen violence to probe the spectator's ambivalent responses and to respond to the social currents of his era, then, was not always consistent. In some films, he simply offered the spectacle and asked from viewers only the most uncomplicated of responses. In this respect, his reliance upon Ardrey as an intellectual mentor entailed, through its intersection with his films, a flirtation with socially repressive ideologies and with antidemocratic tendencies in American society. While Peckinpah may have intended his "we're all violent people" homilies to shock the bourgeoisie in a progressive, classically modernist manner, in actual practice such an outlook may serve to justify violence everywhere. George Gerbner, testifying in 1968 as a social scientist and media analyst before the National Commission on the Causes and Prevention of Violence, made this point forcefully and cogently:

> I am not at all prepared to accept . . . the notion that this is a violent world and there is nothing you can do about it, it is going to go on. That notion I think is an invitation to violence, an invitation both to individual violence, to large social, large-scale violence, ultimately to dictatorship and to a country which is a culture rated by a notion that it will be less able or unable to prevent or to cope with or to resist violence . . . [13]

Through his pronouncements about the inevitability of human brutality, and his seductively beautiful montage renditions of screen violence, Peckinpah seemed to have become one of those in a turbulent era who, in the words of Arthur Schlesinger Jr., "have succumbed to the national susceptibility for hatred and violence, have, indeed, begun themselves to exalt hatred and violence as if primitivism in emotion constituted a higher morality."[14]

This is the conclusion we might reach if we examine, in a somewhat superficial way, the violent montages of Peckinpah's films and isolate them from the surrounding structures of the work and Peckinpah's own statements of his intentions. To some extent, this is what many of his detractors do. We have recognized the problems that these violent montages pose for his work, particularly for his interest in deconstructing screen violence and presenting it to the viewer in a way that would encourage self-reflection.

About his films, Peckinpah remarked, "Someone may feel a strange sick exultation at the violence, but he should then ask himself: 'What is going on in my heart?'"[15] Despite the aestheticizing tendencies inherent in the montage style, Peckinpah conceptualized his work as contributing toward greater psychological health for the spectator and an improved social health for the republic. "The point is," he insisted, "that the violence in us, in all of us, has to be expressed constructively or it will sink us."[16]

In an ABC Network Radio interview that he conducted after shooting *Cross of Iron,* Peckinpah reiterated his view that "Aggression is inborn in man. Without it he could never have survived. The form it takes is what we are concerned with today."[17] Peckinpah was very specific about the manner in which a mode of constructively expressed symbolic violence should work. He felt justified in portraying graphic violence on screen because he believed it would provide a cathartic experience for viewers, promoting social health by purging them of antisocial, aggressive impulses:

> I'm a great believer in catharsis. Do you think people watch the Super Bowl because they think football is a beautiful sport? Bullshit! They're committing violence vicariously. Look, the old basis of catharsis was a purging of the emotions through pity and fear. People used to go and see the plays of Euripides and Sophocles . . . The players acted it out and the audience got in there and kind of lived it with them. What's more violent than the plays of William Shakespeare?[18]

Peckinpah believed that a vital function of art, through the centuries and especially in a time of national crisis, was to provide spectators with the vicarious experience of violence so they would not feel compelled to enact real violence in their homes and on the streets. When hostile reviewers demanded to know whether the extraordinary number of killings in *The Wild Bunch* indicated that he enjoyed violence, Peckinpah replied "my idea was that it would have a cathartic effect."[19] He asserted that the elaborate violence in *Straw Dogs* "serves as a cathartic effect."[20] As late as 1983, in his final film, *The Osterman Weekend,* Peckinpah remained committed to the idea that socially sanctioned violent spectacles, in the form of art or sporting events, offer viewers a vicarious mode for experiencing violence. A vengeance-seeking CIA agent, Fassett (John Hurt), watches on a bank of video monitors the deadly conflict between his team of assassins and their designated victims. One monitor carries a different set of images, a baseball game. Peckinpah juxtaposed the two types of spectacle—the athletic match and the assassins hunting their victims. This juxtaposition is a significant indicator that Peckinpah continued to the end of his career to understand symbolic media violence as a vicarious modality permitting viewers to enjoy a substitute expression of the real thing. However, by this time, Peckinpah had reconsidered the principle of catharsis and its relation to the health of a society. In a 1979 BBC interview, he admitted that his original goal of using graphic violence in pictures such as *The Wild Bunch* to help induce social health via catharsis was wrong.[21] Possibly the well-documented experiences of audiences greeting the violence in his films with excitement and exultation led him to this changed view, although these emotions are actually consistent with what one would expect from a cathartic spectacle. By the end of *The Osterman Weekend,* Peckinpah, through the character of TV celebrity John Tanner (Rutger Hauer), was urging viewers to turn off the television and renounce the vicarious thrills of media-induced experience. Peckinpah seemed now to believe that catharsis, as an apologia for screen violence, did not wash. He was right.

As is well known, the concept of catharsis derives from a brief definition of tragedy in Aristotle's *Poetics,* which states that tragedy chiefly relies upon language and acting to invoke pity (*eleos*) and fear (*phobos*), and in so doing, such emotions are purged from the spectator. From this passage in the *Poetics,* the concept of catharsis has grown in importance to become a foundational concept informing discussions of tragedy and tragic emotion. Extending well beyond them, the concept has become an essential

When he made *The Wild Bunch,* Peckinpah believed in the idea of catharsis, but the images he created in that film were more honest about the effects of viewing violent spectacle. After the San Rafael ambush and massacre, a group of young boys, incited and excited by the violence they have witnessed, rushes to reenact it. Frame enlargement.

prop in debates over violence in the arts. This is ironic for several reasons. Aristotle's own explication of catharsis is singularly unhelpful. As the critic Walter Kaufmann has pointed out, the *Poetics* "contains very few arguments, and the few it does contain are, on the face of them, incomplete and untenable. The celebrated doctrines of the *Poetics* are for the most part peremptory dicta of a few lines, and not theories that Aristotle tries to establish with care."[22]

Although the concept of catharsis has been incorporated into diverse theories about how art works and the psychology of viewer response, Aristotle never offered it as a substantive, clearly worked-out construct or even provided much evidence for it. It remains in the *Poetics* as a tantalizing glimpse of an idea. Peckinpah's resort to the theory of catharsis as propounded by Aristotle was a resort to no theory at all. Nevertheless, his commentators have also found the concept useful and have employed it when discussing the emotional effects of his films. Mark Crispin Miller, for example, refers to "the cathartic holocaust" at the end of *The Wild Bunch*.[23]

Applications of Aristotle's concept to explain how the viewer experiences screen violence are problematic because, as Aristotle formulated it, the concept of catharsis has little theoretical content. Another problem exists, as well, and this is the evident differences between theater and cinema. Aristotle offered catharsis in reference to a performance-based medium—Greek theater—which conveyed its action through language and in which violent action was not directly represented but tended to occur off-stage. The relevance of these differences is obvious. Cinema is a visually based medium in which images, not language, convey action, and it is a medium in which violence is portrayed with explicit detail. There seems to be no essential reason for assuming that Aristotle's concept would necessarily generalize to a medium that can use its elements of style to graphically portray and enhance explicit violence.[24] Empirical researchers studying the relationship between film violence and subsequent aggressive behavior by viewers have noted the importance of these distinctions between the mediums. Singer and Singer point out that

> Even the most dramatic moments in the theater, including the blinding of Gloucester in *King Lear,* or the tragic duel scene in *Hamlet,* cannot compete with the intensity of a scene depicted on television. The Greek tragedies followed the convention of committing all violence off-stage—thus we only hear about these deeds through the chorus or the actor's words.[25]

By contrast, they note, "When you see a violent image on the screen in all its graphic gore, that image intrudes with greater shock as a literal picture, relatively uncontrolled by one's own imagination [or] values."[26]

Because of these medium-specific differences, while Aristotle's concept of catharsis might apply to ancient Greek tragedy, it does not follow that viewers of cinema or television violence necessarily discharge their aggressive feelings or behavior through these spectacles. Aristotle wrote about the audience's feelings of *pity* and *fear,* not about aggression, and empirical researchers on media effects have pointed out that to construe Aristotle's concept of catharsis in terms of the discharge of anger, violence, or aggression is to misapply the term.[27] George Comstock has emphasized that, with respect to media violence, "the catharsis hypothesis is often wrongly attributed to Aristotle, but in fact he proposed only that by arousing pity and fear, the dramatic genre of tragedy would lead to their catharsis. He said nothing about aggressive behavior, and he was prescient not to do so."[28]

The amplification of viewer shock, horror, nausea, or, alternatively, titillation and excitement, achieved through such tools of cinema as montage editing, loud music, or gory prosthetic effects, is unrelated to the emotions and reactions Aristotle described. He discussed the purging of tragic feelings through performance and language, not the enhancement of graphic violence and horror in an image-based medium. To use his notion of catharsis in connection with cinema violence, as Peckinpah did, is a misapplication of the term.

A comparison of Peckinpah's film work with Antonin Artaud's Theatre of Cruelty can be very instructive here. Artaud's work is strikingly analogous with Peckinpah's in respect to its privileging of catharsis, yet it issues from a very different conception of cruelty. Peckinpah, of course, never spoke of cruelty per se, as Artaud did, in defining the terms of the viewer's experience, but both artists believed in the importance of confronting the viewer with cruel (Artaud) or violent (Peckinpah) spectacles that would drain the spiritual abscesses of society. Artaud opened his Theatre of Cruelty in 1935, and, although it was shortly thereafter dissolved, the publication in 1938 of his essays in a volume entitled *Le théâtre et son double* (*The Theater and Its Double)* left a lasting influence on modern theater. Artaud conceived of the theater as a medium that, like a plague, would reveal and release the dark forces at work in society. If "these powers are dark," he wrote, "it is the fault not of the plague nor of the theater, but of life."[29] The theater of cruelty tears off masks to reveal lies and the baseness and hypocrisy of the world. It would be a theater in which "violent physical images crush and hypnotize the sensibility of the spectator seized by the theater as by a whirlwind of higher forces."[30] (This is a good description of what Peckinpah's concluding montage in *The Wild Bunch* does to the viewer.)

Artaud believed that such a Dionysian revelation of life's implacable forces would perform a powerful cathartic function for spectators: ". . . like the plague, the theater has been created to drain abscesses collectively."[31] He argued that viewing violent scenes in the safe confines of the theater would inoculate viewers against their tendency to express violence in the outside world. "I defy any spectator to whom such violent scenes will have transferred their blood . . . to give himself up, once outside the theater, to ideas of war, riot, and blatant murder."[32] Unlike Peckinpah, however, Artaud backed away from any facile equation between cruelty and explicit bloodshed. Cruelty was a more general and mystical concept for him. In his perception, derived from his study of magic and ritual, dark powers animate the universe, which it is the task of theater to reveal. Cruelty is not synonymous with physical sadism.

> The word 'cruelty' must be taken in a broad sense, and not in the rapacious physical sense that it is customarily given . . . It is a mistake to give the word 'cruelty' a meaning of merciless bloodshed and disinterested, gratuitous pursuit of physical suffering . . . Cruelty is not synonymous with bloodshed, martyred flesh, crucified enemies.[33]

Peckinpah's filmmaking has sometimes been interpreted as a modern incarnation of Artaud's aesthetic principles,[34] despite Artaud's own insistence that the cinema is a poor medium for cruelty because it is too mechanical. Artaud believed the cinema to be too literal, too realistic in its imagery to create the kind of poetry essential for cruelty and catharsis. "To the crude visualization [in cinema] of what is, the theater through poetry opposes images of what is not."[35] Literal cinematic images of bloodshed do not constitute a representation of the metaphysical terror and danger that Artaud felt were the essence of cruelty. By insisting upon poetic language and nonliteral visualization, Artaud avoided the conditions that in cinema militate against an experience of catharsis. Like Peckinpah, Artaud believed in the importance of cathartic ritual for maintaining the health of a society, yet, unlike Peckinpah, he did not make the mistake of seeking to apply Aristotle's dicta to images of literal bloodshed.

Despite these problems, Peckinpah's commitment to a drive-based theory of aggression made Aristotelian catharsis seem like a natural and useful prop for his work. Implied in Aristotle's discussion is the idea that viewers carry a fixed charge of emotion which can be discharged in a socially nonthreatening way by the theater experience. Both Ardrey and Peckinpah conceived of aggression as an ever-present current of instinctual energy searching for an outlet. The concept of catharsis was attractive to Peckinpah because it enabled him to reconcile this drive-based view of human aggression with the socially constructive role that art might play in providing a safe outlet for such impulses. But I will argue that violence in the media does not actually perform this function, and that aggression should not be conceived as a drive. As we will see, Peckinpah was ill-informed on both counts, and his errors bear directly upon the highly charged controversies about the social effects of viewing violent films that accrued to his work throughout the period of his greatest productivity.

As noted earlier, media researcher George Comstock has remarked that Aristotle was prescient not to include violence and aggression in his idea of emotional catharsis. We now need to examine the basis for this observation. Its implications extend beyond issues of the applicability of Aristotelian catharsis to cinema, inflecting as well the terms by which we should understand and evaluate Peckinpah's radical screen project. To what extent does the success of that project depend on the provision of a cathartic effect? In the absence of a socially beneficial catharsis, can the project be redeemed? Could Peckinpah have been wrong about catharsis yet still have succeeded with his stated goals?

The Empirical Data on Media Violence

Because of societal concerns about the effects of viewing media violence, viewers' responses to film and television have been subjected to extensive research and experimentation, and the evidence strongly points toward a link between viewing film or television violence and aggressive behavior. A recent meta-analysis of 217 studies on television violence conducted between 1957 and 1990 found consistent and significant correlations between viewing violent television and aggressive or antisocial behavior.[36] Most studies on the viewing of media violence show an aggression-inducing, rather than a cathartic, effect.[37] In 1972, after examining the relation between television viewing and social behavior, the Surgeon General's Committee concluded there was little evidence supporting the catharsis hypothesis (that viewing film or television violence would lessen an individual's propensity to behave aggressively).[38] From an empirical standpoint, the catharsis hypothesis is primarily associated with the work of Seymour Feshback, who has reported some evidence offering conditional support for the cathartic effects of viewing fantasy aggression.[39] Feshback's findings, though, do not represent the consensus of most researchers in this field, and even Feshback reported evidence pointing away from the catharsis hypothesis.[40]

The bulk of the empirical evidence points toward the aggression-inducing properties of media violence, and these properties have been evaluated in terms of the specific content characteristics that are most likely to be associated with subsequent aggressive behavior. When the aggression-evoking characteristics of film victims match the characteristics of available targets in everyday life, aggressive responses toward those real-life targets may become more likely. The incineration of a Manhattan subway-token clerk following the release of the film *Money Train* (1995), which depicts a similar incident, would seem to exemplify this principle, but it has also been demonstrated experimentally.[41] A second content characteristic that has been shown to correlate with subsequent antisocial behavior involves the consequences of depicted screen aggression. When aggression is rewarded within a film or television show, it tends to elicit more imitative aggression from viewers. Albert Bandura, who has argued persuasively in favor of a social learning theory of aggression (which we will examine in a moment), points out that the persuasive example of successful villainy in a show or film "may outweigh the viewers' value systems."[42] Summarizing his experimental work in which he found young viewers imitating the aggressive behavior of a film character whose behavior was rewarded, Bandura noted that children watching television "have opportunities to observe many episodes in which anti-socially aggressive behavior has paid off abundantly . . ."[43] In light of this, the villain's routine punishment at the end of an episode "may have a relatively weak inhibitory effect on the viewer."[44]

Bandura has also demonstrated the modeling functions of aggressive media content—that is, the tendency for observed filmic aggression to shape the form of a viewer's subsequent antisocial behavior. Children's play activities and choice of toys tend to assume forms imitative of the aggressive activities seen on film. Seeing film aggression not only heightens the kids' aggressive reactions but offers a model that serves as a source for imitative learning.[45] When aggression is rewarded in a show, the salience of this modeling is increased. In a similar fashion, when a show or film presents aggression as a justifiable response, it may have a disinhibiting effect on viewers.[46] When Rocky patriotically pummels the robotic Soviet boxer Drago in *Rocky IV* (1985), or when the Wild Bunch confront Mapache to reclaim Angel, the film narratives present scenarios of justifiable aggression that provide a moral orientation for the explicit violence that ensues. Summarizing the correlations between filmic aggression presented as justified and antisocial responses by viewers, which they demonstrated experimentally, Berkowitz and Rawlings conclude, "Seeing the fantasy villain 'get what he deserved' may make the angered individual more inclined to hurt the villain in his life, the person who had angered him."[47]

Yet another content characteristic that has been empirically demonstrated to increase the probability of aggressive responses by some viewers involves the depicted behavior of the victims of aggression. The presence or absence of a victim's pain cues is highly correlated with a viewer's disposition to aggress. Visible or audible signs of a victim's suffering tend to depress, or inhibit, aggressive responses[48] and may also diminish a viewer's enjoyment of the film violence depending on the amplitude of the expressions of pain.[49] Scenes without expressions of suffering by victims also tend to be perceived as less violent than those where the victim's pain is apparent. Blanchard, Graczyk, and Blanchard note that viewers tended to rate the violence level as much higher in *The Deer Hunter* (1978) than in either *The Bugs Bunny Movie* (1979) or the James Bond film *For Your Eyes Only* (1981), because the latter two films present relatively pain-free violence, unlike *The Deer Hunter,* which presents scenes of physical and emotional suffering.

> This suggests that suffering of victims is a major constituent of perceptions of violence. This interpretation is supported by the reliably lower ratings on violence of the Bond film, which contained relatively little emphasis on suffering of victims although several dozen characters appeared to be injured or killed as the result of a nonstop action episode. It is also congruent with the very low suffering ratings for the cartoon, which was rated much lower in violence than any of the live-actor sequences despite portrayals of exaggerated physical violence, including physical consequences such as heads being shot off.[50]

It is important to emphasize in this connection that a viewer's perception that a film contains a high level of violence does not necessarily entail a corresponding inhibition of aggressive or antisocial impulses, even in cases where pain cues are evident in the material. In the Blanchard et al. study, for example, the Russian Roulette scene from *The Deer Hunter* was rated the least enjoyable and most violent scene of all the material under study, yet that scene was associated with 31 violent incidents involving use of a handgun in rituals of Russian Roulette between 1978 and 1982.[51] Despite the evident pain cues in *The Deer Hunter* sequence, some viewers evidently incorporated the exciting sequence as a model for imitative behavior. (Arousal of excitement in viewers, in itself and independently of specific program content such as violence, has been shown to correlate with subsequent aggressiveness by several studies.[52]) To understand such variations, we need to remember that the empirical evidence indicates a statistical probability that aggression will occur if certain conditions are met and is never addressed to, or predictive of, how a given individual will process film violence.

It is clear that the catharsis hypothesis fails to square with the available evidence on how specific features of violent film or television programming correlate with subsequent viewer aggression. That evidence, demonstrated consistently and empirically, tends to show an opposite reaction to what the catharsis hypothesis would predict: namely, a correlation between viewing film violence and increased antisocial behavior. In addition, the measurable phenomenon of viewer desensitization to violent material points toward a different dynamic operating between viewers and film violence. The theory of catharsis presupposes a viewer will experience continuous arousal by film violence, which is then discharged by the fantasy outlet afforded by the film. Contrary to the catharsis hypothesis, however, are data that show that regular viewers of violent media material react with *less* emotion to the material than do occasional viewers, and that viewers demonstrate a measurable desensitization—a lowered physiological response—to the film violence.[53] Catharsis presupposes arousal, yet a steady diet of media violence tends to suppress viewers' sensitivities to the depicted mayhem, and, for a statistically significant percentage of viewers, the demonstrable outcome is an increased propensity to behave aggressively.

The catharsis hypothesis makes intuitive sense. The belief that viewing violence enables a discharge through fantasy of aggressive impulses is deeply ingrained in popular thinking, but it is not supported by the empirical evidence. Moreover, the hypothesis is based on a drive-reduction theory of aggression—a viewpoint shared by Peckinpah and Ardrey—that itself does not have much credence among many social scientists. The traditional view of aggression as a fixed current of energy that needs periodic draining—the terms through which Peckinpah conceived the value of his work for viewers—fails to take into account that which separates humans from animals: the ability through cognition and culture to modify the biological bases of behavior. As Vernon Reynolds notes, "There's nothing in the brain stem, limbic system, hypothalamus etc. that man cannot, with his neo-cortex learn to control."[54]

Rather than conceiving of aggression as a drive (which, despite intensive study, researchers have been unable to isolate), psychologist Albert Bandura has become the widely known and influential proponent of a social learning view of aggression. In contrast to Peckinpah and Ardrey, who viewed aggression as unidimensional and drive-based, Bandura approaches it as a multidimensional phenomenon with many determinants and purposes and as behavior that is learned. "People are not born with preformed repertoires of aggressive behavior. They must learn them."[55] Bandura acknowledges that people have neurophysiological mechanisms that make aggression possible but stresses that social learning factors determine if, when, and by what form aggressive behaviors may come into play. Through observational learning, people develop expectations about the anticipated consequences of aggressive behavior. This, then, serves to channel emotional arousal from aversive experience into a range of behavioral outcomes, including aggression, but also encompassing such other modalities as withdrawal, dependency, and constructive problem-solving. "Frustration tends to provoke aggression mainly in people who have learned to respond to aversive experiences with aggressive attitudes and conduct. Thus, after being frustrated, aggressively trained children behave more aggressively, whereas cooperatively trained children behave more cooperatively."[56]

Bandura's approach places great emphasis upon the observational learning of behavioral cues, the social and cognitive mediation of those cues, and symbolic modes of behavioral expression. Of the latter, the mass media function as powerful models for the observational learning of aggression. According to Bandura, film and television violence has four chief effects upon the viewer, none of which is cathartic. It teaches aggressive styles of behavior, weakens personal restraints over acting aggressively, desensitizes and habituates people to violence, and influences the pictures of reality (e.g., beliefs about the likelihood of personally encountering violence or about the incidence of violence at large in society) that people carry with them in everyday life and on which they base much of their behavior.[57] All of these effects have been empirically documented, and they point considerably away from the catharsis hypothesis and the assumptions of aggressive drive reduction through fantasy that underlie it.

We are now in a position to see that Peckinpah was seriously wrong about the social value he ascribed to his films via the experience of catharsis. It is important to disentangle his work from the traditional belief in cathartic release that surrounds it (and movie violence in general), because neither the progressive, humane focus in that work nor its aesthetic complexity may be found in that belief. A defense of Peckinpah's work through appeals to catharsis is a dead end. Thus, we should be highly skeptical of critical attempts to argue that the gunfire sequences in contemporary films offer subversive and emancipatory pleasures ("They give us a highly stylized spectacle in which are played out genuine dramas of mastery and loss."[58]), just as we should disagree with attempts to condemn Peckinpah's work as a mindless appeal to violence. To my mind, the signal, and morally responsible, qualities of his work in its treatment of violence lie in its ability to disturb and/or offend the viewer.

As noted earlier, his screen violence has an unpleasant edge that persists despite the aestheticizing use of montage and slow motion. Social scientists, as well as aestheticians and film critics, have argued that seriously disturbing screen violence may have merits that the more routine and sanitized violence found in most films and television shows does not (as when James Bond or Rambo can blow up a room full of people without a trace of human feeling or physical and emotional pain). Summarizing the empirical work on the effects of violent media, George Comstock notes, "It would be wrong to conclude from all this that the expression of hostility or aggression is never reduced by exposure to television or film portrayals of aggression. In fact . . . [it may] do so when the portrayal is sufficiently disturbing to inhibit such responses."[59] John Fraser, in his influential discussion of violence in the arts, concurs, arguing:

> For all their violences, violent entertainments normally involve a blanking out of the really unpleasant, and tend to promote a sense of security and invulnerability in the reader or viewer. I wish to suggest that a very important way in which certain violences shock us—and shock salutarily—is that they undermine the yearning for invulnerability that violent entertainments cater to.[60]

The former British censor Enid Wistrich concluded that "the most disturbing films are unlikely to be those which produce antisocial effects. If the violence in the films upsets us, it is likely to be stimulating our capacity to reject it, not reproduce it. It is more likely to be undermining our resistances when we can laugh at it or easily accept it."[61]

This principle—that the more disturbing the violence, the less likely its antisocial effects—needs extensive empirical support before it can be accepted as a valid descriptor. As yet, this research is lacking. But even in the absence of needed empirical verification, there are other problems with this supposition. The perception that some film violence is disturbing is a relative one, personally and socially. In its day, *Bonnie and Clyde* was the exemplar of graphic, disturbing violence. Testifying before the National Commission on the Causes and Prevention of Violence in 1969, social scientist Leonard Berkowitz suggested that the film's graphic images might have a salutary effect by showing people that violence can have horrific consequences. The film, he said, may have "a good effect of dampening the likelihood of the audience member acting aggressively himself, if he says to himself, yes, it can have this effect."[62] Today, *Bonnie and Clyde* is shown unedited on broadcast television. The standard of what is disturbing is relative and changing.

Nevertheless, if we scrutinize the violence in Peckinpah's films, we find that his work goes well beyond the reassuring violences of most popular film. It does this by employing the montage style to aestheticize, pleasurably, scenes of violence and then by projecting onto that aestheticized pleasure two additional frameworks of perception and analysis. The superimposition of these frameworks gives the films their structural complexity and their disturbing force. The resulting structural design demonstrates the seriousness and legitimacy with which Peckinpah pursued his screen project. It also suggests that, even if Peckinpah was wrong about catharsis, we cannot simply foreclose on his stated goals by dismissing the work as an unsuccessful realization of those goals. The failure of catharsis notwithstanding, if his work does disturb the viewer by connecting violence with an experience of moral and psychological horror, then that work meets the moral and artistic challenges that he set for it.

Peckinpah's Mournful Stance

The first of these imposed frameworks, which will concern us for the remainder of this chapter, is the melancholia that accompanies Peckinpah's representation of screen violence. This melancholy has many sources that account, in part, for its power. It inheres in the genre of the Western, forever focused upon the vanishing of the West, a lament for the loss of a frontier whose passing has left the modern era immeasurably poorer. Peckinpah was drawn to stories of losers, outcasts, and misfits, and he was troubled by the loss of his grandfather's ranch: "I grew up on a ranch. But that world is gone . . . I feel rootless, completely. It's disturbing, very much so. But there's nothing you can do about it, nothing."[63]

The Western's culturally coded melancholy suited Peckinpah's personal sense of rootlessness, isolation, and disenchantment with the twentieth century, as well as serving as a focus for his reveries for a lost boyhood on Peckinpah Mountain and the Denver Church Ranch. Accordingly, he inflected the Western's autumnal spirit with great imaginative power. Steve Judd (in *Ride the High Country*), Pike Bishop, Cable Hogue, Pat Garrett—all wage a losing battle against history, and, with the general exception of Judd, Peckinpah's most straightforward hero, they are defeated by the accumulated weight of their own wrong choices. Peckinpah's Westerns are studies in diminishment and defeat, and they move us because of the enormous empathy he feels for these compromised, doomed characters, whose sometimes tawdry examples are so much better than the venal, corrupt, and savage world that surrounds them.

The melancholy of Peckinpah's films, though, extends well beyond the locus of a single genre. A twilight spirit haunts the graveyard narrative of *Alfredo Garcia.* This spirit is the end point toward which the revelation of emotional and physical cruelty in *Straw Dogs* has been moving. It yields up the battlefields in *Cross of Iron,* stripped of political ideal and glory, to the conqueror worm. It judges and condemns, with a terminal weariness, the internecine worlds of the killer apes in suits, enacting endless scenarios of betrayal and duplicity in *The Killer Elite* and *The Osterman Weekend.* The buoyant geniality of *Junior Bonner* seems an exception to these darker films, yet below its spirited surface, the narrative traces the disintegration of the Bonner family, as each member heads in separate directions, toward alternate destinations, leaving only a shared past and a shared trove of memories. The melancholic tone of Peckinpah's films is deeply felt and powerfully registered on screen. It is one of his signal elements as a filmmaker, yet its importance has often been minimized or neglected by Peckinpah critics—especially by his detractors, who see him celebrating, rather than mourning, the violence he depicted. As British director Alex Cox has cogently observed, "That was the great thing about all of Peckinpah's films, the *sadness* that the characters have inside them."[64]

This sadness has important implications for the place that violence assumes in Peckinpah's work, for the manner by which he represented it on screen, and upon his own attitudes toward it. One rarely finds in Peckinpah's work the sort of gross manipulations of viewer response that are routine in Stallone or Schwarzenegger films, scenes in which viewers are invited to applaud an especially sadistic dispatching of the villain. We must be careful, though, in discriminating among Peckinpah's films, and some-

Junior Bonner returns to his father's house, but Ace is gone, and the house is decrepit and empty. Junior finds a photograph of Ace, a haunting reminder of older and better days. Beneath its genial surface, *Junior Bonner* laments the loss of a past that sustained Junior and his father. Frame enlargement.

times even within the same film, as we seek to delineate the ways violence operates in his cinematic universe. Peckinpah was not a programmatic director, and his attitudes toward the characters, narratives, and images of his films were always mixed. Peckinpah's films are not intellectually coherent in a systematic way, but they are poetically powerful, which is the surer index of artistry. As a result, while the work that we are about to examine ruthlessly presents violence as a spiritual and emotional cancer, in other films Peckinpah was less judicious and more complicit in pushing the aesthetic and emotional pleasures that may be afforded by the representation of violence and brutality. The violence in *The Getaway* is largely mechanical and dehumanized; it operates without the emotional pain and trauma that are its familiar accompaniments elsewhere. Furthermore, as Robin Wood notes, in that film Peckinpah cannot seem to detach himself from the brutish Rudy Butler (Al Lettieri), a professional killer pursuing Doc McCoy, and the elaborate tortures he inflicts upon a veterinarian whom he has kidnapped. (Wood finds the humorous approach to the latter character's suicide, and Butler's response to it, to be "in all Peckinpah's work to date the moment that is hardest to forgive."[65])

Presented with elaborate montage editing and slow-motion inserts, the battlefield violence in *Cross of Iron* functions mainly as spectacle because the film lacks the systematic antiwar focus and careful selection of detail consistent with a picture like Lewis Milestone's *All Quiet on the Western Front* (1930). At the end of *Cross of Iron,* when Steiner compels Captain

Stransky, with whom he has been at odds throughout the film, to join him in the German retreat before the advancing Russian army, Stransky promises to show Steiner how a Prussian officer fights, and Steiner promises to show Stransky where the iron crosses grow, an exchange of conventionally heroic sentiment whose tone seems inconsistent with the battlefield horrors and the treachery that the narrative has emphasized. At the end of *The Killer Elite,* the climactic martial arts bout on the battleship in Suisan Bay has no moral resonance and works only as spectacle, as does the barroom brawl in *Junior Bonner,* which is edited like the climactic shoot-out in *The Wild Bunch* and is presented as an occasion for laughter and high spirits.

We must acknowledge fully those moments in Peckinpah's work that are no longer critically disengaged from the violence on screen and are crafted as conventional, at times celebratory, responses. Those moments, though, tend to be exceptions to the more consistent and significant tendency to present violence within a narrative tone of melancholy or despair and to associate it with the crippling or diminishment of human identity. A marked evolution occurs in Peckinpah's work toward a greater maturity in his handling and understanding of screen violence. In this respect, Peckinpah moved toward an emphasis upon the emotional pain and trauma of violence and away from an artistic attachment to the aesthetic pleasures and energies afforded by it. *Ride the High Country* predates Peckinpah's elaboration of a complex montage style, and the climactic gunfight between the heroes, Steve and Gil, and the villainous Hammond clan offers the straightforward pleasures of conventional heroism and the righteous violence that often attends it. The end is melancholy. Steve, Peckinpah's most beautiful hero, dies, but only after he has affirmed his principles and entered his house justified, as he had said he wished to do. Watching the shoot-out that precipitates Steve's death, the viewer feels no conflicting emotions, but sides wholly with Steve and Gil.

By contrast, *The Wild Bunch* utilizes montage editing to deconstruct the old conventions of movie violence (and help create new ones), and it places, in the words of Martin Scorsese, "no-good bad guys"[66] at the center of the narrative. The violent holocaust that concludes the film, when the Bunch attack General Mapache's troops at Agua Verde, was unprecedented in American cinema for its duration and ferocity. As we have seen, the spectacle is so overwhelming that the viewer can do little but submit to it. Peckinpah, however, situated his kinetic set-piece within an immediate context of sadness and despair. It is preceded by the extraordinary, largely wordless scene set in the bedroom of a young woman at Agua Verde, where Pike ruminates silently on his past failures as the Gorch brothers squabble in an adjoining room over the price of their whore's services. As many critics have pointed out, the scene works by way of implication and indirection, with reference to the earlier narrative evidence of Pike's failure to live up to his code of sticking together with one's comrades. The narrative has delineated so clearly Pike's tendency to abandon or desert his comrades, and has so clearly pointed to the bitter disparity between Pike's opportunism and his desperate perception of the ethical code that eludes him, that Peckinpah chose, with remarkable artistic temerity, to play the crucial moment of Pike's epiphany without dialogue. As Paul Seydor notes, "This scene, the most delicately inflected in the film, is the pivot point, and not the least of its attractions is how little it says explicitly, how much it draws together and concentrates."[67] To understand Pike's painful awakening to his own failure as a human being, the viewer must contextualize this scene with the earlier narrative material. Peckinpah offered few explicit guides for doing so, merely a series of sustained close-ups of actor William Holden's eloquent, ruined face as he glances about the shabby room and measures his alcoholic years against the youth of the woman and her baby. Pike's painful awareness of his moral cowardice and personal failings prompts him to lead the remaining members of the Bunch in the suicidal effort to rescue Angel from Mapache.

The explosion of violence which follows Pike's decision to reclaim Angel from Mapache is the consequence of his newly-found enlightment. It makes for a powerful and visually brilliant climax to the film, but, as the register of a character's moral growth, the resolve that precipitates the slaughter of hundreds of people remains a dubious one, especially since its implications remain largely unexamined in the short narrative time that remains. The film, though, does return after the bloody shoot-out to an explicitly bleak landscape and tone. The maimed and displaced survivors shuffle out of the village and head into the empty desert beyond as vultures settle on the corpses that litter Agua Verde. Jerry Fielding's dirge underscores the funereal aftermath of the Bunch's last stand. This is an extraordinarily poetic sequence, one that shows the viewer the aftermath of destruction and the nullity of death. During this sequence, only the vultures win. Together with the scene of Pike ruminating on his personal failure, this sequence places the violent shoot-out within a surrounding context of defeat, despair, and decay. In an early cut of the film, Peckinpah did

The frenzied violence of the Agua Verde slaughter is framed by explicitly melancholy sequences: Pike's alcoholic despair as he confronts his failings, and the kingdom of the vultures which inherits the bounty of the dead. Frame enlargements.

end the film here, with Deke Thorton (Robert Ryan) seated against the wall, a mute witness to the carnage. But producer Phil Feldman wrote Peckinpah an impassioned letter urging him to restore the rest of the conclusion.[68]

Had the film ended here, Peckinpah might have had an aesthetic and narrative structure that could control the extended, climactic, violent spectacle. Instead, though, he went beyond the funereal tone and the vulture kingdom to a sentimental conclusion wherein the Bunch is returned to life and laughter via a reprise of earlier imagery, chiefly the lovely exit scene from Angel's village. Several critics have argued that this conclusion represents the Bunch's entry into the glories of legend and myth.[69] While this stratagem may make for a satisfying narrative conclusion, the abrupt change of gears from the vulture kingdom to Valhalla also represents a failure on Peckinpah's part to think through systematically the aesthetic application of his stated goals of showing how "bloody fucking awful" violence is. Their entry into folklore and song makes the Bunch's violence righteous and rewarded aggression. The ending of the film oscillates uncertainly between the aesthetic celebration of violence (achieved through the extended montage editing of the gun battle), the moral endorsement of imaginary bloodletting (implied by making the Bunch's violence righteous and rewarded), and a critique of the climactic violence by attenuating it through the context of alcoholic despair and physical decay which immediately surrounds it. These contradictory aesthetic and moral tendencies at the film's conclusion help make it a highly charged experience for viewers, one that provokes them into passionately differing responses. These contradictions are also a sign of Peckinpah's own uncompleted position as an artist on the subject of human violence. *The Wild Bunch* represents an early point in Peckinpah's evolving relationship with screen violence and one that he would surpass in later work by reaching a point of greater maturity in his reflections on this subject and problem.

In his next film, *The Ballad of Cable Hogue,* he largely set aside his concerns with human violence but not his preoccupation with examining flawed and failed relationships within a melancholic historical frame. Cable, a prospector after gold, is abandoned by his partners, Taggart and Bowen, because they have enough water for two but not for three. Cable, though, survives because he finds a water hole where none ought to exist. He builds a thriving business around his water, servicing the stage lines that regularly cross the desert. He even falls in love with a prostitute named Hildy, but he cannot let go of the desire for revenge against Taggart and Bowen. Peckinpah made Cable pay for this desire and thereby inflected the narrative with a melancholy tone. By seeking vengeance against the partners who left him in the desert to die, and by putting a dollar value on love and friendship, Cable forfeits his chance at happiness with Hildy and dies a victim of the modern world, run over by a car. The desert reclaims Hogue, who is buried there, and it closes over and obliterates his miraculous spring. Like Pike Bishop, Junior Bonner, and Pat Garrett, Cable is a loser to modernity, ignominiously flattened by a motorcar. *The Ballad of Cable Hogue* is atypical of Peckinpah's features for being relatively violence-free. By temperament, Cable is a nonviolent man.

With *Straw Dogs* (1971), however, his next work, Peckinpah returned to the subjects of anger, violence, and aggression and created a ruthlessly brilliant film that does not equivocate on these issues as *The Wild Bunch* does. *Straw Dogs* presents violence as a multidimensional phenomenon (we see its psychological, emotional, sexual, and physical components) and as a transaction both horrifying and cruel. Its expression reduces the characters, and its explosions produce not redemption and glory, as in *The Wild Bunch,* but devastation and destruction.

That *Straw Dogs* has been Peckinpah's most misunderstood film is curious, but the reasons for this misunderstanding are clear. The film has been generally perceived as Peckinpah's most notorious celebration of brutality, a work that promotes a caveman ethic of dominance by the strong. The narrative of mild, meek mathematician David Sumner (Dustin Hoffman) returning to his wife's native Cornish village and arousing the animosity of some local thugs has been taken as an illustration of Ardrey's territorial imperative, especially since the climax of the film shows David defending his home and his wife, Amy (Susan George), against the thugs and successfully maiming or killing all of them. Reviewing the film upon its release, Stanley Kaufmann wrote that its point was that "even a mathematician has killer instincts and will, presumably, be a more courageous mathematician after killing a few beasts in defense of principle."[70] Pauline Kael concluded that it is a film whose philosophy is "Neanderthal" and whose goal "is to demonstrate that David *enjoys* the killing, and achieves his manhood in that self recognition."[71] Joan Mellen believed that the film says that "only violence against other men can prepare a male to be a lover skillful enough to satisfy a sexually alive woman. . . . If a man does not naturally possess the requisite capacity for authoritarian control won through violence, he must either rapidly learn it or, as a eunuch, lose his child-woman."[72]

The tendency for critics to perceive the film in terms of such caricatured statements has been influenced by Peckinpah's own self-presentation in the press as a brawling, hard-drinking, womanizing renegade. Furthermore, Peckinpah's statements about the film were calculated to inflame passions by baiting his critics. He used the occasion of his *Playboy* interview to act the bad boy by taunting his gallery of self-perceived feminist and liberal critics. This resulted in some truly asinine remarks which damaged the film and his own reputation. The worst of these was his comment that there are two kinds of women: "There are women and then there's pussy."[73] Amy, in the film, Peckinpah said, "is pussy under the veneer of being a woman."[74] Furthermore, Peckinpah contended, "She asked for the rape," referring to the scene where two of the locals, Charlie Venner and Norman Scutt, rape her after luring David out of the house on a snipe hunt. During the rape, there are moments when Amy responds sexually to Charlie, leading many critics to view this scene, as Weddle's biography claims, as "the ugliest of male-chauvinist fantasies" and one that would earn Peckinpah "a foremost place in the feminist hall of infamy."[75] Faced with such seemingly inflammatory material in the film and with Peckinpah's own outrageous remarks, critics unsurprisingly felt compelled to reject and condemn *Straw Dogs.*

All of the mystification that has surrounded this film is unfortunate because it obscures one of Peckinpah's greatest achievements as a filmmaker and casts a shadow on one of his most sophisticated and uncompromising excoriations of violence. When he was not baiting his critics, Peckinpah could be candid about the design of the film. In interviews, he continuously insisted that David Sumner was the villain of the film.[76] Peckinpah drafted letters to critics Richard Shickel and Pauline Kael protesting their negative reviews. In his letter to Shickel, Peckinpah wrote, "I was astonished in your review that you didn't pick up that Dustin was the heavy."[77] In his letter to Kael, Peckinpah explained why he considered David the villain of the picture. He wrote, "I was distressed that you didn't pick up that David was inciting the very violence he was running away from."[78] David is a villain because of the unarticulated rage which consumes him. By being out of touch with his anger, by chronically repressing it, David not only cannot control it, he cannot even recognize its existence.

David's rage surfaces in a behavior pattern marked by smug self-righteousness, by rudeness and contempt displayed toward Amy and the Cornish villagers whom he considers beneath him intellectually, by a petty selfishness, and by his sadistic treatment of Amy's cat in a displacement of the anger he feels for her. David affects an air of condescending amusement when he witnesses a scuffle in the pub between Tom Hedden, Charlie Venner, and the bartender and is oblivious to how culturally alien he appears to them, dressed as he is in sneakers rather than work boots and requesting "any American cigarettes." He maintains the difference in social status between himself and Norman, Charlie, and Chris Cawsey, the laborers working on his garage, by not suggesting they call him anything other than Mr. Sumner. He drunkenly baits Reverend Hood in a parlor game of intellectual one-upmanship by arguing the morality of science and Christianity, besting Hood with a smug smile after quoting Montesquieu on how no kingdom has been so given to bloodshed as that of Christ. When Hood asks David's occupation, David devises an absurd title of astromathematician and then boasts that he just made it up. He plays blaring music which Amy eventually shuts off. Responding to David's unmistakable contempt, the Reverend Hood tells his wife, "I think we'd better leave these good people." The reverend and his wife had come to invite David and Amy to an upcoming church social and to extend a more general embrace into the social life of the village. David spurns this offer through his rudeness, preferring to remain isolated with his equations and with his chronic, displaced aggression.

David cannot bring himself to confront Venner, Scutt, or Cawsey, even after their tricks nearly involve him in a traffic accident. Instead of denouncing them, David engages in his own head-trip of imagined machismo by buying them all a drink at the local pub. (An early cut of the film ran 126.5 minutes, and included a scene in which David does angrily confront Venner and Scutt in the pub after being abandoned on the moor during the fraudulent hunting trip. Upon the recommendation of the film's producers, Peckinpah deleted the scene because its placement erroneously implied that David knew about Amy's rape, which had occurred while he was detained on the moor. Deleting the scene also strengthened the climax of the film, when David finally does confront his antagonists.[79]) David does, though, attack Amy's cat, repeatedly throwing fruit at the animal until the fruit basket is empty. When David's anger finally erupts at the climax, in his attack on Hedden, Venner, Scutt, and Cawsey, it assumes terrifying proportions and destroys them and the house he has pledged to protect. The film demonstrates not the conversion of an egghead intellectual to a real man, as many critics have argued, but a nightmare vision of a pathologically repressed man finally losing control of his rage.

Peckinpah knew the subject of rage only too well, and after seeing it corrode marriages and friendships, he courageously insisted that this film depict David Sumner not as a hero but as a despicable, deeply flawed man. David has pledged to protect the house from the invasion efforts of Hedden and his gang by identifying himself with the house: "I will not allow violence against this house. This is me." Understood in psychodynamic terms, David's defense of the house is a denial of what Venner and the others represent—namely, himself, in all of his fury. They are David's worst nightmare, representing through their unrestrained physical appetites those threatening impulses of his own that he has tried to banish from his compulsively ordered life. As Rory Palmieri points out in his excellent discussion of this film, Venner, Scutt, and the others "are organized around the figure of David as projections of his repressed desires. Hence, David's entrance into the village is simultaneously his passage into his own unconscious."[80]

It is no wonder he identifies with the house. By defending it as a fortress, by seeking to keep it intact and the thugs outside, David aims to secure his own psyche against the irruption of his fury. But he cannot do so. The house is breached, its windows smashed, curtains burned, doors blasted, and floor left crawling with rats and covered with corpses. After all the carnage is over, David superficially, futilely tries to restore order. He uprights an overturned chair and sets it in the corner. But the house has been violated, Amy is traumatized by shock, and David leaves her and the house and drives into the darkness with the village idiot, Niles, who murmurs that he does not know his way home. The editing of this last scene accentuates its symbolic presentation of David's psychological disorientation and estrangement. In the 126.5-minute rough cut, the scene in the car between David and Niles was longer, with additional dialogue and action revolving around Niles' attempts to turn on the car radio. This material was deleted so that the action of the scene begins with Niles saying "I don't know my way home," and ends with David replying, "That's all right. Neither do I."[81]

The mise-en-scène of the film's concluding sequences, then, is heavy with carnage and destruction, and the narrative ends with David's extraordinary abandonment of Amy and the house in favor of a drive into the darkness. The film would seem not to need defense against the charge that Peckinpah was applauding David's acts. Its final sequences seem quite clear in their equation of violence with horror, destruction, and loss and in their demonstration that David has lost everything for which he said he was fighting, i.e., home and marriage. The home is now uninhabitable, and David and Amy are physically separated and emotionally estranged. The ambiguity of the last scene is appropriate. David cannot know where he is now headed, since the world he thought he knew has ended.

The film depicts—clearly, I would think but for the legacy of mystification that surrounds it—the destructive consequences of David's aggression. It is not the film that Peckinpah, in his moments of greatest perversity, claimed to have made. It is not an antifemale film, not a film that shows Amy as "pussy," and not a film that endorses the cruelties and violence that are visited upon her. If David is the villain of the narrative, which depicts his consuming hatred for everything around him, Amy is the chief character through whose suffering the film condemns the brutalities inflicted by David, Charlie, and Norman.

This condemnation is developed through the sustained visual attention given throughout the film to Amy's pain and misery, to her responses to

(Facing page and above) Peckinpah's images draw explicit parallels between the brutality inflicted on Amy by David (her husband) and by the rapist Charlie Venner. Note the similarity between each man's cruel expression as he looks at Amy, and her anguished response to their brutality. Amy's emotional and physical suffering is the center of the film. Frame enlargements.

David's psychological cruelty and emotional coldness, and to Charlie and Norman's physical attack. In Chapter 2, we examined how the editing replicates Amy's anguished emotional perspective. To appreciate the film's melancholic view of human destructiveness, we now need to enlarge our understanding of Amy's function in the narrative and its representation of her distress. Susan George's extraordinary performance makes Amy's suffering quite palpable, and Peckinpah continually turned his camera to her anguish, gave her the camera in order to delineate the impact upon Amy of the male aggression that the film depicts as so ugly. This attention to Amy's distress was not accidental or inadvertent. Peckinpah wrote in a memo to producer Daniel Melnick, "The emotional havoc that happens to Amy is the basis of our story."[82]

The film's attention to Amy's suffering is unremitting, and, again, I would argue that the evident audiovisual design is clear enough. She is hardly a prize that David wins through a violent rite of passage into manhood. She is, instead, a vulnerable wife whom he treats with contempt, whose affections he spurns, and whose loyalty he loses by the end of the film. Through its sustained depiction of Amy's emotional havoc, the film demonstrates that the psychic consequences of violence and cruelty are as horrific as the physical ones. The revelation of these consequences is accompanied by, and productive of, the film's icy melancholia, so different in its sharp concentration from the softly enveloping elegiacs of *Pat Garrett.*

When the narrative of the film commences, Amy and David's marriage is already in an advanced state of disintegration. As Peckinpah wrote in his draft letter to critic Richard Shickel, "This is the story of a bad marriage, marked by their training and environment."[83] They have come to Cornwall not just so that David can do his research and avoid the campus unrest of the Vietnam years but also because Amy has suggested they might be happier together in the village where she grew up. For Amy, at least, the return to Cornwall is part of her attempt to sustain the marriage, but, once there, she finds that David remains as aloof and as emotionally closed to her as ever. He secludes himself in his study and rebuffs her attempts to reach out to him. Angry, she retaliates with small acts of sabotage. Searching for her cat, she enters David's study and hears him say, from another room, that if the cat is in the study, he'll kill it. She then changes a plus to a minus sign in one of David's blackboard equations. Her act is not one of perverse spite. It follows clearly as a response to David's expression of hostility toward her pet. In a later scene, Amy again defaces David's blackboard by drawing a chalk line through the equations and sticking her gum on the board. This, too, is not a perverse act but is clearly motivated. David has again rebuffed her ("I love you, Amy, but I want you to leave me alone"), and she acts in angry response to his rejection.

Throughout the argument, he remains cool, unresponsive, and emotionally inaccessible to her. Amy, by contrast, is distraught. Her anguish is visualized. It distorts her face, and Peckinpah emphasizes this with several close-ups. Amy clearly has made a greater emotional investment in the marriage than has David. Her discovery that the trip to Cornwall has not changed David's chronic pattern of emotional withdrawal thus has terrible psychological consequences for her. Not only does David pull back emotionally from her, he treats her with the same intellectual contempt he feels for everyone around him, though in her case it is especially intense. When Amy begins to explain David's occupation to Charlie Venner, David cuts her off, saying, "Good try. Why don't you put this in the truck, Amy," handing her a box of groceries. Later, when she tells him that she grasps the concept of binary numbers, he cuts her down, saying "Hey, that's right. You're a bright lady. You know, you're not so dumb." David displays the same arrogance and contempt with the Reverend and Mrs. Hood. He begins to explain his work to them only to stop and ask, "Am I boring anyone?" That David does this to others besides Amy demonstrates that it is a character disorder in David and that the film is not endorsing his ill treatment of Amy in this respect, as some critics have maintained, but is showing the chronic and widespread nature of David's pathology. Amy is certainly flawed in her general acceptance of David's intellectual spiteful-ness, and he continually undermines her sense of self-worth. Nevertheless, by the end of the film, she has withdrawn her loyalty and love from David. She does this slowly and belatedly, but it is a direct consequence of David's indifference to her emotional needs and his animosity towards her.

Amy's withdrawal from David, which is readily comprehensible given his treatment of her, has been widely misconstrued by critics, who have condemned her for behaving like a bitch toward David and like a sluttish tease toward Charlie, Norman, and Chris as they work on the garage. Joan Mellen calls her "a feline tease" who craves to be overpowered by a power-ful man,[84] and Lawrence Shaffer, writing in *Sight and Sound,* calls her a "bitch-tease of a wife."[85] The conventional interpretation of Amy sees her as teasing the workmen with sex kitten moves until she succeeds in incit-ing their passions to the point where they rape her, an act that she enjoys. For Pauline Kael, "The rape scene says that women really want the rough stuff, that deep down they're little beasts asking to be made submissive."[86] For Joan Mellen, "The violence of the attack itself excites, decisive ev-idence that women respond most deeply to being taken; male violence be-comes essential to female need."[87] I don't know what movie these critics have seen, but their remarks demonstrate the tendency for discussions of *Straw Dogs* to opt for easy caricature and neglect the remarkable nuances of the film. Since Peckinpah was supposedly saying in this film that women are turned on by rape and brutality (an absurdity which he did verbally parrot in his *Playboy* interview, thereby discrediting his film), let us examine what actually happens to Amy and why.

Amy does have a palpable sexuality which is not itself a crime and should not be held against her. She does not flirt with the workmen. She knows them as fellow villagers and therefore behaves in a more familiar way with them than does David, who remains alienated from everyone around him. Despite the problems in her marriage, Amy intends to remain faithful to David. Early in the film, when Charlie Venner, an old lover, at-tempts to renew their relationship, she discourages him without a trace of flirtation. Charlie asks if Amy remembers when he took care of her, and she replies, "But you didn't, remember?" Charlie then roughly grabs her neck, saying "There was once a time, Mrs. Sumner, when you were ready to beg me for it." Amy tells him, forcefully, "Take your hands off me." Later, the workmen get a peek at her panties when she drives up to the farm and fixes her pantyhose before getting out of the car. She is unaware they are watching, and when she does realize it, her facial expression clearly denotes her disgust with them. She goes inside and complains to David about their presence and their unwanted attentions to her appearance.

Her only act of blatant provocation occurs when she exposes her breasts to them from an upstairs window, but the context in which this action occurs is important. The nuances and subtleties of this context make her act psychologically credible and complex. Immediately before she exposes herself, she and David have had a terrible argument in which she accuses him of being a coward, afraid to commit to anything outside his study, confronting him in a displaced way about his inability to deal with her and the problems in their marriage. Stung by her accusations, David says "I'm here [in Cornwall] because you once said you thought we could be happier here." Amy apologizes, and David immediately begins his manipulative games again. He asks if she's just sorry or is "sorry sorry" and tells her to come over to him on the sofa. She complies and sits uneasily beside him, the camera framing them from behind and from a distance, its physical remove a register of their lack of intimacy. David awkwardly embraces her, and Amy says, significantly, "I'm going to take a bath." David tells her she doesn't need one, and she says "I think I do." Amy is going to wash David off of her. She feels soiled by him and by their irresolvable problems. She goes upstairs, strips off her sweater, passing the window through which the workmen see her. She doesn't at first know they are watching. This is a key point since it goes to her intent. When she does turn and finds them staring, she lingers a moment at the window before walking off. But her gaze at them is cold, angry, and defiant, not sultry or inviting. As so often before, she acts from her anger at David, and also, in this case, from her disgust at them. Her brief nakedness at the window is a gesture of defiance, not invitation, of anger, not seduction. Peckinpah created a scene of disturbingly complex psychodynamics, not the simplistic caricatures that critics have perceived.

The same complexity is evident in the film's infamous rape scene. For most critics, the conventional interpretation of Amy's rape by Charlie, and then by Norman, is that it sexually arouses her, thereby exemplifying male fantasy myths that women enjoy being raped. With his customary verbal stupidity when granting public interviews, Peckinpah endorsed this idea, saying, "Most women do" enjoy rape.[88] There are certainly enough scenes of unreflective brutality toward women in his films to make one think that Peckinpah was thoroughly, and simply, a misogynist. The whore who takes a second slap from Pat Garrett because "I owe the Kid that much"; the Mexican woman Pike Bishop calls "Bitch!" and then shotguns; and the sluttish, imbecilic Fran (Sally Struthers) in *The Getaway* represent moments of unredeemed misogyny in Peckinpah's work. But the rape scene in *Straw Dogs* is not such a moment. Far from being a leering celebration of male subjugation of a secretly desirous woman, as Joan Mellen and others have contended, the sequence is presented as a scene, primarily, of terror that causes Amy the most extraordinary anguish. As in the near-rape of Elsa Knutsen by the Hammonds in *Ride the High Country,* the sequence is visualized internally, and subjectively, from the woman's frenzied, panicked perspective. We have studied this subjective visualization in detail in Chapter 2. We now need to consider the scene in terms of its broader dramatic structure. Amy does not behave seductively in a manner that indicates her secret desire to be raped. She tries to discourage Charlie in unambiguous terms. When he arrives at her door, Amy is not glad to see him. She coldly invites him in because she intends to ask him about her cat, which had been strangled, Amy suspects, by either Norman or Chris Cawsey. When Charlie begins to kiss her, she tells him nervously, "Please leave me." He kisses her again, and she does respond, briefly, before pulling free of him, slapping him and crying, "Get out." Charlie is an old lover, a man she's known longer than David, and she is, at this point in the narrative, feeling significantly estranged from David. Her ambiguous response to Charlie, her brief return of his kiss, says more about her shared past with him and her present loneliness than it does about her alleged desire to be raped.

Charlie responds brutally to her rejection. He hits her face, and the film cuts to a slow-motion shot of her agonized reaction, as Jerry Fielding's music underscores the terrifying direction in which the scene is now going. The slow-motion shot explicitly emphasizes Amy's pain and fear, not any exultation over Charlie's greater physical strength. Charlie then grabs her by the hair and drags her to the sofa. During the siege near the end of the film, David replicates Charlie's actions, thereby identifying him once again (as the subliminal editing during the rape had done) with Amy's attacker. Angered by her failure to remain loyal to him during the siege, David slaps Amy and pulls her by the hair. Peckinpah's instructions to his editors explicitly called for a close visualization of Amy's reaction to this abuse in place of the more distanced framing that was initially used in the early cut of the film: "Use second cut of Amy reacting to slap in close-up rather than the two shot."[89] During the rape, as Charlie strips off his shirt and enters her, Amy sees David atop her. The montage intercutting of Charlie and David, as we have noted, filmed in low angle from Amy's visual perspective, conveys her panicked psychological response—a woman alone, violated by the two men she has held dear. The subjective montage, in which she sees alternately Charlie, then David, conveys not just her alienated frame of mind, but also underscores the powerfully ambivalent feelings she has for each man, an old lover who now rapes her and a husband who has emotionally abandoned her. She then asks Charlie to go easy, and in her emotional pain there is a measured sexual response that elicits a belated tenderness from him.

This mixed set of emotions and responses gives the sequence a provocative and disturbing power, and it is certainly responsible for the critical condemnations that we have reviewed earlier. The brief, sad, and tender exchange between Amy and Charlie in the midst of this horrifying assault serves to intensify the alienation from love and tenderness that Peckinpah dramatized as the consequence of aggression and violence. This alienation from tenderness and beauty was one of Peckinpah's abiding themes, and we shall consider it in greater detail shortly. The subjective imagery from Amy's lacerated consciousness during the rape makes concrete her estrangement from tender emotion and her all too tragic familiarity with brutality and emotional cruelty. Her brief, sensual response to Charlie is one of the saddest indices of her estrangement, and it quickly vanishes, replaced by an even worse violation when Norman arrives and subjects her to a second rape. The scene ends with her agonized screams.

As it is visualized more extensively in the European cut of the film, this second rape changes the scene's moral and emotional dynamics and renders Amy's character less coherent and convincing. We need to consider these differences here because they demonstrate the volatility of the material that Peckinpah chose to work with and how difficult it was for him to find the right balance among the scene's many disparate emotional and psychological elements. The memos between Peckinpah and his production supervisors demonstrate the refinements in the scene's emotional emphases as it progressed from story outline to final editing. In a memo to Peckinpah discussing general story elements prior to filming, producer Daniel Melnick emphasized that the scene should arouse the viewer's compassion for Amy. "In any case there is no question but that we should feel terribly sorry for her both physically and psychically at the end of the scene."[90]

The initial editing of the rape scene failed to adequately convey this perspective and diminished the scene's psychological nuances, particularly because the editing relied on an injudicious use of camera positions. ABC Pictures executive Lewis J. Rachmil wrote to Peckinpah to complain that the editing failed to convey Amy's ambivalence toward Charlie and that too much emphasis was given to such physical details as Charlie fondling Amy's nipples. Rachmil also objected that too much of the scene was cut using long shots or medium shots that revealed more explicit sexual activity than was required.[91] As the scene was revised and now exists, most of the sexual activity is implied, and the rape itself plays in medium shot and close-up to delineate, principally, Amy's emotional responses and only secondarily to show the sexual acts that are transpiring.

In the European cut of the film, the second rape of Amy by Norman Scutt is considerably more detailed and extended. The American release ends with Norman's entrance and a flurry of disorienting shots that imply that Charlie passively permits Norman to rape Amy, although the scene concludes before this second rape occurs. The longer version explicitly shows Charlie pinning Amy to the sofa with his arm and Norman raping her anally. It also devotes considerable attention to Amy's vocal expressions of pain, and these shots are intercut with additional images of David on the moor. The longer version emphasizes the complicity between Charlie and Norman, whereas the American cut barely even suggests this, and it escalates the violation of Amy to a newly appalling and extremely unpleasant level. Indeed, the extra footage intensifies the brutality of the rape to a degree that unbalances the film—the savagery does not seem justified by narrative requirements or recuperable by subsequent story events. Furthermore, the extra footage makes Charlie an explicitly willing participant in Norman's attack on Amy and renders her character's final actions less coherent. Given Charlie's behavior in the longer version, it makes no sense for Amy to switch her loyalties to him and away from David during the siege. In addition, given his earlier cooperation with Norman, Charlie's later shooting of Scutt when he tries again to rape Amy seems less motivated. But in the American cut, which suggests that Charlie is a reluctant observer of, but not a participant in, Norman's rape of Amy, these later narrative developments are more credible.

In evaluating these two versions of the scene, the shorter and less explicit version achieves greater emotional and moral coherency, and it integrates in a more satisfying way with the subsequent narrative. Perhaps Peckinpah felt that the additional footage would intensify the depictions of Amy's brutalization, but in this case, less is certainly more. The differing versions of the scene, and its shaping during the editing process itself, indicate the extraordinary difficulties presented by this material in its conceptualization, design, and execution, as well as marking those thresholds that make the difference between a design that controls and focuses its violence and one that does not. To exploit violence on screen is a very simple matter and need not require much talent or intelligence. But to employ graphic brutality in a way that does not imply endorsement or approval of that violence is extremely difficult, as the evolution of this notorious and ruthless scene from the film demonstrates.

Amy's ambivalent response to Charlie in the rape scene is grounded in the film's careful attention to her psychological predicament, caught as she is between a failing marriage and her past allegiances to Charlie. Her responses are those of a clearly individuated character, whose psychodynamics are complex and whose violation the sequence presents as a terrible act. Peckinpah was unsparing in presenting Amy's physical and psychological violation, but he emphasized her anguished response to the violence perpetrated upon her by concentrating on close-ups of her facial reactions. These close-ups, coupled with the subjective montage imagery of Charlie and David, entail that the sequence is visualized from Amy's emotional perspective, and its keynotes are terror and despair. This is a mournful sequence, melancholy in the extreme, with its few moments of tenderness perverted by the poisoned context in which they appear. The ruthlessness of Peckinpah's approach to, and design of, this sequence lies precisely in the way it grants the viewer no comforting emotional space from which to watch the assault on Amy. By visualizing the scene from Amy's perspective, Peckinpah placed the viewer inside the sequence, on the interior of the action where the violence done to her is experienced with an intensified savagery. Peckinpah then accentuated the scene's disturbing impact by introducing a complex emotional transaction between Amy and Charlie, the brief unexpected tenderness that accompanies the violence and that is immediately alienated by it. Peckinpah introduced this tenderness in the midst of a terrifying assault, and his point was the perversion and corruption of such feelings by violence and aggression. Peckinpah introduced Amy's emotional vulnerability and then showed its brutalization. He portrayed sensitive human feelings and then their mutilation and destruction.

Peckinpah coldly showed the awful cost that violence exacts from its survivors and made the viewer a suffering witness to this lesson. The film's coldness principally lies here, in its attack on the privileged emotional space the viewer wishes to occupy in relation to the screen action and the character. In a film that was more nurturing of the viewer's feelings, David as the protagonist would not be such an awful person and Amy would not be hurt so badly and irreparably. The melancholia of the film lies not just in the joylessness of its narrative but in what it does to the viewer—the emotional and moral gratifications that the narrative denies the viewer as the price of contemplating violence close up. John Fraser has suggested that the radical potential of violent art lies here, in its "ruthless interrogation" of the order of existence and in the intellectual cruelty it inflicts upon its viewers.

> The true mental daring and hardihood are those displayed when the artist simultaneously acknowledges the worth of what is being violated and yet presents unflinchingly its violation. And it *hurts* the reader or viewer to be involved in that process and to feel the broader implications of the violation.[92]

Peckinpah insisted, intensely, that the viewer suffer from witnessing the aggression and brutality that the narrative of *Straw Dogs* unleashes. The narrative is coherent (barring the complications that the extra footage introduces in the European cut) and is uncompromised by the sentimentality that surrounds the violence in *The Wild Bunch*. *Straw Dogs* is a controlled film in which Peckinpah commanded his material and lacerated the viewer with a punishing vision of the savage costs of violence. Like *The Wild Bunch*, *Straw Dogs* concludes with an extended violent montage, but with a signal difference indicative of the greater sophistication with which Peckinpah was now approaching the subject of violence and its artistic representation. The montage showing the siege and David's response to his attackers is not an extended, uninterrupted visual spectacle, as is the final montage in *The Wild Bunch* where the climactic shoot-out at Mapache's headquarters is so visually overwhelming that it demolishes the possibility of the viewer's adopting a critical perspective on the action. The viewer can only submit to its ferocity.

In *Straw Dogs*, Peckinpah interrupted the violent action of the siege with interludes in which David quarrels with Amy and treats her brutally and converses with the attackers outside. As the differing moral perspectives of the characters collide during these interludes, Peckinpah was able to open up the violent action through irony and by sustaining David's character disorder through the siege itself. As a result, though the siege is harrowing, the viewer is granted a more critical space from which to witness the violence, something Peckinpah failed to provide in *The Wild Bunch*. When, for example, Amy withdraws her loyalties from David and threatens to open the door to Tom Hedden's gang of assailants, David grabs her by the hair and brutally pulls her back. His action, and her pained response, visualized in slow motion, identify David with her rapist, Charlie, demonstrating David's own viciousness. By punctuating the power of his montages with these critical interludes, Peckinpah was able to avoid losing control of his material as he did in *The Wild Bunch*.

Peckinpah followed *Straw Dogs* with the genial, relaxed, and delightful *Junior Bonner* and with *The Getaway,* a rare attempt to make a solidly commercial picture. In *Junior Bonner,* he celebrated, via comedy and nostalgia, the vanishing West, the wranglers and riders he remembered from his boyhood, and offered a sustained and compassionate portrait of a memorably dysfunctional family. With these shifts of focus, Peckinpah moved away from the inquiry into violence that had brought him such explosive attention on previous productions. As an action picture, *The Getaway* features abundant violence, some of it quite nasty, but here Peckinpah subordinated style to narrative more completely than in most of his other films. As a result, *The Getaway* offers visceral images of violence but does not inquire into, or explore, their meaning. The violence in the film is mainly, and merely, physical. It lacks the interior correlates that he so brilliantly provided in his other films.

With these pictures behind him, Peckinpah returned to the violence theme in his next two works—*Pat Garrett and Billy the Kid* (1973) and *Bring Me the Head of Alfredo Garcia* (1974)—and authenticated the integrity of the perspective he had developed and dramatized in *Straw Dogs.* These films are among Peckinpah's most substantial works, and stand as proof that his engagement with issue and emotion was passionate. With *Straw Dogs,* they form his great trilogy on the toxic nature of violence. The tone of each film is quite different. *Straw Dogs* is all ice and control in contrast to the lush elegiacs of *Pat Garrett* and the black despair of *Alfredo Garcia.* Yet the moral perspective that Peckinpah sustained through these works is consistent and demonstrates that the excoriation of violence he offered in *Straw Dogs* was not inadvertent or an accident of form but was, instead, his core position and outlook.

In *Pat Garrett and Billy the Kid,* Peckinpah eschewed the use of montage to construct visual spectacle. This, too, is a clear index of his evolving perspective. As we noted in Chapter Two, the only extended montage set-piece—intercutting Garrett's death with Billy's gang shooting the chickens—elicits an intellectual response from the viewer, who is stimulated by the design to search for the thematic and historical principles guiding the atemporal associations between the shots. In place of elaborate montage spectacles, Peckinpah offered a slowed and attenuated narrative that circles around Garrett's death and his inevitable confrontation with, and killing of, Billy. The attenuation of the narrative entails that the violence that occurs lacks the qualities of transcendence or heroics. It is, instead, symptomatic of the themes of defeat, loss, and diminishment that the narrative expresses. The film's remarkable narrative structure—opening and closing with Garrett's death—predetermines all of Garrett's choices and actions, which to him seem freely chosen and rationally enacted, as steps in an inevitable movement toward his own destruction. By beginning with Garrett's death, the narrative forecloses his apparent options and contextualizes his behavior in terms of this penultimate event. In fashioning a parable that sees conspiracy as the motor of history (see Chapter 1 for discussion of the preconditions of this outlook), Peckinpah sharply constrained Garrett's own free will. Its apparent exercise by Garrett proves to be limited by, and expressive of, the historical forces that are operating through him: i.e., the Santa Fe Ring of business and political leaders with their visions of economic progress conjoined with authoritarian political control. In *The Wild Bunch,* Pike and his gang chose to reclaim Angel from Mapache knowing that they would die in the process. But by making this choice, they were able to reaffirm their residual humanity, thereby giving the ensuing violence a heroic dimension. Garrett, though, loses his remaining humanity through the choices he makes, the friends he betrays, and the comrades he kills. Thus, it is appropriate that the last shot he fires in the film be directed at himself. The film's extraordinary melancholy and its critique of violence are tied, then, to its historical and its existential vision. Its dark view of history is conjoined with an antiheroic presentation of violence as a symptom of individual defeat and loss of freedom. By predetermining the narrative in this fashion, Peckinpah vitiated the film's violence of heroism and excitement.

The narrative structure, then, encloses Garrett in a web of historical forces that he cannot control. One of the Santa Fe Ring leaders tells him, "In this particular game, there are only a few plays left. I'd advise you to grab onto a winning hand while you have a chance." Garrett believes that he has done so, but his explanations of his choice to ally with the Ring have a double-edged irony. He talks of wanting to grow old and prosper, but these sad hopes are clearly foredoomed. Impatient with Garrett's slow progress toward capturing the Kid, the Santa Fe Ring assigns Poe, one of their hired guns (and one of the men who subsequently kills Garrett), to accompany him. Speaking the mantra of progress, Poe tells him, "Country's got to make a choice. Time's over for drifters and outlaws and others who've got no backbone." Incensed, Garrett tries to assert his dignity and independence as a free man undeterred by the power of his employers. He angrily tells Poe, "This country's getting old, and I aim to get old with it. Now the Kid don't want it that way. He might be a better man for it. I ain't judging. But I don't want you explaining nothing to me, and I don't want you saying nothing about the Kid and nobody else in my God-damned county." Garrett's reassertion of self is impassioned but futile. This scene ends with a composition that re-inscribes Garrett in the networks of history and power that he cannot escape. After his declaration to Poe, the scene cuts to a long shot of Garrett riding away. In the foreground, through which he is glimpsed, runs a barbed-wire fence belonging to John Chisum, a powerful rancher who is part of the Santa Fe ruling class. Earlier in the film, Billy explicitly equated Chisum's fences with an encroachment upon individual freedom via an excessive privatization of the land. Now Garrett's eloquent defiance of the Santa Fe Ring's power is recuperated and reduced by this imagery of Chisum's empire as Garrett, riding away from the camera, has a fence literally thrown around him.

Garrett's most poignant exchange comes with Sheriff Baker (Slim Pickins) whose help he enlists to flush out a pack of Billy's friends who

Garrett cannot face Sheriff Baker. Haunted by his moral failings, Garrett turns away from Baker and tries to justify his betrayal of Billy the Kid. Peckinpah gave the film to Garrett and his tortured conscience. Frame enlargement.

may know where the Kid is. This beautifully observed scene features Peckinpah's characteristic use of implication to reveal motive and emotional conflict. Baker expresses disapproval of Garrett's new employers: "I understand you've been riding for Chisum. I'd rather be on the outside of the law than packing a badge for that town of Lincoln and that bunch that's a-runnin' it." Sensitive to this reproach and its impugning of his behavior, Garrett wearily moves away from Baker. He stands at a distance, fortifies himself with a drink from his hip flask, and offers his self-justification. But, significantly, he does so with his back turned to Baker, whom he cannot bear to face. "It's a job," he says with fatigue. "There comes an age in a man's life where he don't want to spend time figuring what comes next." Embittered at Garrett for choosing the wrong side, Baker then effectively says Garrett has voided their friendship. What he actually says is, "Well, it's going to cost you some change. I got to the point where I don't do nothing for nobody unless there's a piece of gold attached to it." Stung by this insult, Garrett turns and looks intently at Baker, but he swallows the insult and flips him a gold piece.

It is a small, smarting defeat, but a much bigger one soon follows. Baker is mortally wounded in the attack on the cabin where Billy's friends are holed up. The magisterial sequence detailing the attack and its aftermath is among Peckinpah's finest creations. Its emotional tone is unrelievedly sad, and it depicts the violence as squalid and wasteful of life and friendship. Dying, Baker staggers off to collapse next to a pool of water while Garrett finishes with Black Harris (L.Q. Jones), the last of the gang in the cabin who remains alive. Badly wounded, Harris reminds Garrett that they were once friends and says, in the film's key piece of dialogue, "Us old boys oughtn't to be doing this to each other. There're ain't that many of us left." Peckinpah intercut the final moments of Garrett's fight with Harris with shots of Baker shambling slowly toward the water and with images of Baker's wife (Katy Jurado), also a law enforcement officer who has accompanied them on this attack, dropping her shotgun, deserting Garrett, and rushing to comfort her dying husband. In some of Peckinpah's loveliest and most wrenching images, she stares tearfully, smiling sadly and compassionately, as she watches her husband die. Dazed, he looks blankly at her, clutching his bleeding belly, then turns away and gazes at the mystery of death which is rushing toward him.

The intercutting of these lines of action intensifies the sense of waste to which this violence has led. In his final moments of life, Harris taunts Garrett by saying he knows where the Kid is. "I'll tell you when you're lying

The dying Sheriff Baker and his grieving wife gaze sadly at one another while Garrett watches them, grimly aware of what he has precipitated. Frame enlargements.

proper on the ground. It'll be the last word you ever hear." Defiant of Garrett's treachery, he tells him, "Paris, France." Black dies an ugly, awkward death, lather from an unfinished shave on his face, sprawled in the mud on the ground. Garrett's grim expression illuminates the depth of his recognition of what he is perpetrating. By moving on the Kid, he is destroying his past by wiping out its living links in old comrades like Black Harris and

Sheriff Baker. Garrett is a man doubly dead. He has no future, and now, increasingly, his past is vanishing, too, willingly forfeited by Garrett in his losing gambit. Peckinpah explicitly equated violence with the absence of will and choice and the loss of social connection to others, each a vital component of human identity. Peckinpah thus presented violence as a phenomenon that is corrosive of humanity.

The many acts of violence in which Garrett is implicated witness the steady erosion of his humanity, and its loss is emblemized in the last shot that he fires at his mirrored self after killing the Kid. Peckinpah stripped the Western genre of its fundamental, underlying myth of beneficent historical progress, and the violence here does not offer a ritual of cleansing and purgation. It registers personal dehumanization and social corruption in a parable of historical and existential loss. Through this cyclical narrative of betrayal and defeat, Peckinpah identified the paroxysms of violence through which history moves with a deadening of the spirit and the dawn of a dehumanizing era that is to be dreaded and feared.

In the intensity of its ugliness and hopelessness, *Bring Me the Head of Alfredo Garcia* marks an ultimate point in Peckinpah's explorations of human barbarism. As such, it completes and intensifies the investigations that were commenced uncertainly in *The Wild Bunch* and carried on more surely throughout *Straw Dogs* and *Pat Garrett*. Peckinpah's obsessive re-exploration of this terrain in these films demonstrates the depth to which the violence question resonated for him and the importance he attached to it. Yet in *Alfredo Garcia,* Peckinpah went places he had never gone before, as if to get closure on the subject and theme of human brutality. In the film's weird narrative, Benny (Warren Oates), a seedy piano player in a run-down bar, agrees to dig up the corpse of Alfredo Garcia and turn in his head for a bounty of ten thousand dollars. Benny's quest to find and mutilate Alfredo's corpse forms Peckinpah's most extreme statement on the corrupting influence of money. Peckinpah described the theme of this film as a grim one, the darkness of which was intended to strike a cautionary moral tone. He wrote,

> This is the story of a man caught up in the brutality of the world around him, who loses all sense of morality with one act of violence begetting another, until there is no return to respectability, only retribution. The lasting theme of the film is that such acts only end in disaster for those involved.[93]

The narrative hovers about a graveyard and ends in death, not only Benny's but that of nearly every character whose path he has crossed.

Benny loses everything and betrays every principle that gives life distinction. Peckinpah concentrated here on loss, on showing dehumanization; his art, therefore, assumes its positive value, dialectically, from its preoccupation with negation and destruction. While on tour promoting this film, Peckinpah told Barbara Walters that it was not in his power to present constructive values in his work.[94] Were he more articulate, he might have said, more truly, that he could not present constructive values directly but rather only by indirection, by showing the awful void their loss leaves behind. *Alfredo Garcia* is such a demonstration, and, significantly, therefore, Peckinpah also described the film as "a little picture about human dignity."[95]

The film opens with a brief prologue offering images of tenderness, love, and fecundity, everything which the remainder of the film will negate. Theresa, a beautiful young woman pregnant with Alfredo Garcia's child, lies by a calm body of water dappled with sunlight that gives her and the landscape a golden aura. Ducks and geese swim slowly by as Theresa lovingly caresses her stomach, swollen with her baby. She dips her feet in the water and tilts her head with contentment, in love with the small life that she carries. Peckinpah presented this gentle idyll in five reverse angle shots of Theresa and the landscape. These are linked by dissolves to convey a languid, relaxed tone. The idyll is brief, however, because in the next moment her father, El Jefe (Emilio Fernandez), summons her and demands to know who the father is, commanding that her arm be broken when she refuses to say. Significantly, Peckinpah elided this moment of brutality by cutting to a long shot of the hacienda exterior at the moment the arm is broken, an elision that registers his own pained relationship to this event. (It is not the only moment of visual discretion in this chronicle of human barbarity. We will explore the significance of Peckinpah's discreet approach to presenting violence in our final chapter.) When his daughter gives up Alfredo's name, El Jefe promises a bounty for Garcia's head, thus setting in motion the chain of events that will expose Benny's desperate venality and consequent loss of humanity. It is this loss that is the film's principle subject. El Jefe's representatives promise Benny $10,000 for the head, the same sum of money that Pike Bishop in *The Wild Bunch* said could cut all family ties.

Benny's venality is conveyed primarily through his relationship with his girlfriend, Elita (Isela Vega), who loves him in a genuine way that Benny cannot reciprocate. Elita accompanies Benny on his trip to the distant graveyard where Alfredo is buried because she at first does not know what he intends to do. For her, as she tells him with emphasis, it is important that they are together. Benny begins to tell her of his intentions when they stop by the roadside for a picnic in a scene that is one of the gentlest and most desolate passages Peckinpah ever filmed. Several viewers at a studio sneak-preview of *Alfredo Garcia* were so impressed with this scene that they remarked upon its tenderness. One viewer wrote that this scene "seems to be the emotional core of Peckinpah himself, his relationship to women, his tender side . . ."[96] Certainly, no other scene in his work presents so nuanced and sad a portrait of failed intimacy, of the yearning for closeness and the bitterness that accompanies its collapse. Benny speaks only of money while Elita speaks of her love for him. Elita says happily that they will marry in a church, and she is shocked to discover that Benny will only agree to do so after he has secured his bloody treasure. When Benny tells her they're going for Alfredo's head, she is visibly upset and pulls away from him, though she still does not fully grasp Benny's plans. He puts his arm around her, and she sits stiffly under his embrace, as Amy does under David's arm before going upstairs to shower. Benny asks Elita to marry him, and she cries sadly in response because the proposal has come too late, in too degraded a context, and without deep feeling from Benny. As commentary on Benny and Elita's progressive estrangement, Jerry Fielding's music grows dissonant and leaves its melodic statement unresolved and incomplete. The scene ends with Elita in tears, the relationship, always fragile, now ruptured. As he did in *Straw Dogs* during the scene where Amy and David embrace while sitting on the couch, Peckinpah brilliantly captured the dying intimacy and damaged emotional connections between estranged lovers.

In the car the following day, Elita realizes what Benny intends to do, and she screams that it is criminal, that he is asking her to desecrate a grave. But nothing is holy to Benny. "Don't give me that crap," he says. "There's nothing sacred about a hole in the ground or a man that's in it. Or you. Or me." He tells her the church cuts off the feet and fingers of its saints. "Well Alfredo's our saint. He's the saint of our money." Few films, and certainly nothing else in Peckinpah's cinema, have presented so corrosive a statement of cynical opportunism and amorality. Benny is coldly prepared to violate Elita in his quest for the head and its bounty. As in *Straw Dogs,* Peckinpah attended closely to the suffering of a woman who is better than her man. At the hotel that evening, Elita collapses in the shower stall, crying inconsolably. Benny finds her there and tells her he loves her, and Peckinpah filmed his declaration in close-up with a wide-angle lens that distorts Benny's face. The shot is, furthermore, a subjective composition representing Elita's view of Benny.

This angular and subjective visualization of his face links Benny to Charlie Venner in *Straw Dogs,* who, while raping Amy, is presented from her subjective view in an analogous wide-angle, extreme close-up that warps his features. More distantly, it links him to Sylvus and Henry Hammond in *Ride the High Country,* whose lust-crazed faces are shot with a wide-angle lens when they break into Elsa's honeymoon quarters to rape her. Peckinpah presented them in a subjective perspective from Elsa's point of view. This recurrent iconography—of a man's distorted face leaning in close to a woman to manifest love or brute desire—visualizes the man's inner perversity and monstrosity. The angular distortions of Benny's and Charlie's faces, and those of the Hammond brothers' faces, create a recurrent iconography in Peckinpah's work that is expressive of male brutality and of the twisted, crippled spirits that underlie this.

Peckinpah was consistent in his method of presentation. The subjective imagery emphasizes the woman's perspective on this male condition. The iconography visualizes these deformations of male psychology and emotion, qualities to which Peckinpah was powerfully attuned as an artist, and

Benny gazes in despair at Elita. Compare the wide-angle perspective in this composition with that on page 78.

it is consistent with his portrayal of Amy and Elita's (and Elsa's) suffering as a means to expose the rapacity of their men. Elita embraces Benny in the shower, but she does it coldly and without passion because his words mean nothing. He is choosing death and desecration in place of her. Mark Crispin Miller writes that "Elita offers [Benny] a kind of fulfillment that the quest for Garcia's head makes impossible. She is the center of potential, the source in the film of all that Peckinpah holds dear."[97] Elita is the moral and spiritual alternative to the terrible iconography of male desire that the film elaborates.

Peckinpah acknowledged the vital role that Elita plays in the film; as the representation of what is beautiful and positive in life, she is that which Benny negates. About his perceived reputation for being a woman-hater, Peckinpah said, "I have tried to show in *Bring Me the Head* that I adore them. They represent the positive pole of the film, the lifeforce and instinct." Planning the film's promotion, Peckinpah was anxious that Elita's thematic importance be stressed, and he wanted to accomplish this by re-straining the amount of violence contained in the film's preview trailer. He wrote to producer Helmut Dantine that the trailer looked good, but added, "We should cut down the final shootout, in order to accentuate the love theme a little more."[98]

Elita dies because of Benny's quest, and he abandons her, partially buried in Alfredo's grave, to pursue the head which has been stolen before he can get to it. Elita's death seals Benny's doom, and the last section of the film is a dying fall as he retrieves the head and accompanies it back to its source, leaving behind a trail of corpses. Benny's murderous frenzy, which occupies the last act of the film, is a direct consequence of his betrayal of Elita and marks his character as one that is beyond redemption. Responding to this sustained portrait of depravity, outraged viewers wrote on their sneak preview cards that this was "the most terrible movie I've ever seen" and that "to put that inhuman mess on film is a crime."[99]

It is notable that *Alfredo Garcia* could provoke such wrath even though its narrative design lacks tension, suspense, and sustained excitement. The violence here does not have the kinetic charge of *The Wild Bunch* or *Straw Dogs* because Benny is such a completely corrupted character (and also because Warren Oates is a weaker performer than William Holden or Dustin Hoffman). He offers the viewer no rooting interest. As a result, the violence does not become a vehicle for resolving highly-charged emotional or narrative issues. Enacted by a deadened protagonist, the violence is enervated and becomes more so through the repetitive gunfights that cap the

Elita and Benny reach the end of the line, morally, spiritually, and physically in this squalid room that adjoins the graveyard where Alfredo is buried. They will soon join him in that grave. In the film's sordid and ugly world, Peckinpah searched for grace.

film. It expresses a condition of spiritual and moral exhaustion, and its lack of kinetic excitement points toward Peckinpah's attempt to impose an anti-cathartic design upon the film and its narrative. With this design, which he had begun to elaborate in *Pat Garrett* through its attenuated narrative, Peckinpah was clearly moving away from catharsis and the spectacularized use of violence. As a critical means of achieving this anticathartic design, he emotionally disengaged the viewer from Benny's fate by stressing the extraordinary perversity of Benny's actions. Thus, the violence in the film's latter sections loses the hypnotic and compelling qualities that screen mayhem ordinarily possesses. Its exercise becomes as lifeless as the results it produces. Viewers looking for the excitement that screen violence typically provides will not find it in this film. This is a significant point, and it demonstrates that Peckinpah's attitudes toward violence were changing and had changed since the period in which he made *The Wild Bunch*. That film's explosive use of cinema to propel viewers toward an attempted catharsis is worlds removed from the twilit melancholy of *Alfredo Garcia,* with its enervated style, reptilian characters, and prolonged assault on the normative pleasures viewers look for in narrative cinema.

When, finally, Benny himself is shot and killed by El Jefe's men, Peckinpah largely elided his death, denying viewers even this final, explicit element of closure. Peckinpah skipped the death and showed simply the stoppage of Benny's car, riddled with bullets. The final image is a smoking machine gun pointed at the camera, its barrel opening a black void, the eye of violence that emblemizes the nothingness to which Benny has aspired and which has evacuated from his life all that he ought to have treasured.

When Benny shoots El Jefe, he screams repeatedly, defiantly, "No!" *Alfredo Garcia* is Peckinpah's thunderous No. By piling up so much death and spiritual poison, the narrative offers a hideous refusal to the promise of life with which the film opens. But, ever the ironist, Peckinpah's truest refusal was not of life, but of death, not of the initial idyll, but of the morbid narrative that follows. He showed here more darkly than ever before the graveyard of the spirit to which violence of the flesh leads. If he could not present, directly, a constructive vision on film, he could, by indirection, point toward those better things that his protagonists forfeit in their bloody quests for the bounties that cut all family ties. Benny is Peckinpah's ultimate loser, the grimiest and most haunted of his tragic fools. Pat Garrett learns a similar lesson. By turning on the Kid and his former comrades in order to serve the Santa Fe Ring, Garrett crawls inside the eye of violence and finds the same nothingness that destroys Benny. In neither of these films, nor in *Straw Dogs,* is there the celebration of violent death, its configuration with mythic status, that there is in *The Wild Bunch.*

By 1974, with *Alfredo Garcia,* Peckinpah had completed his trilogy. His subsequent films are problematic because the scripts are undistinguished, the productions were chaotic, and Peckinpah's personal problems were eroding his ability to work in a sustained and focused way. Nevertheless, they all demonstrate, with varying degrees of intensity, the familiar melancholia that issued from Peckinpah's attention to matters of mortality and violence. Thus, despite their individual failings, the later films sustain the coherence and integrity of his approach and perspective. To demonstrate this coherence, we should consider these productions in brief fashion.

The Killer Elite (1975) is a generic, formulaic, cloak-and-dagger action film centered on CIA skullduggery and Peckinpah's familiar theme of one friend betraying another for money. CIA operatives George Hansen (Robert Duvall) and Mike Locken (James Caan) are close buddies, but George sells out to a rogue faction within the agency and double-crosses Mike. Intending to disable Mike for life and force him to retire from the agency, George shoots him in the elbow and knee. As written, the film does not delve very deeply into the psyches of either character. Despite Peckinpah's recognition that "I got to hook the audience and the only way I can hook them is to hook them on the relationship between two people,"[100] the motives and emotional reactions of Hansen and Locken to the events around them remain largely unexplored. Peckinpah did, however, attempt to render Hansen's wounding as a physical and psychological trauma with protracted after-effects. Peckinpah felt very strongly that it was important to emphasize Locken's suffering. His script notes contain the following injunctions: "Accentuate Locken's crippled body and suffering . . ." and "Accentuate the fact that Locken is in constant pain."[101] The latter notation was circled in ink and contained six hand-written exclamation marks after it. In keeping with Peckinpah's intention, the film devotes considerable visual attention to the painful surgical treatment of Mike's wounds and to his lengthy physical rehabilitation, a process accompanied by the humiliation he experiences when he collapses several times in public surroundings. These humiliations suggest the psychological scars that the wounding and Hansen's betrayal have left on Mike. Characteristic of Peckinpah's late work, the film's central act of violence—George's shooting of Mike—provokes an extended legacy of suffering and leaves a ruined body and spirit as its consequence. Despite its largely mechanical construction, the film's residual melancholy lies here, in its contemplation of Mike's ruination and of the extinguishment of friendship and ideal which it manifests. For Peckinpah, violence was more than a physical force. It destroyed minds and hearts as well as bodies. This is the abiding conviction of his work. *The Killer Elite*'s chief interest is its demonstration of Peckinpah's attachment to this conviction, even in a film as erratic and mechanical as this one.

The melancholia of *Cross of Iron* (1977), Peckinpah's next film, is inseparable from Peckinpah's complex and tortuous relationship with that film's subject matter, an account of German soldiers fighting the Soviet army during World War II. Peckinpah loathed the barbarism of Nazi fascism and had a keen sense of the murderous consequences of the manic German patriotism that Hitler had stoked. Responding to a schoolchild who had written him complaining of the chicken-shooting sequence in *Pat Garrett and Billy the Kid,* Peckinpah, as he typically did when addressing complaints about this scene, raised the issue of war crimes and made reference

Mike Locken (James Caan) in *The Killer Elite* is shot by his friend George Hansen. Locken's physical and emotional suffering are key to Peckinpah's conceptualization of the character and the film.

to "the mass genocide that was carried out in the name of patriotism in Germany."[102] Elsewhere, Peckinpah argued that the basis of extremist philosophies such as fascism is the suppression of political and cultural freedoms.[103] Pauline Kael's notorious description of *Straw Dogs* as a fascist work of art disturbed Peckinpah precisely because of his historical understanding of this term. He drafted a reply to her in which he pointed out his distress over this analogy. ". . . I don't appreciate the description of the film as a fascist one, because it has connotations which to me are odious."[104]

Despite his sharp historical sense and his loathing for the fascism of Hitler's Germany, Peckinpah nevertheless agreed to go to Yugoslavia and make this film about German soldiers on the Russian front. But his political position necessitated that the material be de-Nazified. Thus, Sergeant Steiner (James Coburn) and his platoon are presented as soldiers bereft of political ideology and who merely want to survive the violence and madness around them. Peckinpah acknowledged that the film had an apolitical design. In a letter to British critic Colin McArthur, he wrote "... the film is very little concerned with politics—it is concerned with fighting soldiers, be they American, Japanese, Scottish, German ..."[105] Colonel Brandt (James Mason) describes the anomie that afflicts Steiner and the others, saying "The German soldier no longer has any ideals. He's not fighting for the culture of the West, not for one form of government he wants, not for the stinking party, he's fighting for his life ..." His immersion in the pervasive violence of the war has made Steiner suspicious of all political ideals and ideologies and, especially, of the military as the institution charged with the violent implementation of a malignant state policy. With weariness and disgust, he tells Brandt, "I hate all officers, all the Stranskys, all the Triebegs, all the iron cross scavengers in the whole German army. God, do you know how much I hate this uniform and everything it stands for?" For Steiner, fascism and communism are both corrupt. He tells a Russian prisoner that both systems are mindless extremes, "and neither works, nor will ever." Without cultural or political ideals to fight for, Steiner dedicates himself to the men in his platoon and their protection, but he fails to secure this, as most are wiped out in the fighting and by a treacherous ambush engineered by Captain Stransky, a Prussian military aristocrat who embodies everything that Steiner hates.

Peckinpah's de-Nazification of Steiner, then, was based on showing Steiner's awareness of the bankruptcy of the German cause and of Nazi ideals as well as on showing the general disillusionment that results from his perception of the war's savagery. Asked if he believes in God, Steiner replies, "I believe God is a sadist, but probably doesn't even know it." The battlefields of *Cross of Iron* become a nihilistic no-man's-land of unceasing violence, and Peckinpah successfully stripped the combat of the patriotic heroism and glory that usually accrue to it in war films. But by drawing the characters at this level of existential abstraction he is left without a coherent social perspective that might connect this war with the other bloody conflicts that are depicted in still photographs at the end of the film—Belfast, Biafra, My Lai, the Arab-Israeli War. This sudden attempt at the end to enlarge the film's historical focus through analogies with more recent instances of organized social violence makes a statement about neither the war nor those other events—except to offer them as instances of the continuing human propensity to commit violence and as examples of history as an ongoing parade of atrocities. Indeed, this latter lesson is precisely the one Peckinpah wished to illustrate. He wrote, ". . . that the end credits represent the suffering of war and is [sic] timeless and in the nature of war is exactly what I wanted to say."[106] The historical setting of *Cross of Iron* is dehistoricized by these concluding photos in favor of a portrait of timeless human barbarism, a vision toward which the film has been moving all along. "What will we do when we lose the war?," Colonel Brandt asks. "Prepare for the next one," his aide replies.

Peckinpah's preoccupation with violence and his determination to confront its ugly truths led him to view it as a transhistorical and timeless phenomenon. His ethical commitment to understand this phenomenon eventually resulted in these consequences for his historical vision. In *Pat Garrett*'s cyclic narrative, history is a deterministic force that ensnares individuals in a web of circumstance and robs them of free will. This view of history is manifest again in *Cross of Iron* and helps give the film its decidedly grim and melancholic tone as a symptom of the philosophical impasse in which Peckinpah now found himself in his meditations upon human brutality. In *Cross of Iron,* the historical process has become an endless series of deaths and destructive conflicts. Given this view of human history, Peckinpah's aesthetic response was to stare resolutely into the eye of destruction and observe its ugly effects on those who are subject to it. The resulting picture is neither pretty nor comforting, but the truth of violence as he had come to see it would not allow otherwise, because it afforded no possibility of escape from the teleology of the history in which it was imbedded.

After the sorry spectacle of Peckinpah's next film, *Convoy* (1978), a comic saga about truckers inspired by a popular song about CB radio, he remained inactive for several years. *The Osterman Weekend,* released in 1983, was his final film. Its narrative of TV talk-show host John Tanner (Rutger Hauer) being blackmailed by a rogue CIA agent named Fassett (John Hurt) into exposing an alleged Soviet spy ring is incoherent and confusing. But Peckinpah's depiction of psychological alienation within modern society is very powerful. In the film, TV cameras and monitors are everywhere, surveilling and recording the characters in their weakest, most venal, or most violent moments. Much of the violence in the film is recorded by these video cameras and subsequently displayed on TV monitors. Peckinpah's point was that in a society with a voracious appetite for

A depoliticized character in a depoliticized film, Sergeant Steiner (James Coburn) confronts the horrors of war in an existential no-man's-land. The melancholy of *Cross of Iron* is symptomatic of the philosophical impasse in which Peckinpah found himself.

media violence the emotional and psychological bonds among individuals are diminished or perverted. Fassett knowingly kills innocent people (Tanner's friends, who turn out not to have been Soviet agents) and justifies this by arguing that modern society, brainwashed and homogenized by television and other media, can no longer distinguish between real death and its mediated spectacle. He says, "We're in prime killing time . . . It's just another episode in this whole snuff soap opera we're all in." In the character of Fassett, Peckinpah again connected the exercise of violence with dehumanization. Fassett's wife has been murdered with CIA approval, and he keeps video footage of the killing, which he repeatedly watches in order to maintain his own psychic pain, requisite for carrying out the murders he has planned.

The film's portrait of modern America is anguished and disturbing. Peckinpah systematically conjoined physical violence with the psychological alienation prevailing among the characters and equated modern surveillance technologies with the loss of freedom, democracy, and interpersonal trust. Suppressing and manipulating information and images, CIA Chief Maxwell Danforth (Burt Lancaster), a neofascist, waits in the wings to seize political power and purge the nation of its internal enemies. Danforth will accomplish this through his control of information and media images. Through the characters of Fassett, TV talk-show host John Tanner, and, most of all, Maxwell Danforth, Peckinpah denounced the ability of the mass media to create what he believed were ersatz, substitute realities that mystified the true relations of power in society. He bitterly remarked to his script collaborators, "It's the fucking communications that erode you . . ." and he insisted that television be portrayed in the film as a delivery mechanism for advertising and as a means of social control. "I want that said," he insisted. "That's the only reason I'm going to make the fucking picture."[107]

In this respect, the film became a very dark register of Peckinpah's grim perception of the erosion of freedom in modern America. Maxwell Danforth, in particular, became a projection of, and trigger-point for, Peckinpah's rage and fear regarding the political situation in the latter part of the twentieth century. In a preproduction story conference, preserved on audiotape, Peckinpah suggested a potential ending for the film in which Danforth maneuvers Tanner into killing Fassett, whereupon Danforth consolidates his power by announcing on television that Tanner and Fassett were both Soviet spies. In this darker, grimmer version of the narrative, Danforth wins. When Peckinpah finished outlining this ending, one of his collaborators said that Danforth would be acting as if he was in charge, wielding political power. Peckinpah agreed, replying, his voice intense and impassioned, "Like he's in charge, complete control, as he always has been, and that's the danger this country faces."[108]

In discussing Danforth, Peckinpah retained his anger about Nixon's corruption from a decade earlier. "I think [of] Danforth as Alexander Haig—dirty, tricking people, believing the power runs the government . . . Danforth, and we don't need to say this, has reached the point that he's the head of the CIA, considered a Presidential candidate, which is realistic—like Nixon and Haig."[109] Peckinpah, however, now connected this old anger to the then-contemporary Reagan era and reinforced it with his perceptions of that administration's antidemocratic maneuvering. Discussing

Danforth's ability to protect himself by pulling and destroying incriminating files, Peckinpah remarked on the same story conference recording that such behavior is routine in high political office. Continuing, he said, angrily, bitterly, "Fuck, have you forgotten Watergate? And the psychiatrist number and all the shit that followed there? And did you know that Reagan has rescinded the Freedom of Information Act? It's an iron law [this kind of corruption and control], and we're living under it."[110] One of his collaborators asks if this is true and why this effort by Reagan has not been publicized. Peckinpah replied, insisting, "It has been! Nobody pays any attention! [It's] the fucking indifference of the fucking people . . ." He continued warning, "And along with that [the assault on the FOI] is tapping and surveillance, all the laws against that are going out." Peckinpah was wrong about repeal of the Freedom of Information Act, but he was not wrong to sense the animus toward it among some officials in the Reagan administration. Peckinpah was disturbed by the continuities he saw between the Nixon and Reagan eras, and he believed that the *Osterman* project was both topical and timely. "We have a timely script," he said. "I've been saying . . . that we had a timely script. That's the first thing I said. This was written twelve years ago. Today, these things are happening. These things are happening now."[111]

Peckinpah distilled his understanding of Danforth's neofascist identity in a speech that he hand-wrote for the character on the back of a typed list of editing notes. Although it was not used in the film, the speech effectively captures the paranoia that feeds Danforth's megalomania, and, by using a reference to revolution in Latin America, Peckinpah related Danforth to the then-topical obsessions of the Reagan presidency.

> More than crime in the streets the greatest danger to this country—is the indifference of the people—people like you—indifferent to their responsibilities as citizens—tax evaders "citizens" under the pay of foreign governments. Traitors—who are destroying the defense budget of our administration—citizens who laugh at the brush fires sweeping central and South America—well I warn you my job is to destroy any threat to this nation and (pause) if that [illegible] fits, then I'm coming after you. You will be found I promise you that —now you who are guilty look at me.[112]

Informed as a character by Peckinpah's historical perspectives, Danforth embodies Peckinpah's continuing anxieties about the fragility of institutional democracy in America and his contempt for patriotism when it becomes a political tool for manipulating the truth (as he felt had occurred

The object of Peckinpah's animus, Maxwell Danforth (Burt Lancaster) in *The Oster-man Weekend,* personifies Peckinpah's fears about the neofascist potential of the modern corporate state. © 1983, Osterman Weekend Associates.

during the My Lai cover-up). Danforth clearly represents repressive, authoritarian political control as an omnipresent danger to democracy, and fascism, especially, as an adversary that has never been completely vanquished. (Peckinpah wrote, ". . . I feel that people were ready for him [Hitler] and what he did, and certainly they are ready again."[113]) The film's incoherence and coldness notwithstanding, the resulting portrait of modern America is a very sad one that admits of little hope. While Peckinpah's representation of violence is a dialectical one, his presentation of history points toward a process from which dialectical struggle has ceased. Violence, and the darkness which it manifests, overwhelms history. Peckinpah confronted what he saw as a hopeless outcome, and his late work achieves a state of moral paralysis, unable to find an alternative to the darkness of modern society. He ended the film by urging viewers to turn off their televisions, a weak and ultimately despairing solution.

Throughout his work, Peckinpah exhibited a deepening artistic maturity and moral sophistication in his reflections on, and representation of, aggression and violence. Death would never again be the threshold to Valhalla that it is in *The Wild Bunch*. Instead, Peckinpah would come to understand it, and show it, as a cold hole in the ground, prelude to nothing, icy punishment for those who desecrate the ideals by which they should have lived. In his mature trilogy about the cancer of violence, Peckinpah moved far from the excitatory spectacles of *The Wild Bunch* with which he had made his name, and in doing this he came to appreciate the failure of an aesthetically induced catharsis as a means for restoring social health. Disturbed by the vigilante responses his film violence evoked in audiences, he increasingly placed violence within morbid and joyless screen worlds where its spiritual and psychic costs might be rendered with clarity. Thus, though he was wrong about the idea of catharsis on which he rested his early, daring experimentation, he remained true to his overall objective of stripping film violence of the mystification and glamour that surrounded it in the years just prior to the loosening of Hollywood's Production Code, and that still persist in contemporary cinema.

In *Cross of Iron*, when a female Russian soldier kills the youngest member of Steiner's platoon, she weeps. She looks upon him with tenderness and sadness as she drives the knife into his back. She feels compelled to take the life of this wartime enemy, but she understands her task as tragic, one not to be savored or attended with righteousness. This scene is an essential synecdoche for the moral orientation of Peckinpah's cinema toward the violence it depicts. Compelled to explore this subject, he responded with revulsion and grief, and he externalized and visualized these reactions in the characters that he placed on screen. Peckinpah retained an artistic and moral capacity for being shocked and saddened by the violence he dramatized.

Garner Simmons, present on the set of *Bring Me the Head of Alfredo Garcia* when Peckinpah filmed the scene where El Jefe's henchmen break his daughter's arm, reported that Peckinpah's eyes filled with tears while shooting this action.[114] The daughter defiantly endures her father's impious questions about her pregnancy and refuses to be humbled and humiliated when El Jefe's thugs rip the clothes from her body. Unable to get her to speak, they twist her arm until it breaks, completing an ugly assault on her youthful beauty and maternal pride. Peckinpah showed viewers the awful terms of this attack, but as an artist he was not insensitive to the brutality he depicted. His grieving response is an indice of a humane perspective. He never discarded the montage aesthetic to which he gave the most explosive form in *The Wild Bunch*. But he reconsidered the value of a purely kinetic design, and so began to attenuate the kinesis in *Straw Dogs,*

The tragedy of violence makes killers weep. A Russian soldier in *Cross of Iron* executes her German enemy with tenderness and a sad compassion.

and then mantled the action even further in the enervated and anticathartic *Pat Garrett* and *Alfredo Garcia,* in which he placed the irruptions of violence in a melancholic frame that would play against his viewers' desires for simple excitement and that would convey his own sense of the wastage that violence leaves in the lives of those it touches.

Witness to the bloodshed of the 1960s, attuned when sober to the price of his own rages, Peckinpah could not work as a romantic celebrant of violence, a sentimental exponent of gore. Instead, as he said, his best films show its ugliness, the way it diminishes human potential. He saw, and showed, its lacerations of body and spirit. But merely showing these lacerations in a despairing and melancholic context would not be sufficient for countering the aestheticizing tendencies of the montage editing and for accentuating the heuristic effects he wished his films to have. He, therefore, deployed yet a third aesthetic frame around and within his work. This was composed of the self-reflexive designs that he used to control and contextualize the messages viewers were to extract from the violence they witnessed, a concept we will address in the next chapter.

Interrogating Violence

JUST BEFORE the slaughter in San Rafael that opens *The Wild Bunch,* Deke Thornton looks at the street below his rooftop sniper's perch. Down it come the temperance marchers who, in a moment, will be trapped in the crossfire between Thornton's snipers and the Wild Bunch. Contemplating the impending bloodshed, Thornton shakes his head with disgust and a weary resignation. He then participates in the ambush and shoots at least one unarmed townsperson, a man carrying a large tuba who suddenly intrudes into the line of fire Thornton has directed at Pike Bishop. Thornton's brief moment of reflection before the paroxysm of violence that consumes San Rafael helps place that violence within a condemnatory moral framework in which the bloodshed is presented as an outrage perpetrated upon the town by the railroad and the legal institutions it controls. Up on the roof, knowing what is to come, Thornton chokes down the sadness and revulsion that well up within him. Later, when Harrigan, the railroad agent, justifies the killing by declaring that he represents the law, Thornton is overcome again by these feelings and angrily strides away from Harrigan. He leaves the railroad office and goes back outside where the street is covered with corpses. He stares disconsolately at the dead.

These brief character dynamics announce the larger structural forces at work in Peckinpah's cinema. Thornton's reaction on the roof registers the grim and sober attitude toward violence that is the essential stance of Peckinpah's cinema in relation to the bloodshed it depicts. Thornton recoils from what he knows is coming, but, despite this personal revulsion, he nevertheless joins the fray. Thornton's ambivalent relationship with the ensuing slaughter, as a reluctant participant, expresses the deeper levels of betrayal, cowardice, and humiliation that mark his character and to which the narrative events subject him. His use of violence overrides his moral conviction that the ambush is wrong because the people of San Rafael have not been told about the attack Harrigan has planned. Thornton's sorrow before the ambush arises not just from his sick anticipation of the killing but also from his pained awareness that he is about to betray his own humane principles. As so often in Peckinpah's work, violence becomes an index of personal diminishment.

It is not difficult to see in Peckinpah's films the personal cost their production must have entailed. I am not speaking here of Peckinpah's famously stormy relationships with studio executives and the self-destructive battles that he helped provoke. Instead, it is the psychological toll on the filmmaker that I wish to emphasize and that indicates the serious and fundamentally nonexploitative terms by which he interrogated his grand theme and subject. While *The Wild Bunch* relates a grim narrative of disillusionment, betrayal, and violent death, the jovial repartee of the bunch, the bonds of camaraderie between them, and the apotheosis they achieve through death offset the tragic tone of the film and enabled Peckinpah to achieve a spirited connection with his beloved bad men, as opposed to the purely ironic attachment that tends to typify his character presentation in the later films (excepting Cable and Junior, for whom Peckinpah clearly had great regard). Considered in light of the affirmations in *The Wild Bunch, Cable Hogue,* and *Junior Bonner,* it is difficult to imagine a more joyless enterprise than *Straw Dogs.* It is a jewel of a film, sharply cut, precise in its design, yet its vision of life and its treatment of the viewer are unsparing and cruel. Peckinpah perversely built the film around a reprehensible protagonist, David Sumner, and wove a narrative of brutality and debasement in which the Dionysian forces of destruction prevail unconditionally.

Brecht, Artaud, and Peckinpah

The process of filmmaking offers inherent pleasures to directors who are as wedded to their medium as was Peckinpah, irrespective of the content of a particular production. But the grimness of *Straw Dogs,* and especially its studied lack of human affirmation (except by implication), must have entailed that this sustained exercise in cruelty constrained and compromised the psychological rewards derived from working with such material. For similar reasons, the nihilistic landscape that Peckinpah fashioned for his treatment of World War II in *Cross of Iron* must have exacted a continual spiritual depletion intensified by the constant budget and materials resource problems that plagued the production. Could anything have been more depressing after the career debacles of *Pat Garrett, Alfredo Garcia,* and *The Killer Elite* than to go off to Yugoslavia to make a movie about Nazis in a jerry-rigged production put together by a hustling independent producer? Part of the peculiarly abstracted and surreal quality of the film, which strips the German-Russian conflict of a significant social and political context, resides, as I have suggested, in Peckinpah's desire to rehabilitate the Nazi characters he had agreed to represent. By finding some personal affirmation in his task as a filmmaker depicting this world, he could create a way of living with these characters for the duration of the production. But his ambivalence toward the material proved to be aesthetically disabling. The ending of the film clearly demonstrates this. To conclude the film, after the parade of atrocity photos, Peckinpah utilized a quote from Bertolt Brecht's "The Resistible Rise of Arturo Ui" about the danger of another war and a newly resurgent fascism: "Don't rejoice in his defeat, you men/For though the world stood up and stopped the bastard/The bitch that bore him is in heat again."

Peckinpah's lack of intellectual sophistication is evident in this use of Brecht. Brecht fled Germany to escape the Nazi war machine and dedicated his plays and poetry to attacking Hitler and his war crimes. Peckinpah appended Brecht's work to the end of *Cross of Iron* without seeming to understand the ideological violence he does to that work by its inclusion here. Brecht was intent on exposing Nazis as "the perpetrators of great political crimes,"[1] not on making them palatable by portraying them, as Peckinpah did, as weary critics of a pointless war. Peckinpah seems not to have understood Brecht's work or life very well, despite his occasional references to the playwright in interviews. Certainly, as Robert Kolker has remarked, his use of Brecht in *Cross of Iron* amounts to an act of ideological schizophrenia, given the narrative context of the film, which valorizes Steiner and his men.[2] But Peckinpah apparently felt the need to ameliorate the project's general nihilism with a more humanistic and morally-committed statement—one that he thought he could make with the Brecht quotation.

Peckinpah's friend and occasional collaborator Jim Silke said, "By the time of *Cross,* Sam was already into the dark side, and they ask him to make a movie about Nazis. It was too hard for him. He wanted to say something at the end to make it all right."[3]

Antonin Artaud had written that his theater of cruelty would exact a price not just from its spectators but from its creator, Artaud, as well: "'*theater of cruelty'* means a theater difficult and cruel for myself first of all."[4] Discussing the requisites exacted from artists who seriously explore violence and brutality, John Fraser has noted that the artist who depicts violations of body or spirit "has to become a species of violator. . . . Creating the figures who do such things means allowing full play to the darker parts of the mind without fear of what one may unwittingly be revealing about oneself."[5] Peckinpah sustained his explorations of cruelty intensively, through many films and at considerable personal cost. I'm not suggesting that making these films caused his escalating self-destructiveness and eventual creative paralysis. The origins of that breakdown are tangled and multidimensional and, to some degree, unknowable. But the intensive exploration of human darkness and violence clearly did entail some personal risk for Peckinpah, and the production of these works sustained a reflexive cruelty directed inward at their creator as well as the evident cruelties directed outward at the spectator. The nightmarish worlds he dramatized and visualized in *Straw Dogs, Alfredo Garcia,* and *Cross of Iron,* and the dark parables of treachery and defeat he constructed in *Pat Garrett, The Killer Elite,* and *The Osterman Weekend* did not quiet the inner demons that drove him to forfeit his talents. On the contrary, they almost certainly helped reinforce this inner tumult. Cruelty exacts a price from the artist driven to dwell within its awful sphere. Peckinpah paid that price, and he demanded in his films that the viewers drawn to savagery pay it as well.

As we have noted previously, care must be exercised in comparing Peckinpah's cinema of violence with Artaud's theater of cruelty. While his theater incorporated an element of punishment for the spectator, Artaud backed away from maintaining any facile equation between his aesthetic and explicit violence. Cruelty, for him, was a metaphysical outlook rooted in the ontology of being in an implacable, indifferent universe. Of this important distinction, he wrote,

> . . . it is not the cruelty we can exercise upon each other by hacking at each other's bodies . . . but the much more terrible and necessary cruelty which things can exercise against us. We are not free. And the sky can still fall on our heads. And the theater has been created to teach us that first of all.[6]

By eliminating this nonfreedom, by representing the contingent and constrained nature of existence, the theatrical spectacle would cruelly erode the complacency of its spectators. Peckinpah's screen violence thus does not fall squarely within the Artaudian aesthetic of cruelty, since it tends to lack this metaphysical dimension. However, like Artaud, Peckinpah initially believed in catharsis as the affective end point of the dramatization, with spectacle the means for achieving the cathartic release.

With respect to its celebration of spectacle, Artaud's theater is the antinomy of Brecht's, which sought to control the theatrical illusion so as to produce a condition of estrangement in the spectators, who would, Brecht hoped, thereby gain greater understanding of the sociopolitical determinants of their lives. Brecht prized this critical estrangement over the more traditional aesthetic of empathy and catharsis. Brecht's was an explicitly didactic and anti-Aristotelian theater. The estrangement, or alienation effects, that it produced aimed to reveal, by defamiliarizing them, the relations of power in society which, Brecht believed, were habitually taken for granted by the audience. Brecht wrote, "The new alienations are only designed to free socially-conditioned phenomena from that stamp of familiarity which protects them against our grasp today."[7] Brecht, therefore, dismissed catharsis as a means by which the existing theater lulled its audience into a critical indifference by employing representations that mistook social phenomena for metaphysical ones. To the extent that it substituted metaphysics for social praxis, Brecht considered Aristotelian dramaturgy to be antiprogressive. Brecht believed that catharsis resulted from the emotional immersion of the spectator in the dramatic representation. Catharsis could not, therefore, be the goal of his alternative, anti-Aristotelian dramaturgy. The phenomenon of fascism helped make Brecht mistrustful of the mechanisms, whether social or aesthetic, for manipulating mass public emotion, and he considered the cathartic response to be implicated in those manipulations, the worst dangers of which fascism exemplified. Thus, he aimed to defuse spectacle on stage and to make pleasure serve reason by controlling the emotions stirred by the dramaturgy through estrangement-inducing techniques. In contrast to Aristotelian, cathartically based drama, Brecht wrote that his dramaturgy "does not make the hero the victim of an inevitable fate, nor does it wish to make the spectator the victim, so to speak, of a hypnotic experience in the theater."[8]

In contrast with the cooler, controlled distantiation of Brecht's theater, Artaud proclaimed the merits of an immersive dramaturgy which had a more antirational inflection. The theatrical spectacle would bombard and overwhelm the spectator's senses, producing an intensely physical, organic response in the audience. Psychology would be abandoned, magic and ritual embraced, and lights, sound, and movement would be designed, first, for their sensory intensity and then for what they might represent. Artaud urged that his theater exert a kind of hypnotic power over its viewers by virtue of its sensual depiction of extraordinary events and calamities. It would be "a theater that induces trance, as the dances of the Dervishes induce trance . . ."[9] The spectator's consciousness would be swept away by the spectacle.

Peckinpah's elaborate montages of violence in *The Wild Bunch,* as we have seen, approached this Artaudian ideal of crushing and seizing the sensibility of the viewer, and this is why those kinetic spectacles tend to work against his interest in examining violence critically. For a similar reason, the resort to Brecht at the end of *Cross of Iron* does not work because, for the duration of that film, Peckinpah has immersed the spectator in the ghastly sights and sounds of war, engulfed the viewer's senses with deafening explosions and choreographed, large-scale battle scenes. Appending Brecht to the end of this film disorganizes its social perspective and its aesthetic structure, because Brecht's explicit antifascism and hostility to spectacle are incompatible with the film's efforts to de-Nazify its characters and capture the excitement of combat. Though Peckinpah's use of Brecht here is unsophisticated and demonstrates little feeling for the dramatist's work, however, we should not discredit a more general significance that may be found in Brecht's work relative to Peckinpah's films.

In a more general context, the Brechtian example could have been a valuable and productive one for Peckinpah, even if his intellectual understanding of Brecht was undeveloped. Simply put, given the didactic implications of Peckinpah's project to explore and interrogate human violence in ways that could enlighten his viewers, the Artaudian emphasis on spectacle would be a dead end, and Peckinpah quickly reached this end, and realized it, in *The Wild Bunch.* He could go on to endlessly elaborate spectacular montages of slaughter, as a director like John Woo has been content to do, but to his credit he did not. He never again filmed anything with the scale and relentless ferocity of the Agua Verde massacre. As we have seen, his subsequent montages of death tend to be shorter in duration and with a more skillfully controlled moral point of view. Although the attack on the Sumner house in *Straw Dogs* goes on for a long time, Peckinpah continually broke into the spectacle to examine the conflicts among the characters, and the resultant ambiguities and ironies keep viewers off-balance and incline them toward an ongoing reexamination of their allegiances with the characters. In *Pat Garrett and Billy the Kid,* the elaborate montages of death are extinguished in favor of a primary emphasis upon the psychic and emotional components of physical violence, and in *Alfredo Garcia* the montage interludes are brief, because here, too, Peckinpah was exploring spiritual death rather than elaborating on its physical details.

The Artaudian aesthetic, therefore, could not have taken Peckinpah very far in his interrogation of violence. Brecht's alternative would have been much more productive, because it would have enabled Peckinpah to structure violence in a self-conscious way that could open it up critically as a subject and an experience. I do not wish to suggest here that Peckinpah's films are Brechtian. They are not. Nor do I wish to imply that Peckinpah was a student of Brecht. He was not, and, if he were, then the *Cross of Iron* ending shows that he was a bad one. I am suggesting that Brecht's work represents a stylistic direction in which Peckinpah could have profitably taken his inquiries into violence, and we shall see in this chapter that he did so. He seemed to sense that alternate possibilities were available to him.

After *The Wild Bunch,* the stylistic consequences issuing from the montage treatment of violence were clearly understood by Peckinpah. Without some mechanisms for critically reframing the issue of violence, its montage treatment could only result in endless repetition, producing one kinetic bloodbath after another. Peckinpah recognized this danger. So rather than embracing montage as the fundamental frame for organizing the cinematic treatment of violence, Peckinpah moved away from it and employed alternate mechanisms for controlling, containing, and self-consciously examining the dynamics of human violence.

If we take the theories of Artaud and Brecht as presenting ideal and opposing aesthetic possibilities for Peckinpah's work, we now need to trace his movement toward the use of self-reflexive, aesthetic frameworks which constrain the kinetic energies mobilized by the montage approach. These self-reflexive frameworks take his work some way toward a Brechtian aesthetic, even though we must be careful not to identify it with such an aesthetic.

I consider, first, Peckinpah's use of what I will call didactic tableaux: striking scenes and images presented formalistically so that they are detachable from the immediate narrative context. Peckinpah intended such visualizations, I believe, to declaim basic truths or principles of human cruelty. Next, I examine Peckinpah's use of irony as a favored mode for presenting narrative and character, the constructions of violence that irony makes possible, and its strengths and weaknesses for Peckinpah's singular project. Finally, I examine Peckinpah's reliance upon a recurrent visual metaphor for examining the alienated subjectivity that he understood to be a correlative of brutality and violence. These various devices are not necessarily Brechtian, but they collectively incline his work in that direction and constitute the third aesthetic frame through which he approached the grand theme and issue of his cinema.

Tableaux Imagery

The tableaux compositions comprise one of the most striking aspects of Peckinpah's films, and, like so many other features of his screen violence, they derive from the work of Arthur Penn, specifically, that scene in *The Left-Handed Gun* where Billy shoots Deputy Ollinger. In his early work, Penn had begun to explore striking approaches toward stylizing and visualizing screen violence. He had been the first American filmmaker to use Kurosawa's multicamera techniques and slow motion, and, elsewhere in *Bonnie and Clyde,* he demonstrated great sensitivity to the physicality of violence and the small details that convey it. As Buck Barrow (Gene Hackman) lies mortally wounded, Penn moves his camera past Barrow's awkwardly sprawled body to concentrate in close-up on his bloody hands as they jerk convulsively in the dying man's final moments. This unexpected visual detail concretizes Barrow's death in an original and memorable way. Well before *Bonnie and Clyde,* though, Penn was stylizing violence and searching for poetically graphic details. When Billy shoots Bob Ollinger, he blows Ollinger out of his boot. Penn presented the aftermath of the shooting as an extended tableau, captured in a single medium-long shot during which the townspeople display a mixture of fascination and revulsion toward the corpse and toward the spectacular image of his boot, sitting upright, some distance from the body. The absence of cutting enhances the tableau qualities of Penn's design. The boot sits in the foreground of the shot, Ollinger's body in the midground, and from the background a little girl runs excitedly toward the corpse. She stops, points at the boot, and begins to giggle. Her mother promptly appears, slaps the girl, and leads her away as other townspeople gather about the body and one man kneels down in amazement next to the boot and stares at it.

It is not hard to see why this scene exerted such an enormous impact on Peckinpah. It poetically expresses the physicality of violence in an original and disturbing way and begins to move movie violence away from the polite, sanitized exchanges that were prevalent before the late sixties. It portrays explicitly the ambivalent response of spectators, an ambivalence that Peckinpah believed was a fundamental characteristic of audiences watching screen violence. The little girl laughs and is attracted to the corpse, but she is slapped by her outraged mother as others gather uncertainly about the body. Penn visualized the mixed reactions of the crowd of fascinated onlookers in a way that Peckinpah could readily analogize with the responses of a movie audience, many of whom, he knew, wanted to look away but could not. Finally, the scene contextualizes violent death through the reactions of a child who behaves in a way that is far removed from what conventional piety might maintain. Instead of fear, the child is excited. Instead of crying, she laughs. Instead of running away, she dashes toward the corpse. It is her mother who tries to instill in the girl a reaction that she does not spontaneously possess.

In Peckinpah's films, the reactions of children to the death they witness, or are about to witness, exhibit this fascination. In most cases, they find violence exhilarating and react not with fear but with delight, as do the children of San Rafael who maniacally reenact the ambush even as bodies fill the streets. (An additional source for this representation of children's reactions to violence is *Shane* (1952), wherein little Joey Starrett, filled with manic energy, rushes through his house like a dervish, firing his imaginary gun when his father and Shane can no longer delay the final showdown with Ryker. Peckinpah felt *Shane* was the turning point, announcing a more dynamic and realistic rendition of violence in American cinema.[10]) Peckinpah's contextualization of violence in the reactions of children has led some critics to condemn him as perverse for suggesting that the adult propensity for violence is a genetic one, observable early in life in the behavior of children. Peckinpah's screen children torture scorpions (*The Wild Bunch*), play on a gallows (*Pat Garrett*), rush toward a corpse dumped on a city street (*The Getaway*), stride forward to assume the station of an executed patriarch (*Alfredo Garcia*), and torment a puppy in a graveyard (*Straw Dogs*). Their voices, joined in song, accompany images of explosives being planted in a building in *The Killer Elite* and of Hitler's war machine in *Cross of Iron*. This undeniably grim catalogue makes Peckinpah's assertions about his belief in the essential innocence of children seem very strange.[11] While he certainly understood violence as an elemental and fascinating force in human life, he also seized on Penn's representation of the little girl in *The Left-Handed Gun* because it made for striking visual poetry, and he repeated it as variations on a theme in his films because it established a unifying structural pattern to his imagery and a kind of quick, shorthand way of visually describing complex issues of spectatorship, of telegraphing the vicarious excitement afforded by violence, and of explicating the culture of violence he believed was endemic in modern society. (*The Osterman Weekend* is his most expansive statement of this latter issue.)

Peckinpah, then, was sensitive to the didactic implications of Penn's tableau presentation of the aftermath of Ollinger's death, and he incorporated the tableau image or scene as an enduring feature of his own work, most often used as a means for commenting explicitly on the nature and place of violence in human life. The first significant tableau image appears in *Ride the High Country* when the Hammond brothers storm into Kate's Place to beat Judge Tolliver for helping Steve and Gil reclaim Elsa at the miner's court hearing. As the Hammonds march into the back room where Tolliver stays, they pass out of the frame, and the camera moves in to study the reactions of two prostitutes to the beating which can now be heard from off-screen. The camera frames the prostitutes frontally, side by side, to place their different reactions to the beating in formal contrast. One woman turns away from the assault and covers her face in dread while the other stares off-screen at the beating, fascinated, and munches on a cooked chicken leg as she watches. At this point the scene fades out.

Through this tableau, Peckinpah emphasized two very different spectator reactions to a violent event. He was uninterested in the assault itself. Sound conveys the fact that it is occurring. He concentrated, instead, on the ambivalent response to bloodshed. One woman cringes, the other dines with rapt attention. By foregrounding their differing reactions, the tableau announces the mixture of attraction and repulsion that Peckinpah had come to recognize as the essential attribute of the spectator's response to violence, in life and on screen. The tableau announces this component as well as Peckinpah's intellectual, though not yet stylistic, recognition of it. Stylistically, in its cutting and camerawork, *Ride the High Country* is a fairly conventional film. I do not say this to disparage the sensitive anamorphic compositions that keep Steve and Gil on screen together, within the shots, as a visual metaphor for their friendship, or to belittle the beautiful use of autumnal landscapes as a means for visualizing the encroachments of old age, or to deny the surreal style of the scenes at Kate's Place, or to diminish the offbeat manner of filming and staging the final gunfight. But in comparison with the kinetic montage cutting of *The Wild Bunch* and with that film's moral abrasiveness, *Ride the High Country* is

Peckinpah believed that the spectator's response to violence, in life as on screen, was an ambivalent mixture of attraction and repulsion. He proclaimed this principle in this tableau composition in *Ride the High Country*. One prostitute eats her chicken and watches a man's beating while the other woman averts her eyes. Frame enlargement.

clearly a studio picture of the early sixties, though one undeniably inflected with Peckinpah's developing signature. In *Ride,* he intellectually recognized the complicated and complex emotions that grip spectators of violence, but he had not yet begun to explore the stylistic means for provoking those ambivalent reactions. On *The Wild Bunch,* by contrast, he applied this intellectual recognition stylistically, plunging viewers into a graphic violence rendered balletically, beautifully, and placing them in a savage landscape populated by bad characters, in some of whom Peckinpah suggested there might be redeeming, even admirable, features. Stylistically, and in the moral implications of that style for the viewer, *The Wild Bunch* was explosive. It formalized what Peckinpah had announced in his tableau of the two prostitutes in *Ride the High Country*.

As another measure of the immensely more sophisticated formal complexity of *The Wild Bunch* relative to *Ride the High Country,* Peckinpah opened the latter film with what was then, and would remain, his most savagely powerful tableau—the group of children torturing the scorpion with fire and ants. The design and cutting of this sequence were the subjects of several memos from producer Phil Feldman to Peckinpah. Feldman was concerned that an initial cut spent too much time (two and one-half minutes) on the ants and scorpions, seemingly used every take of the children's faces, and, because the opening shot focused on the scorpion and ants, rather than the children, might prove confusing for the audience. (Feldman also wished to discuss with Peckinpah the symbolism of this imagery to determine whether it should be used elsewhere in the film, specifically, before the Agua Verde shoot-out.)[12]

In general, in this initial cut, the picture was getting off to a slow start, with nearly seventeen minutes elapsing before the shoot-out in San Rafael. Feldman specifically urged Peckinpah to connect and integrate the ants with the children by using a shot that panned along a stick that one child was holding in the nest of ants. The pan would connect the children and their prey in an explicit fashion that would be necessary, Feldman believed, if the picture opened, as Peckinpah wanted, on a contextless close-up of the ants. In its revised design, after the children are established, Peckinpah moved to the first close-up of the insects when the boy shoves his stick forward, establishing a matching element for the close-up in which the stick is prominent. In response to Feldman's recommendations, the sequence was reshaped so that the scorpion-ant imagery is integrated more efficiently with the surrounding material, and the children are established first before the close-ups of the insects and scorpion.

Children are intent on their play as the Wild Bunch, in the background, ride into San Rafael. As the outlaws pass by, the children turn their smiling, happy faces toward them. Peckinpah then revealed the object of their play, the savage torture of a scorpion. The tableau is Peckinpah's most resonant symbol of the human appetites for cruelty and aggression. Frame enlargement.

This primitive spectacle greets the Bunch on the outskirts of town as they ride into San Rafael, and the tableau quality of the gathering of children is enhanced by their lack of reaction to, or interaction with, the Bunch as the outlaws ride past. The children say nothing, merely giggle amongst themselves as they torture their prey. Through elaborate and protracted cross-cutting between the circle of children and the members of the Bunch who are watching the spectacle, Peckinpah extended the tableau, and its poetic and didactic associations, for the length of the opening credits and well beyond, finally dissolving from the immolated scorpion to the bloody bodies on the street after the ambush. Escaping from town, the outlaws pass once more by the children, who remain as they were—a speechless tableau incarnate of cruelty and predation (and of encirclement and destruction by superior force, a concept basic to the narrative and the fate of the Bunch and to the visual design that renders this fate).

By visualizing the children and the scorpion as a tableau, Peckinpah ensured that its imagery would be potently metaphoric. The children's speechlessness, the purity of their concentration upon the ritual of torture (i.e., their lack of interest in or address to the Bunch), and the extended cross-cutting that integrates the children throughout the opening act of the film as the major reference point to which the narrative action is compared, all of these structural features work to elicit from viewers a predilection to interpret the children and scorpion as a didactic, metaphoric statement by the filmmaker. Peckinpah had found a way not merely to announce a thesis, as he had done in *Ride the High Country* with the two prostitutes, but to break in on the action in a manner that is stylistically integrated with that action (via cross-cut montage editing, the basic constructive element of the film) and that imposes a didactic level of structure upon the narrative while simultaneously inciting and disturbing the viewer's response. The scorpion tableau remains undeniably powerful and imposes upon the viewer the punishing cruelty of Peckinpah's singular vision as the spectator is invited to reflect upon the tableau's evident metaphoric meaning, is warned in advance of the savagery the film will contain, and is then aroused and exhilarated by the montages of violence. Thereby is the spectator made complicit in the film's world of brutality and death.

Peckinpah recreated and referenced this tableau at the beginning of *Straw Dogs*. The opening credits appear against a fuzzy, defocused image which is gradually, slowly brought into proper focus. The initial frame is so defocused as to appear empty of detail, without articulated features. As the rack focus commences, however, tiny but indeterminate shapes begin to swarm across the screen. This swarming activity, which recalls the nest of ants from the earlier film, continues throughout the rack focus. As the shot attains clarity, the swarming shapes are revealed to be children playing in a cemetery. In both films, Peckinpah employed a slow visual approach to these clusters of kids. In *The Wild Bunch,* the kids initially appear from the Bunch's perspective as the outlaws ride up to the group. Only when the riders come closer to the children is the object of their rapt attention—the scorpion's torture—revealed. (In an early cut of the film, Peckinpah opened with the scorpion-ants as the first image. As noted, partly because of Feldman's objections, this design was revised. Thus, the opening of *Straw Dogs,* with its immediately disorienting and contextless imagery, replicates the initial but unused opening of *The Wild Bunch.*) Peckinpah counted upon the initial images of the children to disarm the viewer, given the general conventions of piety and sentimentality that governed the depiction of children in American films up to that time. The destruction of those conventions via the sudden revelation of the scorpion torture was calculated to have an abruptly shocking and destabilizing impact upon the emotional relationship that viewers would expect to have with a Hollywood Western employing established and respected stars. The impact of that shock and destablization was intended to force a contemplation of the tableau's evident statement about the human appetite for cruelty and its exhibition by the very young.

The slowly focusing image that commences *Straw Dogs* embodies a similar perceptual strategy of gradual approach and recognition. In this film, though, the swarming shapes turn out not to be ants but children, and the viewer is disarmed by the unanticipated and disturbing context of death and malevolence in which the children are placed by virtue of their games and the graveyard location. Peckinpah self-consciously identified his artistic task with the presentation of this disturbing imagery and its metaphoric suggestions of a pervasive human appetite for cruelty and malevolence. When the opening shot attains full clarity, he placed his directorial credit on screen, associating his authorial presence with this revelation. As revealed, the image is a high-angle, long shot of a graveyard. In the upper left of the frame, a band of children, hands joined, encircle and dance around a cluster of gravestones. In the center of the frame, three children encircle a small dog and stalk around it in a menacing way. The shot ends with a quick zoom-in on this activity.

The second shot of the film depicts a gravestone looming prominently in the foreground in the left of the frame. In the center of the frame, a boy sits on a stone abutment as three kids encircle him and romp about the fixture on which he sits. Shot three shows this same action continuing in a reverse angle. A high-angle shot of the graveyard then shows the group of children moving in a serpentine fashion among the headstones. David and Amy Sumner are next introduced as they appear to the village children, who are watching them. The initial shots of David walking toward the camera are intercut with a close-up of two of the children from the graveyard peering intently at him and with a telephoto shot of other children watching him from the gravestones. Amy first appears in a point-of-view shot representing the perspective of several leering boys.

As with the tableau that opened *The Wild Bunch,* Peckinpah used the opening moments of *Straw Dogs* to construct a metaphoric series of images that speak explicitly about the impulses toward cruelty and the attraction to death that he found constituting the deformity of the human psyche. He assaulted the moviegoer's sensibilities by contextualizing this dark vision in the behavior of children, who already manifest these malevolent tendencies. Furthermore, as the scorpion tableau does in *The Wild Bunch,* the cemetery tableau announces and embodies basic structural and thematic principles of the film. These lie primarily in the motifs of encirclement that recur in the opening shots, which are given a sinister quality by virtue of the graveyard locale. As the narrative develops, Venner, Scutt, and their gang draw closer to David and Amy in a predatory fashion. Their presence is invasive psychologically and physically, and in the climax of the film, the gang literally encircles the couple, who are holed up in the house. (The encircling motif, with its implications of predation and invasive control, also resonates with the scorpion imagery of *The Wild Bunch,* since it suggests a victim overpowered by a force of superior strength or numbers.) Furthermore, the initial development of the motif via the children's games in the graveyard imbues the principle with an ontological dimension, makes of it the observation of a fundamental truth of human existence.

Moreover, the imagery of the children would have established a resonance with one of the originally scripted endings for the film, in which young Bobby Hedden and other village children renew the attack and siege of the Sumners after the adult thugs are killed, thereby bearing out on a literal level the implications of the initial encirclement imagery.[13] Peckinpah wisely opted to go with a more ambiguous conclusion that did not reprise the children. Their initial appearance in the graveyard tableau that opens the film, therefore, retains them on the level of metaphor and

declamation, pointing to, and embodying, the essential structure and themes of the work. As in *The Wild Bunch,* the spectator is to be jolted into self-consciousness by this confrontation with ostentatiously perverse imagery that enunciates a clear authorial presence. The surreal combination of kids' games and gravestones is unexpected and provocative. The perversity of the imagery, and the moral disorientation it produces, estranges the viewer from the depicted world on screen during the opening moments of the film. Rather than drawing the viewer into a seductive narrative world, the imagery assaults the spectator and upsets the viewer's moral equilibrium. As in Brecht's theater, the estrangement effect prods the viewer into a more intellectualized assessment of these unexpectedly bewildering and disturbing images.

Peckinpah's next substantive exploration of the violence theme was in *Pat Garrett and Billy the Kid,* and this film contains some of the most numerous and memorable tableaux of Peckinpah's career. As we have noted, by this point Peckinpah was reworking his aesthetic and moral approach to screen violence. In keeping with the film's coherently critical perspective on the violence it depicts, Peckinpah reconsidered the viability of catharsis as an explanation of the spectator's response to observed violence. Two of the film's tableaux offer critical rejoinders to the ideal of catharsis. The first is the tableau of children playing on the gallows that has been erected on the main street of Lincoln for the execution of Billy. Garrett has captured the Kid and left him in the company of Bob Ollinger (R.G. Armstrong) and another deputy. Ollinger is a religious psychopath whose bloodlust is so intense he can barely be restrained from killing Billy while the Kid is manacled in jail. Ollinger identifies Billy's execution with divine justice, and he promises to make Billy repent and say the Lord's Prayer before he crosses the gallows. "Why, good people are coming just to see your poor sinner's spirit meet the devil," he tells the Kid. The ritual of execution is a holy enterprise for Ollinger, and he believes it naturally appeals to all

---

(opposite page)

The encirclement motif, announced in the opening shots of *Straw Dogs* (top and middle), is a basic structural and thematic principle of the film, and it shapes subsequent imagery, as in the bottom shot, where David Sumner faces his antagonists. Frame enlargements.

good people because the gallows is an instrument of righteous vengeance. In his eyes, the gallows is sanctified, and the proof of one's regenerate nature lies in being attracted to this spectacle. The execution of a sinner draws good people to watch.

After the exchange with Billy, Ollinger crosses the street for a drink. Peckinpah then introduced the shots of children playing on the gallows. In the foreground of the first shot, a high-angle framing of the gallows, a boy (played by the director's son) swings on the noose and is pushed back and forth by four other children. After a moment, in the background, Ollinger appears, emerging from the saloon. The camera zooms out slightly to integrate him with the children in the frame. The next shot shows Ollinger looking at the scene and smiling with approval. Next, a low-angle long shot, representing his perspective, shows the children on the gallows swinging their friend on the rope. A sound bridge—the kids' gleeful laughter heard in an audio close-up—extends across all three shots.

Rising above the town's main street, the gallows offers the people of Lincoln and adjoining districts the entertaining spectacle of a local celebrity's public execution, and Peckinpah offered a condemnatory response to this use of displaced violence as social recreation. The appeal of this cathartic spectacle is visualized in the tableau of the children's attraction to the gallows but is then recontextualized through the affectionate reaction of Ollinger, a thoroughly odious character, to the sight of the children playing with the noose. The psychopath approves of the sublimated violence of the gallows because of its righteous appeal to the public, and this approval should strike the viewer as morally problematic, given the tainted status that accrues to Ollinger by virtue of his psychosis and sadism. The social acceptance of sublimated forms of violence, depicted in this tableau, have implications that Peckinpah explored subsequently. After Billy kills Ollinger and escapes from jail, Garrett returns to find the deputy's bloodied body still lying in the street. The people of Lincoln go about their daily chores ignoring the corpse. Three children sit by Ollinger's body, fascinated by the putrefying corpse. The consequence of the social acceptance of sublimated violence is the desensitization of individuals toward the death they witness. Ollinger's death disturbs no one and disrupts nothing in Lincoln. Unlike the mother's response to her child in Penn's *The Left-Handed Gun,* no one scolds the kids who sit by the body or pulls them away.

Peckinpah elaborated this portrait of emotional desensitization in viewers of violence later in the film. One of his most memorable tableaux shows the Horrell family lined up, side by side, as mute witnesses to Billy's

As Peckinpah reconsidered the ideal of catharsis, he began to realize that screen violence desensitizes its viewers. He showed this desensitization in the Horrell family, whose members have seen so much violence they can no longer respond emotionally to it. Numbed, they mutely watch the gunfight between Billy the Kid and one of Garrett's deputies. Frame enlargement.

killing of Alamosa Bill (Jack Elam), one of Garrett's deputies. Moments before, Billy and Alamosa Bill have dined at the Horrell's table—with their hosts in full awareness that Alamosa's badge entails his obligation to arrest Billy and in full understanding of the latter's probable violent resistance. Despite the knowledge of all at the table that bloodshed is imminent, Mrs. Horrell insists on proper table etiquette, admonishing Alamosa and Billy to put aside their quarrel for the duration of the meal. "Won't be having no ill talk at my table. Fill yourself, Billy," she says, handing him a plate. She offers Alamosa another fried pie. Finally, Alamosa says they'd better get to it, meaning that he and Billy need to step outside for the shooting. Mr. Horrell thumps the table with his hand, anticipating the burial work that lies ahead. He says he just got through putting up a new cottonwood door. He used the last one to bury his son, John, killed in a shooting. "He's buried out yonder there," Horrell says casually, without a trace of feeling. He then tells his children to give him a hand with the new door. They take it apart, hand it outside, and then everyone lines up to watch the killing. Ma and Pa Horrell stand among their five kids, with Ma holding the youngest. It is an extraordinary tableau. Deadened by all of the violence they have witnessed or encountered (including the murder of John), the Horrells are unable to respond with any feeling to Billy's shooting of Alamosa. They stand silent, inert, gazing with a stupefied detachment at the murder of the man they have just fed. Even as Alamosa lays dying, they neither move nor speak, and, as Billy rides off, they remain detached, unfeeling, mute.

Instead of catharsis, Peckinpah showed in this tableau the deadening of the sensibilities of spectators of violence. Catharsis requires a response to discharge, but the Horrells have none. Like frequent viewers of movie violence, the Horrells have become inured to the carnage they witness. They cannot summon even a rudimentary affective response. By acknowledging in this tableau that the probable spectatorial response to recurrent violence is not catharsis but desensitization (an outcome which, as we have seen, is supported by the social science evidence), Peckinpah exposed the problematic that compromised his earlier attempts to present violence in a healthy and constructive manner for viewers. Peckinpah clearly grasped, or intuited, this outcome, yet the insight was constrained by the nature of his talent. He was not an intellectual filmmaker, or one who systematically set about the exploration of core issues with entirely coherent and consistent results. As we have seen, he returned to the presentation of violence as spectacle in *Cross of Iron* and *The Killer Elite.* Yet it is to his credit that he glimpsed the psychological dead end to which the recurrent presentation of violent spectacle leads. With the nightmarish Horrells, Peckinpah acknowledged the failure of his early conceptualization of spectacular film violence as a purgative experience. The remainder of *Pat Garrett,* and all of *Alfredo Garcia,* his next film, are congruent with the truths expressed in the Horrell tableau of violence being a depleting and degrading experience.

The other extended tableau in *Pat Garrett* uses violence to reinforce the interpersonal alienation and isolation that recurrently plague Peckinpah's characters and are such significant features of his screen world. Camped by a river, Garrett spots a family on a houseboat drifting with the current. A man on the boat is shooting at floating debris in the river. When Garrett joins in and fires at the same debris, the man reflexively shoots at Garrett, who ducks behind a tree. The scene locks into extended tableau form as Garrett and the man sight each other, suspiciously, silently, along their upraised rifles. The houseboat drifts by, and the scene fades out on this image of reflexive, irrational violence, of Garrett's thwarted attempt at sociality, and of endemic psychological malevolence and mistrust. The man on the boat shoots at Garrett for no discernible reason except that killings are so plentiful and so without reason in the world depicted here that those who would survive had best perceive threats everywhere and fire first, lest they be caught mortally unaware. While the houseboat tableau is one of Peckinpah's most memorable, lyrical, and enigmatic, it elucidates the psychological alienation—the perceived lack of connection or common interests with another—that underlies homicide committed casually and without feeling, as Billy kills and as Garrett is killed, and as the rate of sociopathic homicide in contemporary America demonstrates all too well. Peckinpah here revealed the frightening psychological dynamic that undergirds homicide, and he chose, characteristically, the tableau format to illustrate a principle he felt was so important.

Peckinpah used these didactic tableaux intermittently in his films, and the last significant instance occurs late in *Alfredo Garcia* when Benny, bearing Alfredo's head, returns to the hotel to collect the bounty from his employers. The camera tilts up and zooms out to reveal a tableau of striking decadence. Max (Helmut Dantine), El Jefe's representative, is seated on a tacky sofa, dressed in a suit but without his trousers. Kneeling on either side are two prostitutes giving him a pedicure. Max reads an issue of *Time* with a Richard Nixon cover, and, when Benny enters, he swats one of the prostitutes on the head with the magazine. The tableau is highly formalized. The composition is symmetrical (Max framed by the prostitutes), and the frontality of the grouping is oriented so that the tableau will play explicitly to the camera and the viewer's eye. By placing the portrait of Nixon in this flamboyantly depraved context, Peckinpah was obviously indulging his hatred of that president. But he was also making a connection between the corruption of contemporary American society (as personified by Nixon) and the cold, amoral corporate killers who inhabit this hotel suite. Although this tableau differs from the others in that it is not about violence per se, it points to the institutionalized violence of the modern corporate-political state for which Peckinpah felt a great antipathy, and, though the setting is Mexico, it implicates modern American society in the web of corruption, conspiracy, and murder that the narrative weaves.

The didactic tableaux constitute a category of imagery in Peckinpah's work that is responsible for some of his most sophisticated effects. Despite their intermittent usage, the tableaux's presence in the films demonstrates Peckinpah's efforts to think through, and impose aesthetic control upon, the implications of the material he was dramatizing. These compositions furnished him with a vital and provocative method of visualizing the important thematic, psychological, social, or affective components of violence which he wished to impress upon his viewers. By making the tableau grouping a strikingly pictorial one, and, in many cases, by intercutting the tableau throughout a scene, Peckinpah emphasized the didactic quality of the conception that underlies the design and nudges the viewer toward a recognition of the explicit intended metaphor. Peckinpah did not systematically employ the tableau design as an essential element of structure throughout the body of his filmmaking. He was, instead, an intuitive filmmaker whose creative sensibility tended toward the fragment, the finely crafted detail, rather than toward elaborate and grandly integrated designs (except as noted, of course, in *The Wild Bunch* and *Straw Dogs*). Thus, he used tableau presentations as an irregular, but very important, feature of visual and philosophical design. They enabled him to periodically break in on the narrative, to speak more immediately with the viewer than the dramaturgical stratagems of character and narrative ordinarily permit. Peckinpah's tableaux are not, therefore, Brechtian, but they do reveal a restless, protean, creative sensibility impatient with conventions of narrative and driven to expose not just the look and feel of violence but its underlying psychic and social correlatives. The tableaux concretely speak to the abstraction of these more fundamental components.

The Mask of Irony

While Peckinpah's tableaux tend to intrude on the narrative in order to announce principles more abstract and general than those immediately denoted by the story, his favored mode of narrative construction required a much greater level of sensitivity from viewers because it tended not to announce its intentions or point of view so boldly or didactically. Peckinpah was a thoroughgoing ironist, and he used irony as a means of making his films more provocative in their depictions of villainy and brutality and as a means of preventing his moral point of view from becoming too obtrusive. He used it both to conceal and to reveal, somewhat in the spirit of Nietzsche, who had said that whatever is most profound loves masks. As Northrop Frye has pointed out, irony is a sophisticated mode and requires sophistication from those at whom it is directed: "Sophisticated irony merely states," Frye notes, "and lets the reader add the ironic tone himself."[14]

Many of Peckinpah's critics have condemned him as a celebrant of brutality because they have failed to detect in the films the ironies at work through which Peckinpah distanced himself from the often appalling things he chose to depict. Unlike his critics, Peckinpah retained a properly detached perspective on the often bad characters and behaviors that are at the center of his narratives. He described the Wild Bunch as being essentially a band of killers, as bad men, as people with very little good in them, limited, adolescent, and not very smart.[15] Peckinpah expected that his viewers would supply the critical and moral perspective that is often implicit or latent in his narratives and visual designs. On occasion, viewers did not and were simply swept up by the visceral energy of the imagery and exhibited a bloodthirsty, vigilante response. To the extent that his ironies failed to effectively communicate with viewers who did not perceive their intended meanings, they worked against Peckinpah's artistic designs and helped sully his critical reputation.

Despite these risks, for Peckinpah irony was a crucial means of creating a moral dialogue with the audience and, even more urgently, of insulating and protecting himself from the horrors he relentlessly put on film. As I have argued at the opening of this chapter, violent art, seriously approached, exacts a price from its creator who, driven as Peckinpah was to probe the dynamics of rage and brutality, may become progressively more estranged from those things of beauty and affirmation that hold open the redemptive possibilities in life. *Straw Dogs* is a brilliant film but one that shows little but ugliness, and Peckinpah remarked that he felt sickened by the film he had created.[16] Irony provided Peckinpah with a protective critical and psychic space from which to create his bleak depictions of loss, failure, treachery, and death. The mask of irony conceals the artist's revulsion from subject matter that is ugly and threatening but absolutely central to the screen world the artist is driven to depict. Peckinpah might have cried behind his mirrored glasses during the arm-breaking scene in *Alfredo Garcia,* but irony would provide him with the critical distance needed to prevent immersion and loss of a moral reference point in his films' savage landscapes and the often-perverted desires of their main characters.

The ironies that operate throughout *The Wild Bunch* are especially powerful and have been ably discussed by other scholars.[17] These ironies include, of course, the placement of bad men at the center of the narrative and the creation of an oblique moral perspective on their villainy and brutality. The Bunch are the heroes of the film, but they're also stone killers. Viewers disturbed by the film are upset, in part, by its apparent lack of moral perspective on the Bunch's appetite for murder. Viewers at an early sneak of the film wrote, "There is no theme except bloody senseless violence" and "When a film like yours (and *Bonnie and Clyde*) makes me cheer for the bad guys—it is not a good picture."[18] Peckinpah showed members of the Bunch shooting women, using them as shields in gun battles, and executing their own comrades, and let viewers draw the appropriate conclusions. Peckinpah's moral approach was characteristically indirect, in this film as in others. *Straw Dogs* warns against the destructive effects of chronically repressed rage and hostility by showing what happens when that rage erupts and gains expression. The film does not advocate the expression of violence as a healthy or constructive release, as it has often been misunderstood to say, but shows the horrific and *negatively* transforming results of such violence. At film's end, spent momentarily of the anger that is a core component of his personality, David Sumner becomes again his outwardly repressed, undemonstrative self, except that now the house he metaphorically understood as an embodiment of himself has been breached and violated. His marriage to Amy seems finished, and he abandons her to drive off into the night, acknowledging to Henry Niles that he is lost. There is nothing liberating about this finale, no sense that David has achieved critical insight into his own cruelty and hatred of others or into his complicity in helping engineer the bloody denouement. Instead there is only negativity—loss, destruction, psychic pain, isolation.

Peckinpah's perspective here was oblique. Because David is such an emotionally warped and myopic individual, and is himself so out of touch with his own rage, he is an unreliable moral guide through the narrative. Although he is the protagonist, he is not the exemplar of any affirmative principle that the film wishes to represent. As we have seen, there is no affirmative principle directly embodied in the film by the characters. Instead, through its depiction of David's coldness and hostility and Amy's suffering, and through its dramatization of the results of out-of-control violence, the film gestures beyond these conditions and implicitly questions the quality of a life lived in their presence. Because this is an unusual method for constructing an American film, many critics felt sure that David must be Peckinpah's mouthpiece. Accordingly, they took the film as if it were offering a conventional hero and interpreted the climax as a violent rite of passage through which David was reborn as a more masculine and potent character. The reviewer for *Newsweek,* for example, wrote that the film expresses Peckinpah's belief that "manhood requires rites of violence."[19]

In Peckinpah's view, however, David is sickened by the violence he perpetrates. Nowhere does David manifest the giddy exhilaration of the Wild Bunch just after they have killed Mapache and before the final cataclysm begins. For Peckinpah, David's killing of Chris Cawsey, whom he beats to death with a poker, is the key moment of savagery to which David reacts with nausea and self-loathing. David looks up and sees Charlie Venner leveling a shotgun at him. After killing Cawsey, David tells Charlie the gun is empty, and Charlie mockingly indicates that it is not. Not caring now if he lives or dies, David tells Charlie to pull the trigger so they can both find

David confronts and kills Chris Cawsey by beating him to death. Afterward, David is filled with despair, nausea, and self-loathing. For Peckinpah, this was a key moment in the film's narrative. Frame enlargement.

out if the gun is empty. In his letter to Richard Shickel protesting Shickel's review (which charged that the film was glorifying savagery), Peckinpah wrote, "The horror that Dustin feels after killing Calsey [sic], he feels with total despair, when he turns to Venner and tells him 'pull the trigger.' It certainly isn't with glory and savagery."[20] To Pauline Kael, he wrote, "After the killing of Calsey [sic], he realizes exactly what he has done."[21] He told *Playboy*'s interviewer, "There's a point in the middle of the siege when David almost throws up, he's so sick. . . . He's just used a poker to kill a man who's just tried to kill him. He looks at what he's done with despair and absolute horror and he doesn't care at that moment whether he lives or dies."[22] Peckinpah's tersely written instructions to his editors demonstrate the importance of this moment in the narrative for his conception of David's reaction to the violence he commits. He instructed his editors to expand the interval during which David manifests this self-loathing and indifference to the prospect of his own death: "Hang on David 'The gun's empty.'"[23] Peckinpah had a very precise understanding of this scene and a specific emotional content he wished it to convey, but the viewer has to infer David's internal reaction because it is implied but not explicit. David's outward calm and his flip retort to Charlie to pull the trigger conceal his inner nausea. The emotional dynamics of the scene are oblique and ironic. Peckinpah framed this moment carefully but left it to viewers to grasp the implications.

As an ironist, Peckinpah disengaged himself from David. He was relentless in exposing David's daily cruelties toward Amy and his condescending and myopic treatment of the Cornish villagers. As a measure of his ironic detachment from the character, Peckinpah undercut David's two big moments of self-assertion. Before any blood is spilled, Charlie Venner, Norman Scutt, and Chris Cawsey come to Trencher's farm and try to talk David into giving them Niles. They believe Niles has molested one of the young girls in the village, and they bitterly resent David, this American, this outsider, meddling in village affairs. (Returning from the church social, David and Amy struck Niles with their car. David insisted over Amy's objections on taking him to the house to await medical treatment.) David refuses to hand the man over and tells them Niles is his responsibility. Norman is incredulous that this American would presumptively declare himself the protector of one of their own villagers. He gasps, "Your responsibility? Why?" David does not answer. He cannot answer. He has no real idea why Niles should be his responsibility. He has been role-playing, committed to an intellectual game with them, and he mouthed the reply that seemed appropriate under the circumstances.

Pressed for an explanation by Norman, he cannot give it. Peckinpah drew out the silence by cutting in five reaction shots of the group waiting for David's answer. When David replies, "This is my house," Peckinpah cut to a brief low-angle shot of David. The low-angle view might seem to work, in a conventional way, to heroize him, and it may denote some residual regard from Peckinpah for the character and his stance. But this brief low-angle perspective needs to be situated in the larger context established throughout the film, which stresses David's contempt for the villagers and his culpability in the unfolding violence. The house, of course, is not his. The house and the furniture in it belonged to Amy's father. But David understands his relation to the house in metaphoric terms, not literal ones, and by keeping Charlie, Norman, and the others out of the house, he can protect the well-armored components of his psyche in which he has contained the rage that is too threatening to acknowledge.

Several scenes later, David again declares, this time to Amy, that he will not permit any attack on the house. "This is where I live. This is me. I will not allow violence against this house. No way." He tells Amy that he can-not give up Niles because Venner's gang will beat him to death, to which Amy says she doesn't care. Peckinpah's instructions to his editors called for an expansion of the psychological time of this exchange as a way of in-tensifying its importance.

> 'They just want him' on long shot before David's close shot. Hang on David's turn away. 'They'll beat him to death' hang on David. 'No, I don't' hang on her. Let him look at her longer. Hang on long shot. 'I care' hang on David, extend. Hang on 'No way' before pull out.[24]

While Amy's response that she doesn't care about Niles tarnishes her morally, the fear of attack that underlies it is immediately comprehensible, as is the fact that she, like Niles, Charlie, Norman, and the others outside, belongs to this village. They are her people. David does not and is not. He is the outsider and the cultural alien. Furthermore, while David seems to take the moral high road here, the lack of emotion and passion with which he articulates his reasons for defending Niles and the house tends to un-dermine the certitude of his commitment to those principles. He seems to hold an essentially intellectual, not a felt, understanding of and commit-ment to them.

While Peckinpah wished to expand the psychological duration of Da-vid's and Amy's exchange, it was not to heroize David but rather to dram-atize the *difficulty* with which David elects to use violence in their defense. It is not an easy decision that he makes. Furthermore, the visual perspec-tive that Peckinpah brought to the scene is a counter-intuitive one. David stands below Amy, at the bottom of the staircase, when he makes his grand declaration about defending the house from violence. Consequently, he is shot from an extremely high angle because Peckinpah had positioned the camera on the stairs, midway between Amy and David, during this ex-change. This perspective diminishes David's effective visual presence in the frame and tends to work against the dramatic force of his announce-ment. His big moment is undercut visually. The compositional design pro-vides an ironic frame around his grand declaration of principle, and if Da-vid's declaration is not to be fully trusted, that tends to vitiate the ensuing violence of heroic dimension.

A comparison with Pike's declaration of principle in *The Wild Bunch* can be instructive here. Pike tells Tector Gorch that when you side with a man, you stick with him. Otherwise, they're like some animals, and, without loy-alty, they're all finished. The ironies in this scene are different. Pike fails to

Peckinpah's high-angle perspective on David undercuts David's grand assertion of principle. By contrast, in *The Wild Bunch*, Pike Bishop's declaration of his code of honor is presented without visual irony. Frame enlargements.

live up to this code until the end of the film, but one never doubts that he believes, in his gut, in the truth of what he tells Tector. Thus, Peckinpah films Pike during this exchange with Tector from a low angle to lend authority to his words. Pike's special pain results from the awareness that he has betrayed those principles. When he leads the Bunch at the end to reclaim Angel, he becomes heroic because he honors, at last, his code. David Sumner, though, lacks this commitment to principle. He does not seem to believe in anything very passionately, certainly not with the intensity that causes Pike's personal failures to consume him. Consequently, David is not, and never becomes, heroic. He is striking a pose, playing another game. The high-angle shot that frames his declaration offers the critical rejoinder to it. David is aheroic. His aspirations to moral stature are beclouded, and they are critiqued by the ironic frame that Peckinpah drew about this character.

As his representation of David Sumner indicates, Peckinpah's remarkable artistic courage lay in his willingness to let viewers construct their own moral response to his work and their own evaluation of the characters in the narratives. The appropriately moral and humane response to the savagery Peckinpah placed on screen is often not given explicit voice within the body of a scene. For instance, *Cross of Iron* opens with an extended series of killings. Steiner's men silently stalk and then garrote, suffocate, and knife three Russian soldiers. Steiner's platoon subsequently grenades and machine-guns a larger encampment of Russians. Surveying the destruction, Steiner utters the film's first line of dialogue as a compliment to his men: "Good kill." Peckinpah assailed his viewers in the film's opening moments with this frightening portrait of a morally-inverted world where cold-blooded killing is complimented. The ironies at work in the scene, however, cannot yet be grasped by viewers but only become manifest through the remainder of the narrative which strips the glory from war-time killing. For the sake of letting those ironies work through the body of the film, Peckinpah was willing to risk being misunderstood at the outset. But he trusted his viewers to see what was correct, even if this entailed that he commit an audacious defiance of politesse and propriety in his depictions of human depravity.

The most audacious such defiance, and Peckinpah's most corrosive ironies, occur in his bleakest and saddest film, *Bring Me the Head of Alfredo Garcia*. Benny, the protagonist, disregards the entreaties of his lover, Elita, to desist from the quest, disregards her love for him, and leads her directly to her death. Peckinpah's narrative concept here was so black and perverse that the trust he placed, as an ironist, in his viewers was more thoroughgoing and essential than in any of his other films. Benny moves through a world of greed and debauchery, emblemized by the specter of Fred C. Dobbs, the gold-crazed psychopath from *The Treasure of the Sierra Madre* (1948), whose name is invoked by one of Benny's homicidal employers.

It is a measure of Peckinpah's humanism as a director that he retained a significant degree of compassion for Benny, this pathetic loser and vile opportunist. In no other Peckinpah film is there such a huge, ironic distance between the values embodied in the screen world as states of pure negativity and those affirmations of heart and spirit that are implicitly pointed to by the film through their almost total absence. They can be glimpsed through the alcoholic despair that saturates the narrative and through the example of the brutalized Elita, whose love songs Benny continues to hear after her death. Peckinpah asked his viewers to see past Benny's filth and depravity to find the residual humanity that may still exist in this worst of all losers. But implacable ironist that he was, Peckinpah granted Benny no absolution or opportunity for regeneration. In this respect, Peckinpah's punishing attitude toward his protagonist gives evidence of the moral frame he placed around the narrative rather than of the director's own lack of humanity. The moral voice in the film is displaced. It is ironic and implicit. Benny remains true to the void at his center. He begins and ends in death, and, thereby, becomes the chief instrument through which Peckinpah estranged viewers from this film whose narrative is self-devouring. Benny is not just the emblem of death but the destroyer of narrative, as Peckinpah's ironies are invested with an unprecedented degree of self-reflexivity.

Of Alfredo, Benny says, "The first time I saw him he was dead," and he may as well be speaking for himself. Benny is the walking dead. Peckinpah repeatedly made this equation in the film, between Alfredo and Benny, bound in everlasting, dark partnership. With bleak honesty, Peckinpah reminded his viewers that Benny is a dead man, first spiritually, then physically, reminded them in a way that should enforce a conceptual distance between spectator and character—provided, as always, that the ironies are perceived. When Benny, sitting in his piano bar, first sees the dead Alfredo's picture, a car crash is heard off-screen, and Benny says "You got me." A subsequent scene reveals that Alfredo has died in a car crash. The auto accident heard when Benny looks at Alfredo's portrait may, of course, be occurring in the street outside the bar, in the time and space of this scene. But it is also a nondiegetic sound, symbolically linking Benny and Alfredo. It indicates that Benny's path through this narrative is one toward the grave, toward nothingness.

Benny briefly shares the grave with Alfredo when he and Elita are ambushed at the grave site and are dumped into the earthen hole. Elita is killed, but Benny rises from Alfredo's grave to walk the last act of the narrative, spreading death until he, too, is consumed. Benny's return begins with a remarkable point-of-view shot, below ground, in the grave, opening onto darkness, then with Benny's hand before the camera (his view), clawing through the earth and pushing upward into the light. Announced with this disturbing image, the last part of the narrative turns in a self-reflexive direction as Benny searches for the meaning of the story that he inhabits. He says that he wants to know who is willing to pay such a fortune for a dead man's head and why. Seeking the answer to this question, Benny follows the trail of killers, eliminating them all, back toward that figure—El Jefe, the father of the girl whom Alfredo impregnated—whose commandment "Bring me the head of Alfredo Garcia" set the narrative in motion. Pursuing the trail of henchmen to El Jefe, Benny turns the narrative back on itself, seeking its reason for existing. Destroying those henchmen, learning that secret, Benny destroys the narrative links that have given him existence, and, killing El Jefe, he eliminates the foundational authority for the tale. If El Jefe is the instigator of narrative, Benny is its destroyer and, therefore, his own destroyer as well. By turning the narrative back upon itself through Benny until it is consumed, Peckinpah showed violence and death as forces that return and rebound upon their perpetrators until they are immolated as well. As a measure of Peckinpah's displaced and implicit moralism, Benny cannot be spared. After rising from the grave, he is to die twice more. In a shoot-out with the thugs who hired him at the El Camino Real hotel, Benny darts around a corner to evade the shots fired by one of the gangsters. But his reflection is held in the wall-length mirror behind him, and the bullets strike his reflected body. Seeing Benny's image hit momentarily confuses his opponent. Seizing the advantage, Benny steps out from behind the corner and kills the man. Benny lives again but the poetry of the imagery insists upon his death.

Finally, at the end, after killing El Jefe, Benny has removed the narrative conditions for his own existence. He is ambushed while driving away from El Jefe's hacienda, and, consistent with his status as an already-dead protagonist without a narrative to inhabit, the final imagery omits Benny's actual death, showing instead bullets striking his car which slows and then halts. Since Benny is already dead, only his final stoppage matters, and this is what the last images show. Since there is no longer a structured and coherent narrative, there is nothing to conclude or achieve closure on. The last image is, therefore, a freeze-frame, interrupting the action and holding this end point of time and space until all light fades from the screen. (The end credits that follow reprise a series of freeze-frames from earlier in the film.) The content of this image is significant. It is a freeze-frame close-up of the black opening at the end of the barrel of a machine gun. Overtop

In Peckinpah's self-reflexive narrative design, by killing El Jefe, Benny destroys himself by destroying the narrative that he inhabits and that El Jefe has instigated. Photo courtesy of United Artists Corporation.

this image, Peckinpah placed his director's credit. It is a gesture of defiance and despair, a self-reflexive meditation on the quandary in which he found himself and his art during this period.

We must consider the resonance and significance of this signal image. First, however, we should consider its predecessor in the film, an earlier moment where Peckinpah hid behind his mask of irony and then dropped it to reveal with utter honesty the moral relationship of his filmmaking to the violence it depicts. After Benny rises from the grave, he ambushes the pair of thugs who murdered Elita and stole the head. After killing them, Benny retrieves the head. Clutching this filthy, decaying bounty, he staggers back to one of the gangsters and gratuitously pumps a few more bullets into the man. As he does this, he asks, rhetorically, "Why? Because it feels so God-damned good."

This passage is perverse and horrible, but lyrically so, and classically self-reflexive, using irony to construct a meta-critique of the brutality which is on screen and that is simultaneously visited on the viewer. As with all great ironists, Peckinpah's stated and intended meanings are powerfully divergent. In the early seventies, when the film was produced and released, the critical condemnation of Peckinpah for what was perceived as excessive violence in his films was exceptionally intense. His talent and his films were castigated as "loathsome" and "sick." Reviewing *Pat Garrett and Billy the Kid,* the critic for *Newsweek* attacked Peckinpah's macho style as "adolescent" and "ridiculous."[25] The reviewer for *The Wall Street Journal* called *Alfredo Garcia* "So grotesque in its basic conception, so sadistic in its imagery, so irrational in its plotting, so obscene in its effect, and so incompetent in its cinematic realization that the only kind of analysis it really invites is psychoanalysis."[26] In this hostile critical climate, Peckinpah presented this scene wherein Benny talks about how good gratuitous violence feels. Peckinpah was obviously baiting his critics. He was not obliv-

"Why? Because it feels so God-damned good!" The disparity here, in *Alfredo Garcia,* between what is stated and what is meant has rarely been greater in any Peckinpah film.

ious to the tarnish that now adhered to his reputation and to the stereo-typed terms in which critics had come to see his work. Indeed, as we have seen, his own injudicious commentary in interviews had helped instigate this hostile climate. But this scene is ruthlessly honest. Benny's question is as close to and as far from a glorification of violence as one can find in the director's films. The details of mise-en-scène establish the ironic frame which contextualizes Benny's words. The rotting head, the fly-infested car, the dust that hangs like a curtain in the air, the mud and sweat that soil Benny's clothing, Elita's death, and Benny's own evident descent into mad-ness—all these elements fashion the critique of Benny's remark. Despair and loss have never been so palpable in a Peckinpah film.

Through Benny, Peckinpah examined the attractions and appeals of vi-olence, and he admitted that they exist. But he remained a moralist and re-tained a humane focus even in this most grotesque of films by situating those appeals within a context of regret, madness, and futility. By con-structing a mise-en-scène that insists on the connections between vio-lence, degradation, and spiritual defeat, Peckinpah enabled the spectator to feel for Benny both compassion and condemnation. But the director went even farther than this. Peckinpah located himself and his art in the spiritual lower depths where the characters in this film bottom out. By placing his director's credit alongside the smoking barrel of the machine gun, Peckinpah defiantly identified his reputation and his art with vio-lence and the gun. This was an act of honesty and willful self-destruction. As the narrative of *Alfredo Garcia* shows, the black hole of the gun barrel down which Peckinpah forced viewers to stare in the film's penultimate image is a void, a place of nothingness and one that leads to nihilism. From it, as the film dramatizes, come horrors that we must respect be-cause they are dangerous for artist and viewer alike. We should regard them warily, and only through art, because they may consume those who approach too closely. With the placement of his director's credit at the end of this film, Peckinpah burned any remaining bridges of accommodation that may still have existed between his work and its contemporaneous critics; he acknowledged that his aesthetic and personal preoccupation with violence had led to a position of apparent nihilism in his art, the end point of aesthetic and moral paralysis, and had contributed to the destruc-tion of his critical reputation. This credit is defiant but also melancholy. The project that Peckinpah made his own—to become intimate with vio-lence through its aesthetic rendering while preserving the awareness of its destructive and horrifying consequences—was immensely difficult. If, finally, all the energy and inquiries of his films reduce to the smoking gun barrel, if its black hole is their end point, then, like Benny, Peckinpah and his art are surely losers, come at journey's end not to the high country but the lower depths.

Peckinpah proved unable to extricate himself from the artistic and spiritual dead end that *Bring Me the Head of Alfedo Garcia* signaled. It is a bleakly compelling work, in some ways the ultimate Sam Peckinpah film, but it also marks the terminus of Peckinpah's art and of his career as a filmmaker who could fashion coherent and well-designed films. Subsequent films have their moments, but none is so courageous or unsparing in its confrontation with darkness as is *Alfredo Garcia*. And Peckinpah's subsequent attempts at irony lack the devastating force that he achieved in *The Wild Bunch, Straw Dogs,* and *Alfredo Garcia.* The laughter at the end of *Cross of Iron* juxtaposed with the children's song, the atrocity photos, and the Brecht quotation, fails to cohere into an organized, articulate design. The "Oh, shit," heard in voice-over, that concludes *Cross of Iron* and terminates this last sequence shows that Peckinpah's recourse to irony was here merely a means of dissociating himself from the film he

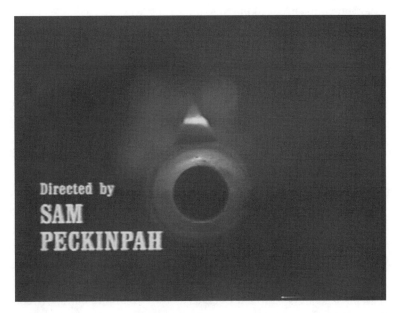

Peckinpah's aesthetic and spiritual dead-end as a filmmaker: the defiant end credit of *Alfredo Garcia.* Frame enlargement.

had made, a cynical maneuver, as is the closing exhortation in *The Oster-man Weekend* to turn off the television.

The attempts at irony in the later films lack the structural and moral complexity of its use in the earlier works and become merely occasions for exercising a reflexive cynicism. We should, then, bid farewell to this self-reflexive modality by noting that scene wherein its appearance is the most singular and striking. This is the scene in *Pat Garrett and Billy the Kid* where the director appears as Will, a coffin-maker, to urge Garrett on toward his historic confrontation with Billy. En route to Pete Maxwell's where Billy is staying, Garrett stops by Will's workshop and offers him a drink, which Will declines. (In the scene, James Coburn, as Garrett, smiles slightly at this. Later, the actor noted that it was the only time he knew Peckinpah to turn down a drink.) Peckinpah, as Will, sends Garrett off to his destiny. "Go on. Get it over with," he says, the director stepping inside the narrative to orchestrate its final act. He did so, though, by condemning his own protagonist, cursing and vilifying Garrett. Garrett, for Peckinpah, was a traitor and a coward for betraying his friends and selling out to the Santa Fe Ring. Will calls Garrett a "chicken-shit, badge-wearing son-of-a-bitch." As Will, Peckinpah admonished his fictional character that, in a world where deceit and treachery are the norm, "you can't trust anybody, not even yourself." Speaking metaphorically, with this scene Peckinpah announced his plans to abandon the Hollywood production system where, he had come to feel, profit worship and personal betrayal were endemic. The tortured production history of this film had reached epic proportions. As Will says, "You know what I'm going to do? I'm going to put everything I own, right here [in the coffin]. And I'm going to bury it, in the ground, and then I'm going to leave the territory." (Peckinpah's next film, *Alfredo Garcia,* was an independent production shot in Mexico.)

In this remarkable sequence, the filmmaker appears inside the scene to condemn the protagonist he helped create and, by identifying his craft with coffin-making, to add a bitter, dark, funereal tone to the film and especially to its climactic act, Garrett's killing of the Kid. By identifying his craft with coffin-making, Peckinpah also identified himself as the American cinema's preeminent explorer in matters of death and violence. Playing Will, Peckinpah portrays himself as a sad dealer in death, and he condemns Garrett for being a company man who has lost his integrity (as Peckinpah believed he had done as a Hollywood filmmaker). Despite the bitterness and antipathy he felt for Garrett, however, he built the film around this character because of his fascination with the dynamics of be-

Peckinpah's supreme moment of irony. He appeared as a coffin maker inside his own film to condemn and curse Pat Garrett, the character around whose suffering he built his film. Frame enlargement.

trayal and self-destruction and because of the empathy he felt for losers. Lest viewers come to feel too much sympathy for Garrett because of the film's attentiveness to his anguish, though, Peckinpah stepped into the narrative to confront his creation and to condemn him. It is an ironic moment, however, because the director had great regard for this character (witnessed in the film's intimate detailing of Garrett's psychic pain) and because, by casting himself as Will, Peckinpah symbolically implicated himself in the narrative scenario of Garrett's duplicity and betrayal.

The ironic mode, as Peckinpah practiced it, places the filmmaker at a critical distance from the situations and images that he or she creates, and it invites an analogous type of critical appraisal from viewers, relative to the film, who are asked to appreciate the differences between stated and intended meanings. As such, irony is an intellectually inflected mode of discourse, and Peckinpah found it especially useful for framing and controlling the volatile kinds of issues that he put on screen. The intellectual distance that it afforded Peckinpah, and that it invites from the viewer, is a key attribute of the self-reflexive aesthetic frame that he placed around his violent materials. In conjunction with the didactic tableaux, irony enabled Peckinpah to speak not only *through* the violence he depicted but *about* it as well. By wearing the mask of irony, Peckinpah was adopting a persona. Behind the mask lay the true self or, at least, an alternate self which chose not to speak candidly or directly but prized, instead, a degree of concealment.

The Mirrored Self

Due no doubt, in part, to his own psychodynamics, Peckinpah was drawn toward characters who display a failure of psychological integration: Pike's betrayal of his ideals, David Sumner's chronic repression, Pat Garrett's existential bad faith, Benny's choice of death instead of love. Peckinpah's ironic perception of life extended to the psyche in his recognition that morals and motives are always mixed and that the personality holds layers and secrets which one might never reveal, or reveal only at the cost of great pain. "I regard everything with irony, including the face I see in the mirror when I wake up in the morning," he said.[27] For Peckinpah, the mirror was a recurring motif and instrument of psychological revelation, and its use in his films, and in his personal remarks, is tied to his ironic sense of the fissured psyche and its proclivity for deceit, self-deception, and bad faith. Such a proclivity, rooted in chronic disparity among those layered components of the personality, can entangle oneself, and others, in the ugly differences between intention and act. ("It's not what you meant to do, it's what you did I don't like," a character says in *The Wild Bunch,* and it's a good descriptor for most of Peckinpah's protagonists.) In all of its ugliness, Peckinpah believed, and said, that *Straw Dogs* offered "a mirror for everybody" in which they might see reflected their own baser impulses.[28] Angered at a writer who criticized the chicken-shooting scene in *Pat Garrett,* Peckinpah, who always considered most such critics to be hypocrites, replied by saying the writer was "incapable of judging his own mirror."[29]

Peckinpah tied his innate sense of the fractured psyche with his developing perspectives on the phenomenon of human violence. From this, he fashioned one of his signature elements as a filmmaker, a key and recurring visual motif that he used as shorthand to convey his complex understanding of human psychology. The psychological correlative of violence in Peckinpah's work, as we have seen time after time, is self-alienation, and Peckinpah employed mirror images as a recurrent means of visualizing the fissured self and of interrogating the consequences of violence. He began to explore the implications of the mirrored self as an embodiment of estrangement and duality in *The Wild Bunch,* and in subsequent films he refined and sharpened the imagery. As a result, it achieves exceptional resonance in *Pat Garrett* and *Alfredo Garcia.*

In *The Wild Bunch,* during the Agua Verde shoot-out, Pike Bishop bursts into a room to find a woman cowering against the rear wall. On the door to his right hangs a full-length mirror. Pike pauses in his survey of the room.

The mirror imagery, as used in *The Wild Bunch,* has not yet attained its full resonance in Peckinpah's work. Pike Bishop fires at the mirror, but it holds the reflection of another character, not himself. Frame enlargement.

He then fires through that mirror, and a moment later a wounded soldier, who has been hiding behind the door, staggers out. Pike then turns to leave, and the woman shoots him in the back. Enraged, he turns and kills her. The scene is intercut with the ongoing battle in the plaza outside, and its complex dynamics partake of Peckinpah's implicit and indirect approach to character development. Pike pauses when he sees the woman and the mirror because it reminds him of the death of Aurora, the woman he loved who was shot by her enraged husband. Just before that moment, as Aurora prepared for bed with Pike, she paused before a multipaneled mirror, which caught her reflection and the image of her husband bursting into the bedroom and firing his gun. Pike's subsequent encounter with the woman in the mirrored room at Agua Verde reverberates with his memory of Aurora's loss, and he initially spares the woman in tribute to the importance of that earlier relationship. Pike pauses upon entering the room because the encounter unexpectedly unleashes the painful recollection of that earlier trauma. ("There's not a day that goes by that I don't think about it," he once told Dutch.) Pike is especially sensitive to the losses and mistakes that have accumulated in his past. Throughout the film, he suffers from the tortured recognition that his opportunism and readiness to betray his comrades give lie to the ideal of loyalty in which he passionately believes and to which he wants to hold himself. He has repudiated his more hopeful and principled self through a lifetime of arrogance, error, and willful desertion of friends and partners. Now, the encroachments of age and declining physical skills and the intrusion of a modern century have combined to make him feel old, used up, and bereft of conviction.

Given Pike's personal anguish and given also the use to which Peckinpah would put mirrors in subsequent films, it is notable that Pike does not see his mirrored reflection in this Agua Verde bedroom. Earlier in the film, Peckinpah had demonstrated in the flashback shared by Pike and Deke at their respective campfires an exploratory recognition of the formal means for enabling a troubled subjectivity to intrude upon and disrupt the flow of narrative events. In subsequent films, he would extend and deepen these irruptions of a disenchanted consciousness in ways that *The Wild Bunch* would only prefigure.

A similar evolution of style and implication is apparent in Peckinpah's use of mirror imagery. As it appears in the Agua Verde sequence, the mirror image is evocative and suggestive, but its fleeting appearance prevents it from being incorporated into the sequence with real denotative force. As with the flashback material, which in later films would be transformed from flashback inserts into intervals of fluid, free-associated imagery, *The Wild Bunch* shows Peckinpah beginning to appreciate the mirror's utility as a means for disrupting the spectator's empathic relationship with a character and substituting in place of this a more critical perspective. But none of this was as-yet worked out in any full or complete sense.

With his next film, *Cable Hogue,* Peckinpah lapsed into a more relaxed and jovial mood. Hildy's upstairs room at the saloon does have a mirror, but neither she nor Cable occupy the sort of psychological landscape which might be caught in that mirror and turned back upon them in a threatening and destabilizing way. But *Straw Dog's* David and Amy Sumner do occupy a precarious and fragile psychological territory—a marriage undermined by buried hostilities—and David's grasp of his own character is frightfully out of synch with the world in which he finds both himself and Amy. *Straw Dogs* achieves its impact from the scale of the awful psychological destruction visited upon Amy by David and from its revelation of just how titanic is David's inner rage, how great is his unacknowledged capacity for violence. Because *Straw Dogs* is about physical violation and psychological rupture, its visual design is amenable to Peckinpah's developing and distinctive use of mirrors to emblemize the fissured self. In the Sumner's bedroom stands a tall, full-sized mirror which catches the couple's reflection on the bed. During the scene where the Hedden children spy on David and Amy as they play in bed and then make love, Peckinpah interrupted the action between David and Amy with cutaways to their reflected selves. As she plays chess, he exercises, then gets into bed and coldly interrupts her affections to remove his watch, set the alarm clock, and then tease her with a lost chess piece; the cutting disrupts their interchange with lengthy shots of the mirror, standing alone in the frame, on which we can see the ongoing action. One shot of the mirror, taken through the bedroom window, simulates the vantage point of the voyeuristic Hedden children.

Neither David nor Amy is distracted by their mirrored reflection in this scene (though Amy is briefly arrested by her reflection in an earlier scene when she stands alone in the bedroom) so that the mirror motif does not function here as an overt and explicit emblem of psychological fragmentation, though it implicitly does so given the subject of the film. Peckinpah used the cutaways to the mirror to disturb and destabilize the spatial configuration of the scene, appropriately enough since the climax of the film exteriorizes the psychological and emotional conflicts of the narrative into physical space, which is disrupted and rent, and since the editing patterns throughout the film accentuate the disaligned angles of view from shot to shot. (But not in a fashion that carelessly violates continuity. The film is

The Sumners as a mirrored reflection in *Straw Dogs*. The imagery visualizes the emotional dissociation that prevails between David and Amy. Frame enlargement.

very carefully designed, and Peckinpah's instructions to his crew indicate how important the maintenance of proper continuity remained for him. "With reference to the insert in which Scutt and Venner open and lock the mantrap, the action on this was much too fast and must therefore be shot again. If you have a look at the rushes you will see that it does not match at all the action in the master."[30]) The cutaways to the mirror alter the viewer's direct perspective on the action by substituting a second-order, more removed perspective mediated via the mirror. The repetition of the cutaways, extended for the duration of the scene, produces a distancing effect.

The interplay between Amy and David becomes disassociated and fragmented by the cutaways to the mirror. These produce a disorienting effect on the viewer since there is no obvious narrative rationale for them. Except for the one shot of the mirror taken from outside the bedroom window, none of the cutaways represent the perspective of the Hedden children, who are watching David and Amy. The lack of a clear rationale for the camera's viewpoint in these cutaways is the chief reason for the destabilization of perspective in this sequence. These cutaways obtrude upon the action, disrupt the viewer's normative relationship with the characters, and, by mediating visual access to David and Amy, they enforce a distancing of perspective on these characters. The viewer's optical relationship with the action is disturbed, and the spatial field of the scene is fragmented. While neither David nor Amy confronts this fragmentation as a psychological correlate within themselves through a direct encounter with their mirrored opposite, the cutting of the scene invites the viewer to make this connection, intellectually, between physical and psychological space and the embodied and disembodied lovers who inhabit it. There is, therefore, more of Brecht in this use of the mirror than elsewhere in Peckinpah's work. Peckinpah used the mirror here not as an immediate visualization of psychological alienation, as he would most typically employ it, but as a third point triangulating the relationship between viewer and character. The precise design is distancing, disturbing, and replicates for the viewer the estrangement between Amy and David in the optical relationship that is structured with these characters.

Peckinpah used the mirror toward a similar end in *The Getaway.* Doc (Steve McQueen) has been in prison for four years. On his first day of release, his wife, Carol (Ali McGraw), takes him to an upstairs bedroom for lovemaking. Doc sits next to Carol on the edge of the bed, and the camera frames them from behind, with their images reflected on a bureau mirror directly in front of them, which the camera sees. They touch tentatively, hesitantly. After the years in prison, Doc is uncomfortable with his wife, especially with the physical and emotional intimacy that she now requires from him. The cutting of the scene alternates between the set-up framing them from behind (with the viewer able to see their faces reflected in the mirror) and a reverse angle close-up on their faces. The mirror creates a distancing effect in the shots where Doc and Carol are filmed from behind. With their backs to the camera, the viewer can see their facial reactions but only as a reflection. Peckinpah used the mirror to split the composition and create a distanced optical relationship for the viewer with the characters. The tensions between Doc and Carol, the fragile exchanges of insecure tenderness that pass between them, are visualized in the mirror composition which splits the couple and creates a visual metaphor consistent with Peckinpah's understanding of married life. It was an important scene for him. In a memo to Steve McQueen, who was fine-tuning the editing on the picture, Peckinpah strongly suggested that this scene, and the earlier swimming sequence, not be recut.[31]

In *Cross of Iron* and *The Osterman Weekend,* Peckinpah again employed mirror images but in a lesser context and without the resonance established in earlier films. In *Cross of Iron,* Stransky learns of Triebeg's homosexuality when he glimpses Triebeg and a lover as reflections caught in his shaving mirror. In *Osterman,* Virginia Tremayne (Helen Shaver) is sickened by the implications of her addiction when she sees her cocaine-smeared face reflected in a bathroom mirror. But in both of these films, the mirror's usage is minor and is relatively uninflected.

By contrast, in *Pat Garrett* and *Alfredo Garcia,* Peckinpah deployed his mirror imagery with its most powerful poetic force to delineate the fissured, alienated self. As we have already noted, in the climax of *Pat Garrett,* Garrett fires his second shot into his mirrored reflection. In the room at Old Fort Sumner in which Garrett awaits Billy's return, a full-length mirror adorns one wall and reflects old Pete Maxwell as a silent witness to the coming ambush. When Billy enters the room where the sheriff waits, Garrett rises from his chair and shoots him. The mirror catches his reflection, and, after he shoots Billy, Garrett realizes his image confronts him across the room. Without pause, on impulse, he pivots and fires into the mirror. The moment replicates and deepens the implications left unexplored in the earlier scene from *The Wild Bunch.* When Pike shot through that mirror, he was not metaphorically annihilating his alternate self, because the door on which the mirror was mounted held not his image but the reflection of a secondary character. Like that earlier scene, the mirror at Old Fort Sumner also holds a secondary and lesser reflection, that of Pete Maxwell, but once Garrett steps into view of the mirror, the glass holds his image relentlessly.

Garrett shoots at himself in an impulsive expression of self-loathing, but this impulse then opens onto tragic self-knowledge. Garrett walks over to the mirror and deliberately positions himself so that the hole in the glass leaves a void, no reflection, in the center of his chest where his heart ought to be. He lingers a moment before the composition in the mirror that he has created, appraising its meaning. Garrett has not only destroyed the finer things in himself by accepting wages to kill his friend, Billy, has not only committed an act of psychological murder against himself, but, worse, he suffers the realization of all this in his tragic and haunted encounter with the disembodied self. Garrett's deliberate arrangement and

The mirrored self as an emblem of psychological alienation. Garrett sees himself in the mirror and fires at his image. Tragically aware of his loss of humanity, he then moves closer to align the bullet hole with his reflection. Frame enlargements.

production of the composition testifies to this inner recognition. The bullet hole at the center of Garrett's tortured reflection is Peckinpah's most poetic and evocative visualization of the self-alienation and psychological diminishment that he had come to understand as the true components of human violence. Pike Bishop is spared the necessity of firing through himself in that mirror at Agua Verde. Pat Garrett cannot escape the obligation of doing so or the self-knowledge that accompanies it. The change in Peckinpah's attitude toward violence, the shift from a commingling of critique and celebration to a more sophisticated understanding of tragic effects, is signaled by the differences of design in these two sequences.

The splintered psyche and violence as a means of self-destruction receive paramount attention in *Alfredo Garcia,* where Peckinpah again utilized mirror images to destabilize space and to comment on psychological crisis. Five scenes employ this mirror imagery, making *Alfredo Garcia* the occasion for Peckinpah's most expansive use of this motif. One scene has already been discussed, where Benny's mirror image is "killed" by one of El Jefe's gunmen in the hotel suite. Much earlier in the film, when Benny goes to the reception desk of the El Camino Real hotel to get the room number of the men who have advertised a bounty on Alfredo's head, Peckinpah filmed his approach in a remarkably off-kilter and weird composition. The camera films the wall of the hotel lobby on which hangs a large mirror. This occupies most of the composition. Appearing in a small area below the mirror and above the bottom frame line are the tops of people's heads, hotel patrons congregating in the lobby. Reflected in the mirror is the distant reception desk. The composition is very bewildering because its center of interest is perplexing. The people in the lobby are cut off by the framing of the shot, except for the tops of their heads. The mirror refracts the light to make the reception desk appear very tiny and far off. Thus, the viewer cannot be sure at first exactly what he or she is supposed to be looking at. Then Benny's profile appears along the lower frame line, and in the next second he moves out of frame. After a moment, he can be seen in the mirror, from behind, a tiny figure in his distinctive white suit walking toward the reception desk. Only his reflected image is conveyed by the shot, centered on the mirror, after he passes through and out of the frame.

This peculiar composition fractures the spatial design within the frame and decenters Benny (and everyone else). In the shot, Benny exists primarily as a mirrored image, a spectral presence. The destabilized design is an exterior correlative of internal psychological distress, and we have seen that Peckinpah employed this expressive modality many times before, particularly in the use of poetic, free-associative montages to convey the sudden eruption of a thwarted or warped subjectivity into narrative time and space. (Peckinpah extended a destabilized composition to the next shot in the sequence, when Benny stands before the desk clerk. The camera is placed at a low angle to create a composition bisected, and split, by pairs of diagonal lines inclining on sharply divergent slopes. The diagonals are formed by the edges of the enclosed reception area and by a wall mural behind Benny. One of the designs on the mural, a blade of bright paint, ends in a point aimed directly at Benny's head and neck. It is an image suggestive of decapitation, fashioning yet another link between Benny and Alfredo and offering yet another suggestion that Benny, as he said of Alfredo, is already dead when we meet him.) As in *Straw Dogs,* Peckinpah destabilized space via the mirror imagery to provide a mediating distance between viewer and character. In *Alfredo Garcia,* though, such distancing techniques are fully deployed throughout the film, as we have already noted, in narrative structure and character design, sufficient to make this Peckinpah's most self-conscious and bleakly playful film.

The next times the mirrored compositions appear in the film, they explicitly denote alienation and psychological disintegration. After Elita realizes the true magnitude of Benny's intentions with Alfredo's corpse and she tells him that it's a desecration of all that is holy and will finish their relationship, she and Benny spend the night at a cheap hotel. As the scene begins, the camera films the hotel room mirror, mounted on a bureau on top of which sits Elita's guitar. Elita is off-screen, in the shower, its noise audible on the soundtrack. Benny appears as a reflection in the mirror. He is out of frame, sitting on the bed loading bullets into his pistol. The juxtaposition of the guitar on the bureau and the mirrored image of Benny with his gun is significant. The guitar emblemizes Elita's connection with life, with art, with things of beauty and affirmation. Early in their journey, before learning of Benny's awful purpose, Elita plays her guitar and sings for him. This hotel room composition uses the mirrored image to underline Benny's isolation and separation from Elita, who is in the next room, and from her music. Benny loads his gun while the guitar rests unused. Furthermore, if Elita represents and chooses life, Benny chooses death. As the guitar is Elita's emblem, the gun is Benny's. The emotional desolation that now prevails between Elita and Benny, and that has long filled Benny's soul, is the essential subject of this brilliant shot. The characters are removed from one another. Elita cannot be seen, and Benny exists, initially, only as a mirrored reflection.

Benny's damnation lies not just in his own relentless and desperate self-destruction, but principally in the way his blind selfishness pulls Elita into the grave. Benny's madness during the last act of the film, as he stalks the narrative like a vengeful ghost pursued by the strains of Elita's music, issues from his recognition that he has discarded his own humanity and has become the instrument of Elita's destruction. Like Pat Garrett, Benny glimpses the void that has opened inside him, but whereas Garrett could sustain the confrontation and even accept its results with melancholy resignation, Benny cannot bear the direct gaze of his mirrored self. After retrieving the head and eliminating several of his employers, Benny returns to the rented room where he had lived and slept with Elita. He ices the head while speaking obsessively to himself and to Alfredo. Passing by a small mirror, Benny pauses. He stands before the mirror, removes the dark glasses he habitually wears[32] and stares at his reflection. But the face he sees and, especially, the direct gaze of his own eyes are too disturbing. He sees perversion and damnation in those eyes, as he had seen them in the eyes of others, earlier, when he screamed at several young men in Alfredo's village because they were looking at him with their "fuckin' eyes." Afraid of what he now sees in the mirror, Benny puts his glasses back on and turns

Peckinpah used this mirror composition to stress Benny's obsession with death and his emotional disconnection from Elita. Frame enlargement.

away from it. He goes to the bed and loads his gun. He belongs to the grave, not to life, and it will soon reclaim him. Subsequently, when he takes the head to Max at the hotel and stands before a mirror over the sofa on which Max had been sitting, Benny, like a vampire, casts no reflection.

Alfredo Garcia is a work of overwhelming negativity. It takes viewers on a trip through hell and creatively dwells in the spiritual netherworld of the film's main character. But Peckinpah found a variety of aesthetic measures to organize the darkness of the film's vision so that it would speak in a controlled moral voice to its audience. Throughout his films he used such measures to organize the physical energy of the violences the films study and to establish a clear and coherent perspective on that violence. As such, these techniques collectively comprise the self-reflexive components of his filmmaking that have tended to be minimized or under-appreciated by critics. These stratagems of control include the use of didactic tableaux that intrude onto the narrative in an explicitly denotative way to announce some fundamental characteristic of violence that is too important to be conveyed through the indirect mediations of narrative or dramaturgy. They include, as well, Peckinpah's recourse to irony as his essential narrative voice, requiring of the viewer a sophisticated appreciation of the disparity between what is stated and what is intended. While Peckinpah's ironic tone has tended to becloud and confuse the popular and critical reception of his films and arguably, therefore, has undermined the integrity and success of his didactic cinema project, the ironic mode was essential for his work because it provided him with emotional and psychological protection from the ugliness to which he was aesthetically drawn. Wearing a dark mask was a means of artistic survival amid the violences he portrayed. Finally, the psychological alienation that is the true spiritual condition of his characters, and is the consequence of the violence they commit, is given poetic and self-conscious visual form in the disturbing evocation of the mirrored self and its ability to fragment and upset space and perception. While these are not Brechtian devices, they are clearly the tools of an intelligent and articulate filmmaker who was cognizant of the moral and aesthetic dangers of the territory he visited. These devices constitute the third aesthetic framework that Peckinpah superimposed upon his violent materials, and they demonstrate the care and the high regard he had for his viewers. These techniques are not just a means whereby Peckinpah could shape his exceptionally volatile material. They also grant the audience a measured space, a critical vantage point, from which to survey Peckinpah's bleak landscapes. They helped give Peckinpah his compass when navigating the disturbing screen exploration of human brutality, and they serve as anchors, as a means for ensuring that viewers might not be swept away by the savagery they are asked to confront. In contrast to Peckinpah's orientation, filmmakers today are unrestrained and undisciplined in their depictions of violence, inundating viewers with a tide of gore. We turn now to a consideration of Peckinpah's work in relation to contemporary ultraviolence.

A Disputed Legacy

IN RESPECT TO the artistic and social goals that he set for his filmmaking, and in terms of its stylistics, how does Peckinpah's work connect with the films of contemporary masters of movie violence, such as Martin Scorsese, Paul Verhoeven, and Quentin Tarantino? This chapter places Peckinpah's work in relation to the contemporary cinematic violence that it has helped inspire. Situating his work thus will enable us to obtain closure on it, as well as on the moral and social project that sustained his cinema. We need to come to terms with the question that now confronts this inquiry: Are Peckinpah's explorations of graphic screen gore invalidated by their legacy of contemporary movie ultraviolence? If we are moved to condemn the exploitation and pernicious social effects of modern movie violence, must we also, therefore, condemn and reject Peckinpah's work?

Before we take up these issues, it will be helpful to quickly trace the final phases of Peckinpah's career so that we may begin to draw the appropriate conclusions from his work. The problems that beset Peckinpah in his later career are manifold. His alcoholism and cocaine addiction (the latter acquired during the production of *The Killer Elite*) proved highly destructive of his ability to work successfully. The endearingly off-center, improvisatory, and meandering quality to many of Peckinpah's films may be due, in part, to his use of intoxicants. Unfortunately, as this use intensified, the later films such as *Cross of Iron* and *The Killer Elite* began to fragment into incoherence. However, an initial slackening of control over pace, dramatic focus, and narrative structure is already apparent in *Pat Garrett* and *Alfredo Garcia*. It is instructive to remember that Peckinpah's two films of hard brilliance and crystalline control in their cinematic design—*The Wild Bunch* and *Straw Dogs*—were made by a man who stayed relatively sober during production. (During the initial shooting of *Straw Dogs*, Peckinpah drank himself into a state of physical collapse after which—and after a warning from producer Daniel Melnick—he straightened out and moderated his use of alcohol for the remainder of production.) Eventually, Peckinpah's drinking and drug use helped clinch his reputation with industry executives as an out-of-control drunk to whom a production ought not to be entrusted. There is a certain irony in this that Peckinpah, great ironist that he was, no doubt appreciated.

The Hollywood industry accepts self-abusive and destructive behavior from actors, filmmakers, and production executives so long as this behavior coincides with a proven ability to generate revenue. Don Simpson, for example, was one of the industry's most successful producers, responsible, along with partner Jerry Bruckheimer, for such profitable hits as *Flashdance* (1983), *Top Gun* (1986), and *Days of Thunder* (1990). Simpson was also a profligate drug user, and when he died of an overdose in late 1995, no one was very surprised. Had not Peckinpah's chemical dependency so compromised his ability to work, and had he been willing to make more formulaic pictures with greater box-office potential, such self-destruction might have been compatible with the continuance of his career.

Things, though, got badly out of hand, and as one sign of the downwardly spiraling career, his choices for projects after *Alfredo Garcia* were uniformly ill-advised. In every case he signed on to projects with profound script problems that could not be solved and that corrupted the resulting productions. On every film from *The Killer Elite* to *The Osterman Weekend*, the transcripts and recorded notes of the story conferences held by Peckinpah and his production teams reveal a floundering, almost desperate search for narrative coherence as differing permutations of story and character concepts were explored and deemed unsatisfactory. (A typical objection that captures the atmosphere of these meetings is "Why? What does it do for the picture? Where is the progression?") A December 5, 1974, step outline of a proposed sequence of narrative events for *The Killer Elite* demonstrates this erratic search for order and organization.

11. Airport sequence. Open. Hansen somewhere near the plane? Catering truck explodes? Mack does something to prevent it. Kwok gets killed????

12. They take the Bay Shore[,] find the road blocked[,] have to return to the city. Mack finds the bomb. Gets killed?[1]

Peckinpah tried to find some structure by conceptualizing the key relationship between Locken and Hansen in *The Killer Elite* in terms of his far more successful work on *The Wild Bunch.* "You've got something working there, that we create sympathy, which I found worked quite well with the Wild Bunch, sympathy for professional killers, which so many fucking people are."[2] But the Hansen-Locken relationship remained unsatisfactorily formulated, and Peckinpah confessed in a subsequent script note, "Of course I shall shoot the picture because I am committed to it, but it is not going in the direction and does not have the quality that I had expected."[3] With the onset of principal photography set for March 17, 1975, Peckinpah cabled Eric Pleskow at United Artists on January 23, warning "As of this date, I am becoming more and more convinced that the starting date proposed is not only impractical but is becoming ludicrous because of the simple fact that we have no script."[4] Peckinpah disliked the eventual shooting script and attempted to turn it into a satire of itself (for example, by shooting an ending in which a character who was killed earlier in the narrative reappears in the last scene), but it was a lame effort, and the finished film bears the clear marks of its conceptual disorganization.

Peckinpah's next production, *Cross of Iron,* was also plagued with insoluble narrative problems. The script notes from story conferences complain about a misplaced emphasis upon arbitrary narrative events and an unclear delineation of Steiner, the central character. Steiner "seems to be going through some sort of moral dilemma but at this point his many arbitrary actions mask exactly what that is." Frustrated with the script, Peckinpah offered a flippant solution to the problem of Steiner's poorly motivated character: "Steiner wants to die and yet he lives because he doesn't want to give the assholes the pleasure of life without him."[5] Obviously, this wouldn't do. Peckinpah admitted that he could make no sense out of the script, and last-minute rewrites failed to provide a satisfactory narrative structure. Peckinpah remarked, "The *Cross of Iron* is, was, based on a book by Willi Heinrich, I have no idea what it is based on now."[6] The problems on this picture were compounded by producer Wolf Hartwig's chronic inability to fund the production or to provide Peckinpah with sufficient resources, such as costuming and props, necessary to make a World War II picture. Of this experience, Peckinpah wrote, "In any case, we have learned a great deal *again* about how not to make films."[7] That Peckinpah would embark on such a rag-tag project in the first place says much about the lack of care he was giving his talent and career during this period.

Convoy was adapted from a popular song about truckers and CB radio, and the script was so devoid of the attributes that one would associate with the work of a major director that Peckinpah's agreement to do the film was widely perceived as a terminal error and further proof of a career beyond salvage. The script notes and cutting memos on this production make for very sad reading, because they demonstrate the chronic inability of the production team to determine what the film was about. Peckinpah again tried to recycle some *Wild Bunch*-derived themes of honor and loyalty but could get nowhere with them, and the gesture was, in any event, one born of desperation. He eventually decided, near the end of shooting, that a coherent conceptual design and organized dramatic structure were incompatible with the film that was emerging. He wrote, "the picture is a Montage. . . . This picture is a Happening, not the well-made play." The concept unifying the film was so badly out of focus that Peckinpah considered using out-of-focus shots to portray the convoy and to suggest that the political movement it symbolized was fatuous. He told his editors, "Use out of focus shots, maybe out of focus collage, then one at a time to come in clear. Convoy . . . a myth."[8] Furthermore, at this late point, Peckinpah proposed that the film be taken in a new and previously unplanned direction. He suggested to executive producer Michael Deeley that the material be drastically reshaped to emphasize the mechanics of the convoy itself because he felt the narrative's principal characters were so badly conceived and so poorly acted by the performers.

> I would also like to remind you of our discussion, after viewing certain dailies and certain fragmented pieces of the assembly, that we both felt the emphasis (for the picture's sake) might well be better put on character moments of truckers, the movement and dynamics of the convoy itself rather than the dialogue of some principle actors, which, unfortunately, when they finally had a scene that was playing, if even to a limited degree, was ruined by technical problems . . .[9]

Peckinpah's recommendation constitutes an admission of a badly focused and failing production. In terms of his career, this film was very nearly a killer.

After *Convoy,* he would not direct a feature again for five years. During this time, he was once more in the position of an exile and outcast, as he had been during the interval between *Major Dundee* and *The Wild Bunch.* But this time there would be no spectacular return from the brink. *The Osterman Weekend,* his last feature, was adapted from a convoluted Robert Ludlum novel. Alan Sharp, whose rewrite on the script garnered him screen credit, remarked that he never felt it worked as a script and was surprised to see his rewrite actually go into production. During preproduction story conferences, no one seemed to understand what the character Fassett was up to in the story (a confusion this author shares), and Peckinpah remarked, "It's the first completely unmotivated motion picture . . ."[10]

Fatigued, much older than his years, and with his career in eclipse, Peckinpah is shown here conferring with actor Rutger Hauer during production of *The Osterman Weekend.* © 1983, Osterman Weekend Associates.

Peckinpah's maddeningly bad choice of scripts in the last phase of his career foredoomed his efforts to make something good out of those scripts once they were in production. His awareness of this must have been chronically painful and dispiriting. Writing to his old cinematographer, Lucien Ballard (*Ride the High Country, The Wild Bunch, The Ballad of Cable Hogue, Junior Bonner, The Getaway*), Peckinpah sadly acknowledged the place that *Osterman* would occupy in his career. "My dear and sometime only friends. I am in my fourth week of an exploitation picture, non union, but the best I could get. Cast and crew are okayed by the completion guarantors. It's madness and I doubt my judgment in doing it but it was this or nothing."[11] In another letter to a different correspondent, Peckinpah reflected, "Currently, I'm doing an exploitation film which I have been unable to rewrite. Consequently, I am a little discouraged but forge ahead."[12] In a memo to his editors on *The Osterman Weekend,* he acknowledged that the film is a failure and that the viewer effectively has no character to empathize or bond with in the narrative. Sadly, because it came so late in production and recognized so elemental an insufficiency in the film, Peckinpah asked his editors to try to produce some rooting interest for the viewer who, he suspected, would find the material much too cold and aloof. Peckinpah wrote, "Bottom line: This is not a great flick. I appreciate the efforts to make it so but it really is not. 1) give me somebody to hate. 2) give me somebody to love."[13] The emotional engagement with the material that Peckinpah failed to manifest during filming could not be created in the editing as a late, post production addition.

Osterman thus shares the characteristic weaknesses of Peckinpah's late films. If we now consider that film's opening scene in some detail, we can begin to position Peckinpah's presentation of screen violence in relation to the notorious work of subsequent filmmakers. Although it was adapted from an espionage story by a best-selling novelist, Peckinpah's film of *The Osterman Weekend* offers viewers few of the conventional pleasures of this form. The film is extraordinarily cold and impenetrable, and its opening scene is Peckinpah's last, sustained attempt to assault and engage the moral sensibilities of his viewers in a didactically self-conscious manner. Its main character, Fassett (John Hurt), a CIA agent, makes love to his wife and gets up from bed to take a shower. Two men abruptly enter the room, inject a drug into her face and quickly leave. When Fassett returns from the shower, his wife is dead. The disturbing power of the scene lies in the way it systematically disorients the viewer. The scene appears on screen as video footage, which accentuates the voyeuristic qualities of the action. Because of the video imagery, the viewer knows that the action is either being surveilled simultaneously with its occurrence or that it is the surveillance record of some event that has already occurred. In either case, the intimacy between Fassett and his wife has been despoiled by an eavesdropping surveillance camera, and by watching the footage, the film viewer becomes complicit in this invasion of privacy. The voyeuristic experience of watching the video is intensified by the nakedness of Fassett's wife and by her sensual responses as she recalls their recent lovemaking. The sudden intrusion of the two dark-clothed strangers, the unanticipated violence, and her terrified expression (shown in close-up, as the needle goes in) are disorienting and disturbing because nothing has prepared the viewer for this coldly alienating violence and because it is such a reversal of the tenderness between Fassett and his wife with which the scene opens. The desaturated color of the video images emphasizes the ugliness of the murder and the despairing response of Fassett when he finds his wife's body.

In the opening moments of the film, Peckinpah assailed his viewers with a harrowingly gruesome scene and presented it in a style that accentuates its visual and emotional ugliness. As the video footage ends, the camera pulls back from a monitor before which sits CIA head Maxwell Danforth (Burt Lancaster). When Peckinpah's directorial credit fills the screen, Danforth mutters, "Nasty piece of film," evidently seconding the director's own judgment about what he has just shown viewers and about what is still yet to come. Fassett engineers an elaborate and murderous vengeance upon those he holds responsible for the death of his wife, in the process of which most of the characters in the film are exposed as venal opportunists or moral cowards. With his abiding sense of irony, Peckinpah told his editors that, despite the character's bloody thirst for vengeance, "The only person who is innocent is Fassett."[14] This assessment is significant and instructive. It tells us a great deal about Peckinpah's capacity for registering human suffering. Peckinpah found this character compelling precisely because of his anguish. For Peckinpah, Fassett was "a human being tortured into unconscionable acts . . ."[15] Peckinpah's assessment of Fassett demonstrates how essentially uncommercial were his moral and artistic inclinations and reveals how those inclinations were guided not by an accountant's sense of what viewers would like and would respond to but by his ability to inhabit the blasted souls and psyches of those twisted by violence, both perpetrators and victims.

Peckinpah felt a special empathy for Fassett (John Hurt) in *The Osterman Weekend* because of that character's tortured emotional suffering. For Peckinpah, suffering and anguish were the essential consequences and accompaniments of violence. © 1983, Osterman Weekend Associates.

Suffering and Anguish in Peckinpah's Films

Peckinpah's regard for Fassett was predicated upon that character's psychological torture, as was his regard for Amy in *Straw Dogs*. This regard would not endear his work to many viewers or prove commercially viable in the terms that the industry covets. His empathy for debased individuals, such as Fassett or Benny, even as they are prodded by extraordinary suffering or desperation into unforgivable acts, requires an exceptional fortitude from viewers and asks, in many cases, more than some are willing to give. Peckinpah did not merely look at the physical ugliness of violence. He was drawn to search for the residual traces of humanity in those individuals, like Benny or Fassett, who have surrendered to a bleak rage and spiritual void. Finding this humanity in their suffering, Peckinpah suffered with them as an artist committed to understanding their capacity for unconscionable acts and as a director committed to retaining his own capability to be horrified by what his camera might reveal. We need to explore the significant issue of human suffering in Peckinpah's work and then consider how this compares with the violences of later filmmakers.

Suffering, for Peckinpah, was the central psychological effect produced by violence and its core component. His work adheres to this recognition. "Accepting the fact that violence is part of our lives," he wrote, "and being a realist I am unable to portray violence in any way except in the way that it is. Death by violence is slow, tortuous and terrible."[16] Honoring this outlook entailed adopting a nonexploitative approach to visualizing violence, and the measure of this approach lay in systematically curtailing the normative pleasures that conventional cinema offered to viewers. Peckinpah was very clear about how this assault on the viewer's pleasure might be carried out, and the consequences of this assault for the commercial performance of his films seem equally clear. He insisted that portrayals of violence on screen would be morally and artistically honest only if the filmmaker stressed the terrifying and unpleasant components of the experience. As Peckinpah surveyed earlier decades of American cinema, he found these qualities lacking. Violent death was quick, attractive, and carried no pain. It was this tradition that he demolished with such epochal results in *The Wild Bunch*. "*The Wild Bunch* was my way of reacting against all the films in which violence seemed facile, factitious and unreal. I was always fascinated to see how one died easily in the movies . . . People die without suffering and violence provokes no pain."[17] In Peckinpah's mind, violence and pain were inseparable as the outer and inner manifestations of an indivisible experience. To use film in a way that denied this connection, he believed, was inexcusable.[18]

In the films of other directors, scenes which stressed suffering and pain resonated for Peckinpah as honest explorations of violence. He cited two sequences from Hitchcock's later films that struck him as disturbingly honest in their representation of death. The first was the murder of the Soviet agent Gromek in *Torn Curtain* (1966). The assault on Gromek is protracted and escalates in its savagery. Despite being beaten, stabbed, and strangled, Gromek stubbornly clings to life. Only when his assailants thrust his head into a kitchen oven and turn on the gas do they succeed in killing him. Hitchcock staged the violence with a brutality that was unusual for films of that period. In particular, his attention to detail gives the violence a rawness that struck Peckinpah forcibly. A knife blade breaks off in Gromek's shoulder, his legs are smashed with a shovel, and his fingers spasm as he succumbs to the gas from the oven. Hitchcock told Truffaut that his design for this scene was intended to get away from glamorous movie style and draw closer to an authentic experience of violent death. "In doing that long killing scene, my first thought again was to avoid the cliché. In every picture somebody gets killed and it goes very quickly. . . . And I thought it was time to show that it was very difficult, very painful, and it takes a very long time to kill a man."[19]

Peckinpah appreciated the existential point Hitchcock was making through the scene's close attention to the physical details of Gromek's murder. He believed, "This is one of the rare films in which one can really see death at work. Hitchcock, with all of his immense talent, shows us that it is not easy to kill a man and that the human body has an extraordinary power of resistance to physical aggression."[20] Peckinpah showed again and again in his films this power of resistance. Peckinpah's insistence that violent death not be quick, that the taking of life not be easy, demonstrates his humane principles as an artist, his regard for the sanctity of life, and constitutes an affirmation toward which all of the destruction in his films points. Only one committed to life would care so deeply about the agony of its loss. Those filmmakers who lack this commitment in their art tend to show violent death as quick and painless or they tend to show it in a graphic but dispassionate manner. Thus the physical and emotional pain that Peckinpah placed on screen have their basis in a compassionate and empathetic response toward the tragedy of human violence and the loss of life it entails. This pain is a clear index of his humanistic orientation.

The other Hitchcock sequence that resonated for Peckinpah is easily the most grotesque and graphic act of violence in all of Hitchcock's films —the murder of Brenda Blaney (Barbara Leigh-Hunt) in *Frenzy* (1972). For most of his career, Hitchcock had labored under the restrictions on movie content imposed by Hollywood's Production Code which prohibited detailed attention to crime and violence. The murder and dismemberment of Thorwald's wife in *Rear Window* (1954), for example, occur off-camera. While Hitchcock pushed against code restrictions with the shower murder in *Psycho* (1960), it was not until *Frenzy* that he had the opportunity to take advantage of the new climate of freedom in American cinema inaugurated by the CARA system. Accordingly, the film visualizes Brenda's rape and murder in vivid detail, juxtaposing her terror-stricken cries and anguished prayers to God for deliverance with the audible sexual pleasure of her attacker as he slowly strangles her. Hitchcock showed her face in close-up, contorted in death, her tongue protruding. Peckinpah was impressed by Hitchcock's attention to the physical aspects of dying and to the intense anguish of the victim. He said:

The murder of Barbara Leigh-Hunt in *Frenzy* is just as remarkable because Hitchcock really causes us to feel the intensity of the suffering of a person who decomposes under our very eyes. I am not a Hitchcock fanatic, but all the same one has to admit that he knows how to render tangible . . . human suffering.[21]

It was precisely the ugliness of this sequence and the pain of its victim that impressed Peckinpah as being true to his own conception of the physical and psychological response of individuals subject to extreme duress. He said, "Violence and suffering should be very intimately bonded. In almost all the films made before *The Wild Bunch,* the characters died without distress."[22] He condemned films that sanitize their violence with comedy. He believed that such sanitized films please viewers because the spectator is left unconcerned with the violence depicted on screen. Such films, he argued, that amuse instead of upsetting their viewers, show violence "with

Because of its stress on the suffering of the victim, the scene of Brenda Blaney's torture and murder in Hitchcock's *Frenzy* held a special resonance for Peckinpah, who found the scene remarkable for its brutal honesty. Photo courtesy of Universal Pictures.

no social or moral perspective."[23] As we have seen throughout these chapters, a constructive social and moral perspective on violence was immensely important for Peckinpah and was an essential foundation of his work. Peckinpah complained that the United Artists executives who hated *Bring Me the Head of Alfredo Garcia* nevertheless wanted lots of blood and guts and vulgarity: "They [the studio executives] want it more bloody and the graphics more explicit. They [want] sensationalism and vulgar effects [to] arouse the interest of the public."[24]

The social science research reviewed in Chapter 3 bearing on the effects of viewing media violence asserts that depictions of a victim's anguish within scenes of violence lessen a viewer's tendency to respond to such scenes with simple excitement. The victim's anguish may call attention to the unpleasant consequences of violence and thereby complicate the viewer's response by pulling it in a direction counterposed to a simple excitatory reaction. This finding has obvious significance for Peckinpah's films, which use their multiple aesthetic frames to make the viewer's response a subjectively problematic experience. Peckinpah's work uniquely renders the experiences of a victim's suffering and anguish in multifaceted ways. These include the extended poetic and subjective interludes when a character's lacerated consciousness breaks in on the narrative, disrupting its contours and reorganizing them according to the dynamics of a specific trauma, as Amy's consciousness does at several points in *Straw Dogs*. Or the entire narrative may be refracted through the increasingly deranged and anguished persona of a debased and alienated character, such as Benny in *Alfredo Garcia*. In this case, the complication of the spectator's response works differently. While little pity is felt for the corrupt thugs and businessmen that Benny kills, the entire narrative is rife with depravity, and, once Elita is murdered, the viewer is left with no character who does not warrant approbation. As the killings in *Alfredo Garcia* spiral on in a world of ugliness peopled by repellent characters, the violence as spectacle turns against itself, becoming increasingly alienating to the viewer, coldly distancing, and unexciting. The lacerated spirits and dissociated selves, the psychological perversion that Peckinpah understood as the internal correlative of physical violence, are eloquently conveyed as well in didactic and self-reflexive imagery, as in Pike's, Pat's, and Benny's confrontations with their mirrored selves. Through these confrontations, Peckinpah poetically acknowledged the fundamental principle of violence as he understood it. Its commission entails a loss of humanity, in part because violence represents a failure of rationality and language, fundamental attributes of hu-

man nature. To perpetrate violence is to violate the human capacity for reflective thought and, thereby, to forfeit one's human identity. Peckinpah
noted this connection, emphasizing that "Violence grows from frustration,
from the inability to communicate on a verbal level, when one can no
longer make oneself understood on an intellectual basis."[25] We will explore
the importance for Peckinpah of the rational basis of human identity later
in the chapter.

Before we turn to an examination of Peckinpah's legacy, in order to accentuate the contrasts we will uncover, it will be helpful to briefly sum-
marize what we have learned about the moral design of Peckinpah's work.
As we have noted, the melancholic framework that contextualizes the violent exchanges in the films announces Peckinpah's own suffering and saddened moral perspective on the violence he depicted. But that framework
also enabled him to sidestep the powerful myth of regenerate violence
which is so ingrained in contemporary filmmaking. Because his return
from oblivion in *The Wild Bunch* was so spectacular, and because this film
does affirm that myth, the more sustained and truer tendency of his work
to reject it has not been sufficiently appreciated. The Bunch's entrance into
Valhalla at the end of the film subscribes to what Richard Slotkin has
argued is a defining American cultural mythology of violence, which he
has termed "regeneration through violence." Films conforming to this mythology—most frequently, though not exclusively, Westerns—present violence as a singularly transcendent and transforming experience that re-
generates individual and society. The myth of regeneration through
violence implies that "violence is an essential and necessary part of the
process through which American society was established and through
which its democratic values are defended and enforced."[26] Rocky's patriotic
beating of the Soviet boxer in *Rocky IV* (1985) clearly partakes of this ideology. To be sure, *The Wild Bunch* is highly critical of American society and
personifies its economic and moral stages of development in the ruthless
capitalist Harrigan and the gutter-trash thugs he hires to protect his property. However, by building the narrative toward the Bunch's ennobling last
act of violence, Peckinpah rather uncritically subscribed here to the ideal
of regenerate violence. This does not harmonize well with his intent to reveal and expose the tawdry and inhuman aspects of violence. It is, therefore, significant that in his other major films—*Straw Dogs, Pat Garrett and
Billy the Kid,* and *Alfredo Garcia*—he backed away not only from the kind
of extended and uncontrolled montage set-pieces that are on display in
The Wild Bunch but also from the notion that violence may be morally,

spiritually, or socially regenerative. *Straw Dogs* has been misunderstood in this respect as we have discussed in earlier chapters. The violence in these later films is explicitly associated with loss, despair, and dehumanization. It follows from these conditions and, in turn, reproduces them. Even in the comic *The Ballad of Cable Hogue,* Cable forfeits his chance at happiness with Hildy by remaining in the desert to seek vengeance against his former partners. When he at last has the opportunity for revenge, the experience is neither purgative nor transfiguring, and he loses interest in it midway through, sparing the life of one of his antagonists. In the films of this period other than *The Wild Bunch,* only *The Getaway* with its plot-driven characters offers a sense of regeneration and deliverance through violence as Doc and Carol manage to patch up their marriage and escape to Mexico. Peckinpah regarded this film, though, as one for the money, and it lacks the resonant complexities of his other works of this period.

The Wild Bunch, therefore, is an anomaly in Peckinpah's screen treatment of violence. Critics have generally failed to perceive the shift of attention and emphasis in Peckinpah's work after this film because the immediate stylistics of that work—montage editing, slow motion, exploding squibs—seem so continuous. But by shifting his moral orientation regarding the screen violence he depicted, Peckinpah was better able to honor his underlying philosophical and artistic intentions. As I have suggested, however, this was a risky undertaking. The shocking cinematic experiences to which Peckinpah wished to subject his audience entailed, and exacted, a considerable toll on his own career and well-being as an artist. This is part of what I meant when earlier I observed that Peckinpah did not remain aloof from the awful visions he conjured on screen but suffered through and with them in his empathy for victim and victimizer. The price was apparent in the belligerent mask he often adopted as a means of dealing with the objections of press and public that his work was sadistic and gratuitously ugly and violent. No matter an artist's intentions or designs, public vilification must remain an intensely painful experience capable of stoking bitterness if an artist is already inclined in that direction.

To continue working, Peckinpah had to absorb and negotiate within his own head and heart the extreme denunciations of his work from viewers and industry executives. The preview cards for *The Wild Bunch* filled out by a Kansas City audience after a sneak preview in May 1969 include such savage remarks as "It's plain sadism. Only a sadist or one who is mentally deranged would enjoy this film," and "Peckinpah should put his own features on the vultures; he must crave human carrion."[27] The preview audience at a sneak of *Alfredo Garcia* responded with judgments that the film is "decadent and lacking in meaning and content. It doesn't relate to my life or anybody else's"; "This picture should be burned—a waste of money—where did you get this idea?"[28] Peckinpah might have taken solace in the conviction that if viewers were not upset by his treatment of violence, then he had failed. Still, for an extremely sensitive individual such as Peckinpah, this excessive approbation must have been difficult, especially as it accumulated over the years. Furthermore, Peckinpah knew that dislike for his work came not just from viewers but from industry executives. He remarked during the release of *Alfredo Garcia* that United Artists, its distributor, hated the film and considered it uncommercial: "They say it will never bring in the crowds in the moviehouses. According to them, it is not commercial enough." He added that the constant battles to keep working in his own way had left him extremely fatigued, the effort required was too great, and he sensed that an end of some sort was approaching. "I am an aging and tired man. I know that this all won't last much longer. . . . I am too worn out."[29]

To the frequent chagrin of his industry employers, Peckinpah did not approach cinema as if it were fundamentally a form of entertainment. I do not believe it is an exaggeration to maintain that Peckinpah approached cinema as a medium for exploring ideas. Such an approach is more in keeping with the manner in which European artists have used the medium. His orientation, though, was not an intellectual one but was attuned to the affective and sensory components in the *idea* of violence. His use of cinema actively transcended its entertainment function, and with films like *Straw Dogs* and *Alfredo Garcia,* Peckinpah came close to nullifying the appeals of popular cinema. He wanted the experience of watching his films to constitute a voyage of self-discovery for the viewer, who, like David Sumner at the end of *Straw Dogs,* would emerge adrift and estranged from prior understandings of self and world. Of this process, with respect to *Straw Dogs,* he remarked that the film

> concerns a seemingly peaceful man's discovery of the violence within himself, and indirectly his innate penchant for inciting violence and I hope that this discovery is shared by the audience as they watch the film [and that the film] makes the audience . . . fearful and very, very uncomfortable about their own potential for violence.[30]

Responding to a viewer who wrote to him protesting that the violence in *Straw Dogs* was sickening and distasteful and rendered the film impossible to enjoy, Peckinpah wrote back, saying "I didn't want you to enjoy the film, I wanted you to look very close at your own soul."[31] Upon seeing *The Wild Bunch,* Paul Staniford, a lawyer and close friend of the Peckinpah family, wrote to Sam and in a gentle, nonaccusatory way condemned the film's brutality. In reply, Peckinpah declared that for him capturing truth on film was more important than entertainment. "I personally feel it's time Hollywood quit glamorizing violence and let people see how brutalizing and horrible it really is. This is what I tried to do. I'm afraid the truth, to me as I see it, is more important than entertainment for its own sake." Peckinpah then added, presciently, in view of the path his career would subsequently take, "The unfortunate thing is, I suppose, I see a certain kind of truth only too clearly."[32]

Peckinpah, then, acknowledged and understood the reasons why his films caused the furor they did and why many viewers felt antipathetic toward them. "I understand how some people can find my films difficult and even terrifying, but they cannot ignore our world today. I feel that people throughout the world must face the fact that modern society has its uglier side. We cannot hope to correct the abuses without facing up to them."[33] Peckinpah pressed on and continued making films he knew would be difficult and unpleasant for large sectors of the movie-going public, disregarding the outcry surrounding the work, its limited commercial appeal in comparison with films that aimed to please their publics, and the toll that his artistic defiance was taking on his health and his ability to keep working successfully in an industry whose products must ultimately satisfy and please their audience. Making the perverse *Alfredo Garcia* was his ultimate act of artistic defiance, and it helped destroy the prospects for continued employment as a major filmmaker within the system.

Peckinpah's films, then, offered an alternative to the normative pleasures of commercial America cinema during the period in which he worked. If movie violence was sanitized and polite, he made it raw and ugly. If movie entertainments offered a narrative world of crime and violence that constructed a safe and comforting viewing position for the spectator, Peckinpah used screen violence to destroy this comfortable position and to implicate the viewer in the mayhem on screen. By making his screen violence both fascinating and repellent, he sought to prod viewers into a recognition of their own moral and emotional relationship to that violence, of their complicity in it by virtue of their tacit decision to seek out violence and experience it vicariously on screen. Peckinpah's films aim to produce a spectator who is enlightened. In a similar fashion to the way that Brecht con-

ceived of enlightenment, Peckinpah's viewers are first subjected to alienation and estrangement and, from there, ideally, viewers are led to a more
reflective understanding of their relationship to the violence depicted on
screen. The alienation and estrangement are produced by Peckinpah's remarkable ability to arouse within the viewer a powerfully ambivalent
response to screen violence. By aestheticizing violence using dynamic
montage editing and complex temporal manipulations (as discussed in
Chapter 2), Peckinpah portrayed screen mayhem as sensuous and kineti-
cally appealing. Yet by situating that violence in a narrative context
marked by despair, melancholy, and suffering and by placing a bad protagonist at the center of the narrative, Peckinpah aimed to alienate viewers
from their own excitement and enjoyment of the aestheticized violence.
The self-consciousness that might result from this alienation—the awareness of one's own fascination with violence and the excited emotional response to it—was intended by Peckinpah to be disturbing, painful, at
times terrifying. By holding a mirror up to the soul of the viewer, Peckinpah aimed to produce the same kind of psychological destabilization that
he visualized on screen in his scenes of the split and mirrored self.

"My films can be understood and grasped at several levels," he said.[34] By
virtue of their expressed intent to impart a lesson, Peckinpah described
them as modern versions of the ancient morality plays. "If I had to compare them to another artistic form, I would compare them to the Morality
Plays of the Middle Ages. They are all constructed of a series of stages and
rituals which lead to a conclusion from which one draws a lesson."[35] The
lesson that many of his films would try to impart, as Peckinpah stressed
again and again, would be a caution against violence coupled with a visualization of its seductive appeal and of its pervasiveness in human life. The
latter qualities made the cautionary stance the more urgent.

Ultraviolence in Contemporary Film

As he became more successful following *The Wild Bunch,* instead of moving closer to the normative conventions and pleasures of commercial
American cinema, Peckinpah moved away from these norms with his insistence on portraying the depravity of violence. While this would cost
him his career and a large, gratified audience, his stylistic design of violence and attention to the mechanics of its visualization would prove to be
massively influential upon subsequent filmmakers. As one critic has
noted, Peckinpah's cinema helped open the "bloodgates" of American film,
which has never stopped bleeding since.[36] Peckinpah's stylistics have been

a seminal influence on such later filmmakers as Martin Scorsese, Walter Hill (who included a series of explicit references to *The Wild Bunch* in his neo-Western *Extreme Prejudice,* 1987), and Quentin Tarantino, but the constructive moral vision that underlies his work and that work's didactic engagement with the viewer have not been so influential. These attributes, which are the crucial elements of Peckinpah's project to use cinema in a socially progressive fashion, are generally missing from the work of subsequent filmmakers, despite their eagerness to borrow Peckinpah's visual grammar and syntax.

Peckinpah's techniques—the squibs, slow motion, and montage editing—have been removed from the contexts in his work that gave them meaning and have, thereby, been rendered superficial and mechanical. The scope of the contemporary ultraviolence in cinema that has flowed, or bled, from Peckinpah's work is so vast that an entire book might be devoted to this tradition. In this respect I should emphasize that Peckinpah's influence has been international in scope. The films of Hong Kong director John Woo (*A Better Tomorrow,* 1986; *A Bullet in the Head,* 1989; *The Killer,* 1989) feature the familiar combination of montage editing, multiple cameras, and slow motion to transform ferocious gunplay into elaborately choreographed, spectacular set-pieces. Woo has generated tremendous fascination among Western critics because of the sociological complexity of his work, a striking amalgam of Eastern and Western cultural, religious, and cinematic traditions and styles.[37] In the brilliance of their staging, though, Woo's gun battles function like Peckinpah's Agua Verde sequence, as purely visual spectacle, and Woo has taken that sequence as a model for his own work. Woo is now working as a successful filmmaker within the Hollywood system, and Hollywood today will accept vastly greater amounts of carnage and mayhem than it would in Peckinpah's time. Woo slaughters scores of characters in *Face-Off* (1997), coldly and with moral indifference. Their deaths are, at best, an exercise in stylistic pyrotechnics.

The Italian director Carlo Carlei points to Peckinpah's international influence when discussing his own approach to filming the gunplay in *Flight of the Innocent* (1993). He says, "There is a chain of inspiration like the Bible. . . . Everything comes from Peckinpah."[38] It is now virtually impossible to see screen violence that has not been aestheticized along some parameter deriving from Peckinpah's work. Slow motion, for example, is an ubiquitous means of stylizing gunplay in contemporary film. Filmmakers use the device even when they display a gross failure to understand it, as in the shoot-out that climaxes *State of Grace* (Phil Joanou, 1990) in which slow motion takes over so extensively that the scene is voided of kinetic energy. It is not possible to chronicle here, in a comprehensive way, the myriad films and filmmakers who represent what I will suggest is the distorted Peckinpah legacy in modern cinema, nor would such an expansive focus be appropriate in a study of Peckinpah's work. Instead, I will specify the significant differences between what Peckinpah was aiming for and achieved and the regrettable design of more recent films.

The most immediate and obvious difference lies in the level and explicitness of the gore itself, but, beyond this, there is an important difference of moral emphasis. In comparison with today's films, Peckinpah's work seems quite restrained, but its sustained ability to disturb and provoke modern viewers testifies to the success of his achievements and to the importance of the multiple, superimposed aesthetic frames that we examined in earlier chapters. Peckinpah's images of violence are remarkably discrete. This discretion follows from his regard for the sensibilities of the viewer that he did not wish to bludgeon and destroy. This discretion was often

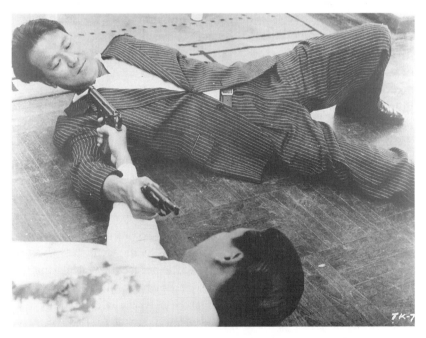

Peckinpah's visual stylistics have influenced cinema throughout the world. Hong Kong director John Woo (*The Killer*, pictured) is the most famous example of a foreign filmmaker whose choreography of violence was inspired by Peckinpah.

achieved by a careful pruning and cutting away of more graphic imagery that had been shot and assembled in initial rough cuts of the films. In an initial cut of *Straw Dogs,* the details of Venner's death—the jaws of a steel animal trap are clamped around his neck—were unduly emphasized in close-up. Peckinpah eventually discarded this in favor of briefer, long-shot framings. Production executive Lewis J. Rachmil found the lingering attention to Venner's agonies to be excessive and unnecessary. In his notes based on the 126.5-minute cut, he suggested that Venner's death throes were overly detailed.[39] Peckinpah concurred and instructed his editors to use a wider framing in order to de-emphasize Venner's death: "Do not like Venner in c/u with trap, let him die in full shot."[40] As a result of this change, Venner's death becomes a more distanced event. It is not thrown into the viewer's face, but transpires in the background of a wide-framed shot. Instead, a close-up emphasizes Amy's horrified response as she watches him die. The focus of the action becomes her anguish and not the mechanics of slaughter. This is a crucial distinction which we will need to keep in mind when we examine the work of today's filmmakers.

In other ways, throughout his work, Peckinpah judiciously selected and shaped his materials to avoid pandering to the salacious interest of viewers. The decapitation of Alfredo Garcia is elided by the narrative. This barbarous event occurs off-screen. Peckinpah spared the audience close-ups of the head itself, showing it only when covered by a sack. As we have noted previously, Peckinpah cut away just before El Jefe's henchmen break his daughter's arm. Moreover, the raw, unedited footage of this action was inherently discreet in its presentation. Peckinpah originally filmed the action by panning the camera away from Theresa to her mother and another woman as Theresa's arm is broken.[41] The latter part of the shot, which includes the pan, was omitted in the editing in favor of a cut to the high-angle camera perspective outside the hacienda. During filming, therefore, Peckinpah averted his camera from this act of brutality, and, while editing the film, he elected to be even more discrete by cutting away to a perspective that was entirely outside the physical space of the scene. Elsewhere in the film, he framed Benny's gratuitous shooting of a corpse by placing the camera behind an open car door that obscures what Benny is doing. These examples point toward an important feature of Peckinpah's work. Despite the exploding squibs that became synonymous with his work, his films lack the leering attention to viscera and gore that have become normative in the films of later directors. Brian De Palma has blown characters up like pulpy, exploding balloons (*The Fury,* 1978) and skewered them with a

Peckinpah opted to delete from *Straw Dogs* many details of Venner's death in the animal trap and to use a full-figure framing rather than closer views. Close-ups stressed Amy's horrified reactions to the violence. Frame enlargements.

powerdrill (*Body Double,* 1984). In *Wild at Heart* (1990), David Lynch blows a character's head off with a shotgun and shows it arcing through the air. In *Henry: Portrait of a Serial Killer* (John McNaughton, 1990), a character's eye is impaled with a pair of scissors, and the character is subsequently dismembered in a bathtub. Nothing even remotely like this exists in Peckinpah's work. Peckinpah's interest in violence was never prurient, and it was never conceived to stoke the extravagantly gory fantasies of its audience. But these characteristics are routine in the films of today's directors. Peckinpah's ground-breaking work clearly opened the door for their excesses, and many directors have consciously placed their work in reference to his to form an unfortunate and misguided stylistic tradition, one uniformed by the tortured moral complexity of his films.

Martin Scorsese, for example, has acknowledged the importance of Peckinpah's films for his own work, particularly, as we have noted, in giv-

During filming, and again during editing, Peckinpah turned away from a direct presentation of the arm-breaking scene in *Alfredo Garcia.* His visual tact shielded viewers from this horrific moment.

Al Pacino as Tony Montoya in Brian De Palma's *Scarface* (1983). Killers with huge guns awash in a sea of blood are everyday features of contemporary cinema, but this glorification of death represents an inversion of the principles on which Peckinpah based his work.

ing him the courage to film raw and ugly characters and episodes. Scorsese is capable of sensitively portraying the spiritual and psychological pain that accompanies physical violence. His best portrait of this occurs in *Raging Bull* (1980), in which he vividly captures the inarticulate despair and anguish of boxer Jake La Motta (Robert De Niro), who realizes that the rage he channels so powerfully inside the ring has effectively destroyed his life. Scorsese's depiction of La Motta's emotional devastation is quite harrowing, and it humanizes this extraordinary character in unforgettable terms. In his work, Scorsese seems to be drawn to topics of violence and brutality out of a genuine and nonexploitative interest in these phenomena. However, his depictions are usually unaccompanied by a rigorously controlled moral point of view, ironic or otherwise, though they are accompanied by a level of detail that verges on the sadistic. In *Casino* (1995), for example, two thugs are beaten to death with clubs in an extended scene that shows their gradual transformation into bloody but still living pulp. The arm-breaking scene in *Alfredo Garcia,* already discussed, bears instructive comparison with the scene in Scorsese's remake of *Cape Fear* (1991) wherein psycho Max Cady (De Niro) breaks the arm of a woman whom he has just taken to bed. Unlike Peckinpah, Scorsese shows the actual breaking, and he leads up to it with close attention to Cady torturing the woman and biting off a piece of her face, a degree of cruelty not found in the Peckinpah scene.

In the intensity of its carnage and the detailing of its violence, Scorsese's work quickly topped that of Peckinpah. The rapidity with which the American cinema surpassed what Peckinpah felt was decorous to put on film is demonstrated by Scorsese's *Taxi Driver* (1976), released a mere two years after *Bring Me the Head of Alfredo Garcia,* which was widely considered to be the nadir of Peckinpah's savage cinema. Like Peckinpah's film, Scorsese's concerns a borderline personality whose aberrance and destructive behavior the filmmaker studies in close detail. But whereas Peckinpah was clearly suffering with and through Benny (and Elita), Scorsese's relationship to his material is cold and clinical, and Travis Bickle (Robert De Niro) remains unaffected by the despair and anguish that humanize Benny. *Taxi Driver* concludes with an exceptionally bloody shoot-out during which Travis massacres three people in order to rescue a hooker whom he erroneously believes wants his help. Scorsese's visualization of the gunfight includes shockingly graphic details. These include the spectacle of a man's fingers blown off by gunshot, replete with pumping, arcing blood spurts; a man's face shot apart at close range; and the first man's fingerless stump impaled by a knife that goes all the way through and sticks out the other side. Travis then shoots this character in the head, spraying blood and brains across the back wall. The blood dribbles audibly on the soundtrack.

Such sustained attention to the physical facts of dismemberment and mutilation cannot be found in Peckinpah's work. Peckinpah used squibs to visualize bullet strikes and montage editing to kineticize the imagery of bodies dehumanized by violent death, but these techniques also defined the boundaries beyond which he would not go. When in *Straw Dogs* David Sumner beats Chris Cawsey to death with a metal poker, Peckinpah avoided showing the impact of the blows on Cawsey's body and, particularly, the progressive mutilations of Cawsey's face and head which must be occurring to produce death so quickly. Instead, he kept the camera on David, because, as we have seen, he considered David's slaughter of Cawsey a pivotal moment in the narrative, and because he was primarily interested in the revulsion and horror that this act produced in David. Peckin-

De Niro always portrayed as psychotic violent social outcast in Scorsese's films.

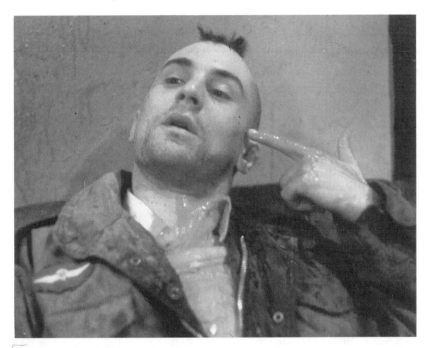

The baroque and abundant gore of *Taxi Driver* demonstrates that the trend toward graphic violence that Peckinpah had helped instigate quickly surpassed his work, transgressing limits beyond which Peckinpah would not go.

pah's attention here, as it often did throughout his work, focused on the psychological and emotional response to violence and touched only secondarily on the physical manifestation of violence. It is David's reaction that Peckinpah considered crucial, not detailing the physical destruction of Cawsey. To say this is to recognize that Peckinpah retained a principled focus on the violence he depicted. Watching his work, we can usually tell where he stood, morally, emotionally, and artistically, in relation to the carnage he presented.

By contrast, in the conclusion of *Taxi Driver,* Scorsese attends chiefly to the mechanics of slaughter. At the end of the massacre, he cuts to a baroque high-angle shot (derived from Hitchcock) as the camera, mounted to the ceiling, tracks through the room to survey the destruction below. The bodies are arranged artfully, and the blood splatters on the wall look almost like a Jackson Pollock collage. In the next series of shots, the camera tracks through the hallway and down the stairs, past an endless series of blood splatters. The visual design of the shots plays to the spectacle of the film's concluding violence, as Scorsese stops the narrative entirely so the viewer can survey and appreciate the elaborateness of the staging and effects work, of the violence itself as an effect and a design. Scorsese has arranged his bloody tableau with care, and the slow tracking shots are intended to accentuate the intricacy of the physical staging. Whereas Peckinpah transcended the physical manifestations of violence to probe its consequences for the lives and feelings of the people involved, Scorsese lingers on the viscera and gore because these in themselves command his cinematic interests. At the end, Travis continues on with his life, unaffected by his rampage and ready to explode again. The concluding orgy of violence has no consequences. The climactic massacre produces no shift of moral perspective in the film with regard to Travis and by implication with regard to the filmmaker's view of the material.

If we can almost always tell where Peckinpah is in relation to the violence he depicted, we can rarely tell where Scorsese is. Peckinpah decided that Benny had to die at the end of *Alfredo Garcia* because of the unconscionable things he had done. In this case, the character's fate implies the filmmaker's judgement of that character, much as Jeffries' second broken leg does at the end of Hitchcock's *Rear Window*. Scorsese, though, has the ability to show, in such films as *Goodfellas* (1990), *Casino*, and *Taxi Driver*, the most gruesome scenes of violence in a completely dispassionate way. In those films, characters are shot, bludgeoned, stabbed, and tortured in graphic detail and with minimal emotion expended by other characters in the narrative, certainly without the elaborate mortification and suffering that Peckinpah's characters undergo. Violence in Peckinpah's films occurs within a context of psychological and emotional anguish. By contrast, in Scorsese's films (with *Raging Bull* being a notable exception), the only pain that violence generally elicits is physical, a response of tissue but not mind. This dispassion is a quality that Scorsese shares with other contemporary directors of ultraviolence, and it is the chief psychological characteristic of modern screen violence, typifying the disconnection of filmmakers from the images they craft and from the emotional response these images ask from their viewers. This is the most important area of difference between Peckinpah's work and objectives and the direction in which screen violence has gone since his time.

In *True Romance* (1994), director Tony Scott audaciously blends a romantic love story with hyperviolent gun battles that unleash rivers of blood. After helping instigate the film's climactic massacre, during which a truckload of gangsters and police are killed, the young couple (Christian

Slater and Patricia Arquette) abscond with a bag of money and live happily ever after. The affirmative possibilities of a love story are negated by the fascination with death that runs through this intensively violent film, eliciting a kind of moral and emotional schizophrenia in the viewer. The emotional disconnection that accompanies the killing in *True Romance* is also a hallmark of the violences found in the work of Paul Verhoeven. In *Robocop,* Verhoeven presents the gut-wrenching spectacle of a cop dismembered by gunshot, as well as the slapstick humor of a toxic-waste-covered thug melting into gloop. In *Total Recall,* we see a man deprived of oxygen and atmosphere explode before our eyes. In *Basic Instinct,* Verhoeven offers several spectacularly bloody serial killer–ice pick murders in a narrative that fails to cohere except as a means for staging violence and death.

In Quentin Tarantino's *Pulp Fiction,* a hit man (John Travolta) riding in a car driven by his partner (Samuel L. Jackson) accidentally shoots a passenger sitting in the back seat. When Travolta's gun goes off, Tarantino cuts to a camera position behind the victim to emphasize the exploding head and the shower of blood and viscera that spatters against the rear window of the car. The camera gets behind the head, into the line of fire, so that the head explodes toward and into the viewer's face. Tarantino gleefully places his camera to give the bloody effect its maximum visceral impact. By contrast, as we have seen, Peckinpah often selected a set-up that would minimize the visceral charge of particularly bloodthirsty moments in his films. Peckinpah aimed to contain the responses of his viewers because he was interested in creating a moral dialogue with them. Tarantino is interested in the shock itself, and, like other contemporary directors, he seems cut off from the moral implications of violent images.

This moral short-circuiting is apparent in the aforementioned scene's coupling of Grand Guignol violence and broad comedy. The special effects work emphasizes the considerable mess caused by the exploding head. Tarantino drenches the screen with gore and then uses it as the basis for laughs. The killers squabble over the mess that soils the interior of the car and bicker about who will clean it up. Travolta tells his partner that he must have hit a bump in the road and that's why the gun went off. The convoluted action that follows deals with the comedy of scouring the blood and brains out of the car. No recognition is conveyed by the characters or by the stylistic design of the imagery that a human life has been taken. The violence is graphic and is without serious emotional consequences for the characters in the film, for the filmmaker who has created it, and for the viewer who need only laugh at the ensuing comedy.

As such, the sequence has the attributes of cartoon violence, which can be extremely graphic and destructive in its physical effects but entails no lasting pain or suffering.

We are now in a position to recognize a further consequence of this fundamental distinction between Peckinpah's work and that of subsequent filmmakers. Like many of his peers (e.g., David Lynch, Kathryn Bigelow, Walter Hill, Tony Scott), Tarantino's rendition of screen violence is thoroughly postmodern, whereas Peckinpah's was not. Tarantino's images are pastiches, inflected by the movie and TV culture he imbibed while growing up, and their emotional and moral content is second-hand, derived from, and mediated by, the pop-cultural material that is their immediate referent. Thus, when a character is killed in a Tarantino film, or in Lynch's *Wild at Heart,* or in Walter Hill's *Last Man Standing* (1996), the character does not reference a real human being, but rather only other movie characters. By contrast, violence for Peckinpah was a raw and damning reality. He understood it personally, and he could see that it was a plague infesting the country in the late 1960s. It was too serious a matter

The killers in *Pulp Fiction* are post-modern pastiches that reference movies, not life.

for him to play for laughs. Tarantino, though, is drawn in his work to violence because he knows it as a movie style, and it is one that he finds compelling. The style itself is the subject and form of his work. Accordingly, he has not moved to explore the psychological and emotional dynamics of violence in terms that might reference life apart from the movies. The famous ear-cutting scene in *Reservoir Dogs* (1992) exists on its own flamboyant terms, principally in the striking audiovisual combination of the psychopathic Mr. White (Michael Madson) dancing with a razor to the music of "Back in the Middle With You" by Steeler's Wheel as his victim cowers and screams. This audiovisual mix is so insistently aggressive that it obviously functioned as Tarantino's design concept for the scene and as his principal reason for shooting it. But as a unit of narrative, the scene is isolated and gratuitous. It does not connect with anything else in the story. It is a set-piece. While, in this case, the victim audibly suffers and the violence is painful in its nastiness, this pain becomes as formalistic an element of the total design as the music, the camera movements, and the editing. By segregating the scene from other material in the narrative, Tarantino keeps the design closed, self-contained, and without moral connection to the characters' precipitating and subsequent behavior. By contrast, Peckinpah conceived of his narratives as moving through a series of interconnected stages or scenes from which the viewer was expected to extract a lesson.

Graphic violence is now embedded in contemporary cinema as a formulaic element, endlessly repeated, and often removed from any recognizably human context. It solves story problems by providing talented as well as mediocre filmmakers with an easily-assembled, if mechanical, narrative structure. It also substitutes for thought and reflection. German filmmaker Wim Wenders (*The American Friend,* 1977; *Wings of Desire,* 1987) has observed that movie violence today "is partly a solution to story problems and partly a solution to thinking. Mostly, when violence occurs, it stops the thinking process in the audience, as well as the film-maker's. It solves the problem in your plot as well as the one in your attention span." As one critic has recently suggested, "Far from being difficult and challenging, violent movies tend to be highly routine. Righteous violence and self-defense is the predictable *structure* of violence, in which killing becomes casual and arguments are normally settled by fists or gun."[42] In the slaughter epics of Sylvester Stallone and Arnold Schwarzenegger, the hero suffers some grievous offense, which then motivates an extended scenario of righteous, lethal vengeance. In *Cliffhanger* (Renny Harlin, 1994), for example, Stallone is a mountain-climbing guide whose friends are kidnapped and killed by the villain and his cohorts, and the narrative devolves into a frenzy of mass killing as Stallone hunts down and dispatches his enemies. When he runs out of people to kill, the narrative ends. Stallone and Schwarzenegger have helped popularize a seriocomic approach to ultra-violence, which combines over-the-top mayhem, preposterous in its out-sized dimensions,[43] with a winking, tongue-in-cheek attitude toward the bloodshed. Taking their cue from Clint Eastwood's Dirty Harry, they taunt the villains with smart-alecky wisecracks just before, or after, the climactic slaughter. In *Cobra* (1986), before knifing and shooting his psychopathic opponent, Stallone announces, "Crime is a disease, and I'm the cure." In *Judge Dredd* (1995), executing a criminal, he mutters "Court's adjourned." In that same film, after slaughtering a group of villains, he proclaims, "This room has been pacified." In *Total Recall* (1990), Schwarzenegger grapples with a villain on an elevator. In the course of the fight, the villain's arms are torn off and he falls to his death. Holding the bloody stumps in his hands, Schwarzenegger contemptuously tells the now-dead villain that he'll see him at the party and then tosses the stumps down at the body. When he shoots and kills his wife, he sneers, "Consider that a divorce." Comedy in these films is an essential means of achieving dispassionate, postmodern violence.

Interestingly, Sylvester Stallone now feels some ambivalence about the bloodfests that he helped popularize, and he has expressed regret for taking the violence too far in some of his pictures. Deformed by their violence, these pictures (*Cobra, Rambo III, Judge Dredd*) become grotesque. "No one had reached the point of saturation yet, so we kept going until we'd eliminated characterizations, eliminated the story, and had only stunts and explosions. We're now in an era when all films must end in a kind of choreographed Armageddon. The bad guy must go up in flames, the planet must explode, everything must end in a bang. If explosions were removed from films of the last five years, three-quarters would have no ending."[44]

Contemporary ultraviolence, taken to such extremes, becomes cartoonish, and its insulation from psychological pain and emotional consequence helps promote a sense of security and invulnerability in its spectators.[45] It comforts those viewers who do not mind its graphic nature. In addition, it requires, and helps produce, the kind of numbness that Peckinpah had come to understand as a concomitant of frequent exposure to random violence and that he had visualized in the Horrell family of *Pat Garrett and Billy the Kid*. As Todd Gitlin has noted:

The action epics of Arnold Schwarzenegger and Sylvester Stallone have made violence a joke. These films exhibit a cartoonish approach to slaughter and a wisecracking response to ultraviolence. © 1996, Warner Bros.

> . . . over the years of chain saws, sharks, abdomen-ripping aliens, and the like, movie violence has come to require, and train, numbness. Anesthesia becomes necessary equipment for steering through the thousands of limb tearings and arterial spurts that the movies have made more common than dependent clauses.[46]

As we have seen, this numbing of response can be empirically demonstrated,[47] and the dispassionate regard for screen violence that underlies it now seems to be shared by filmmaker and viewers alike. Oliver Stone's *Natural Born Killers* (1994) is very instructive in this regard, because it wants to critique a modern America in which the media culture glorifies violence and makes celebrities out of killers and because Stone is a director who has in other films shown respect for the human consequences of violence. Stone intended his film to be an indictment of both screen and real-life violence, yet he could not divorce the style of the film from the targets of his attack so that the movie becomes the very thing it wished to expose. This is an unintended and uncontrolled irony, in contrast to Peckinpah's more shrewdly calculated use of the ironic mode. Moreover, Peckinpah's heartfelt engagement with the issue of violence was very different from Stone's cooler, more intellectualized stance. A brief exploration of the design and flaws in *Natural Born Killers* can help clarify the integrity of Peckinpah's approach, its historical specificity, and its lasting importance.

In other films, Stone has been very successful at locating violence within a recognizably real and painful human context. His treatment of the El Salvadoran death squad killings in *Salvador* (1986), in particular the rape and murder of a group of U.S. Catholic churchwomen, conveys with scrupulous intensity the suffering and pain caused by these acts. In *Platoon* (1986), much of the battlefield violence is conveyed with a palpable physical edge and seriousness of purpose, and particularly horrifying are the savageries some of the soldiers inflict on a group of Vietnamese villagers. Stone's moral point of view ensures that the killings of these villagers register as savageries and not as comedy or as mechanical spectacle. Like Scorsese, then, Stone has proven himself capable of representing the human consequences of violence. But, like Scorsese, Stone's work has also been conditioned by the stylistic imperatives that now govern contemporary cinema violence and that transcend their incarnation in any single filmmaker. Thus, *Natural Born Killers* finds Stone far from the human issues and realities that grounded his representation of violence in *Salvador* and *Platoon*.

Stone's film follows the exploits of two serial killers, Mickey (Woody Harrelson) and Mallory (Juliette Lewis), an outlaw couple whose romantic devotion to one another the film lyricizes in the manner of *Bonnie and Clyde*. In a media-saturated culture eager for tabloid sensationalism, Mickey and Mallory's killing spree earns them celebratory status, and they become media stars with an adoring public. One devoted fan remarks, "I'm not saying, you know, I believe in mass murder or that shit, but if I was a mass murderer, I'd be Mickey and Mallory." Stone aims to capture, visually, the psychotic states of mind of the characters and to correlate this with the adrenaline rush of living in a society that is obsessed with violence and that overdoses on a steady stream of pop-culture images. For Stone, these images from movies, television, and consumer advertising have created a pseudo-reality that engulfs the consciousness of Mickey and Mallory and their public so that they can scarcely tell the difference between real killing and the fictional media violence that surrounds them. Stone has said:

At the beginning of the movie, these two young people are really desensitized to violence. The concept is that they live in a TV world and don't realize the consequences of their actions. They also live in a world of rage and anger because of their abusive parents and because the nature of the Twentieth Century has been very violent. We incorporated those ideas into the movie by using rear-screen images. We wanted to give a sense of the schizophrenic madness of the century . . .[48]

Stone and cinematographer Robert Richardson use the rear-screen imagery as a means of externalizing the uncontrolled, lurid psychology of the homicidal characters and as a way of commenting on pervasive social violence. While staying at a hotel, Mickey watches television, specifically, violent movies, and Stone includes clips from the chain saw killing in Brian De Palma's *Scarface* and the prelude to the Agua Verde massacre in *The Wild Bunch* when Pike shoots Mohr, the German military advisor working for Mapache. The motel room's window becomes a giant rear-screen projection surface onto which other violent images appear, supplementing Mickey's television fare. These images include footage of Hitler and Stalin as well as shots of predatory animals. Mickey's mental world is awash in violent imagery that is externalized into the design of his physical surroundings.

The entire film is saturated with images of violence and death. Stone intercuts the narrative with nondiegetic shots of wolves and rattlesnakes, and Mickey and Mallory respond to all of the bloodshed they perpetrate without remorse. The rear-screen imagery also visualizes the tender regard these killers have for each other. After slaughtering the customers and employees of a roadside diner in the film's opening scene, Mickey and Mallory declare their love for each other and dance romantically amidst the carnage while the rear-screen imagery shows Paris and beautiful fireworks. Stone accentuates the frenzy of their perceptions and adventures by employing a mixture of different film and video formats coupled with abundant self-reflexive imagery. He intercuts color and black-and-white 35mm footage with 16mm, 8mm, and beta video footage. He uses frequent jump cuts, and the camera perspective rolls and lurches crazily. He intercuts animated footage with live action and treats the live action as if it were a cartoon, as when a speeding bullet stops before a terrified woman's face before continuing on its lethal trajectory and splattering her brains on the diner wall. By mixing modalities in this way, Stone evidently hoped to make the point that social violence and media violence have become so intermingled today as to be indistinguishable. The action of the narrative is periodically interrupted by advertisements and by images of TV channels

In *Natural Born Killers,* Oliver Stone aimed to critique the modern culture of violence and to employ Peckinpah's rationale for placing graphic violence on screen. But times had changed, and graphic violence had become an artistic and philosophical dead-end. © 1994, Warner Bros.

being switched as if the whole film, and the culture it satirizes, were just one extended television show. Stone has said that he wanted to combine in the design of this film the ferocity of Peckinpah with the cinematic self-consciousness of Godard.[49] But whereas Godard's use of the medium was extremely controlled and Peckinpah's savage poetry was informed by an abiding moral perspective on its violence, Stone's film lacks these qualities.

The critical voice Stone wished to employ through this film is undermined by the fascination he felt for Mickey and Mallory. They are monsters, but they also exhibit, in their loving regard for one another, the only truly human feeling on display in the film—especially in reference to the gallery of grotesque and depraved characters who surround them. This beclouds the film's point of view and tends to conflate it with Mickey and Mallory, who become the viewer's guides and emotional reference points on this trip through a modern American hell. This confusion over point of view and over the distinctions between social reality and the symbolic realities of media programming (a confusion that is also apparent in Stone's cavalier treatment of history in *JFK,* 1991), prevents a coherent perspective on the problem of violence from emerging in the film. In the motel room scene with Mickey, fictional movie violence and historical footage of real figures blend seamlessly together. The Wild Bunch, Hitler, Stalin, Scarface —no evident distinctions exist between the different fictive, social, and historical registers to which these images belong. In this film's postmodern perspective, as images, there are no viable distinctions among them.

At the end of the film, Mickey kills the television interviewer (Robert Downey Jr.), host of a popular tabloid show called "American Maniacs," who wanted to tell his story. Mickey tells him, "Killing you and what you represent is a statement." After the murder, which Mickey films using the reporter's video camera, he and Mallory stroll off, and the film cuts to footage of O.J. Simpson, Rodney King, the Menendez brothers, and Lorena Bobbitt. It is a bewildering series of images. During the 1990s, these people all became media stars as the result of massively publicized crimes and trials, but beyond this general connection, the film can offer no account of the range of disparate issues that emerged in these cases. The image itself is all things for Stone, and he treats it as freely interchangeable with all other images. The Wild Bunch and Hitler—Why not? Rodney King and Mickey and Mallory—these are images of celebrity criminals, so the editing connects them, even though one corresponds to a real person who was the target of a beating and the others are fictional killers. As happened on Stone's previous film, *JFK,* the distinctions between referentially fictional and referentially real images dissolve in *Natural Born Killers,* such that the film treats them as indistinguishable and interchangeable.

The resulting form is, therefore, postmodern. The realm of the social disappears because it is overwhelmed by the realm of the image. This is crippling to the aims of a filmmaker like Stone who wishes to engage social issues, because it entails a loss of control over the images he wishes to manipulate and entails also that his film become indistinguishable from the phenomenon he seeks to satirize and condemn. The film's cool presentation of horrific violence is inseparable from Mickey and Mallory's own sociopathic response to their deeds. The film's point of view becomes that of the killers, and one searches the mise-en-scène, the dialogue, and the narrative for some alternative perspective on all the killing, some credible point of view that exists beyond the immediate homicidal impulses of the protagonists. It cannot be found.

Cinematographer John Bailey has eloquently criticized contemporary movie violence, charging that it is so pervasive that it has come to seem unreal and routine for the artists who make the films. Of Stone's film, he writes that it places viewers inside the hurricane of violence, but in a way that produces a confusion of perception and response. "Its point of view is that of the killers, not because of a clear critical or moral perspective but because that's where the action is. The defining aesthetic is MTV. . . . The film eroticizes violence, wallows in it and struggles to incite the viewer."[50] The unreality of the violence in *Natural Born Killers* is apparent not only in the style of its presentation but also in the way it fails to represent authentic human responses to violence, namely grief and emotional anguish. Apart from the romantic longing Mickey and Mallory feel for each other, the only emotion the film dramatizes is rage. This dehumanizes the real-life emotional context that surrounds actual violence, but what the film is mainly concerned with, in its postmodern style, is *imagery* of violence, violence as pop-culture iconography. The film, like Tarantino's work or Kathryn Bigelow's *Stange Days* (1996), is preoccupied with a derivative, second-order movie and media-based iconography. In this postmodern style, the filmmaker's images comment on other images, other films, or television shows because the possibility of the image having a referentially real relationship with a representable world is mistrusted by the filmmaker (e.g., Tarantino) or else she or he is simply uninterested in that relationship (e.g., Stone in *Natural Born Killers*). When Oliver Stone, therefore, attempts to put a high moral gloss on *Natural Born Killers* by recycling the terms by which Peckinpah spoke of his own work, the attempt seems not merely hollow and imitative but strangely antihistorical, as if the intervening decades of movie violence have not demonstrated the limitations of that effort. Stone has said that the theme of his film "is that violence is all around us; it's in nature and it's in every one of us, and we all have to acknowledge it and come to grips with it."[51] He added that the film upsets people and makes them think about their own relation to violence.

Today, so many years after Peckinpah's work in this area, it is doubtful that there is anything of interest left for a filmmaker to say with such a theme. Stone's attempt to employ Peckinpah's justification for screen violence is unpersuasive because Peckinpah's work belongs to a very different period in terms of both social and cinema history. Accordingly, his rationale for exploring screen violence cannot simply be transported to a later period. Peckinpah's efforts to work through the dynamics of human violence on screen possessed a social validity and an internal aesthetic integrity that a picture like *Natural Born Killers,* and contemporary cinema ultraviolence in general, does not. By adopting a dispassionate approach to ultraviolence, contemporary films inoculate by numbing their viewers to the graphic displays of gore. This is the antithesis of what Peckinpah wished to achieve, even though such films work from the tradition of explicit violence that he helped establish. They lack the complex ambivalencies of Peckinpah's regard for violence and do not display the contradictory visual, emotional, and psychological perspectives that he employed as a means of provoking the audience into a heightened state of self-awareness.

Peckinpah's best work produces a crisis of response for the viewer because it pulls the viewer's emotional and cognitive responses in different directions. The viewer is torn, and in some cases, appalled by the conflicting responses the films generate, but Peckinpah evidently had an abiding faith in the orderly components of this process—that is, in the ideal viewer's ability to make sense of the experience, to reconcile the disparate responses into a newly integrated understanding of the self in relation to aggression and violence, and to recognize the place of these phenomena in the social world. Peckinpah's morality plays were designed to produce enlightenment, not to stoke chaos. By stressing the eruptive force of human violence, he aimed to replicate in the viewer not primitivism but its opposite, civilized control. Peckinpah valued this control because he recognized that it was fragile, subject to destruction by others, and, because of that, all the more precious and necessary. This outlook entailed a corresponding regard for democracy, liberty, and law as the great achievements of a social life whose basis transcends the anarchic state of nature. We thus arrive at a surprising place. Moving through the darkness and destruction in Peckinpah's work, we find that the intellectual foundation of that work is not a Hobbesian ethic but a commitment to rationality and order. As always, Peckinpah instructed by way of negative example.

Despite his preoccupation with violence, then, Peckinpah was neither a nihilist nor an anarchist. He quoted Robert Ardrey, but the model that influenced his conception of the ideal viewer of his work was a rationalist one. In a 1982 BBC radio interview, he stated "I know that anarchism has little to do with any philosophy that I entertain."[52] On an ABC Network Radio program conducted after the shooting of *Cross of Iron,* he spoke expansively about his concept of freedom, law, and justice in relation to a democratic society. He stressed how fragile are the benefits of democracy and how essential law is to human dignity. These things are achievements to be protected because they are not qualities inherent in the struggle for life.

> I believe very deeply in freedom. I abhor censorship and restrictions on human endeavor and human liberty in any shape or form, while still believing strongly in law and order. I believe that freedom and just law are not some-

thing that is given to man, but are something he must fight hard to attain and equally hard to retain. Even when such liberty is attained, the battle has only begun—the most important battle—to keep it and let it grow without destroying or degrading the rights of your fellow man.[53]

Peckinpah's filmic explorations of the dark side of human life reinforced his appreciation for those human achievements that negate primitivism and brutality, because these latter conditions are the antithesis of the rationalism on which democracy and liberty rest. He noted that the Hitlers of this world rise to power on the blind and unquestioning assent of their publics,[54] and, as an artist, he opposed censorship because it represented a kind of intellectual rule-by-force that he believed correlated with antidemocratic and authoritarian social impulses. He wrote, "Censorship is the cor-

Peckinpah confers with Dustin Hoffman on the set of *Straw Dogs,* his most horrific film. Peckinpah's explorations of the human heart of darkness were predicated upon a commitment to rationality and order. Ever the ironist, he could only present constructive values by showing their opposite. © 1972, ABC Pictures Corp.

nerstone on which extremist philosophies have built their empires, fascism, communism, the burning of books, the suppression of artistic freedom, the indoctrination of the people by the bigoted, the prejudiced and the narrow-minded."[55] As we have seen, Danforth, the neofascist in *The Osterman Weekend,* represents the ongoing threat to freedom and democratic life, as Peckinpah understood it, and against which constant vigilance is required.

For Peckinpah, democratic rationalism was the answer to violence and brutality on the social level. The social unrest and crisis of political authority in the late sixties were frightening, because while they might produce much needed changes—"America has just lost a president because of his attempt to suppress the truth," Peckinpah wrote in 1974[56]—they might also undermine and erode the republic. Even though his films do not deal explicitly with that era's problems of social and political authority, this crisis nevertheless provided an immediate horizon of experience on which he based his cinematic project. That project had two major points of reference. These were the social phenomena of human violence, resonating through late sixties culture, and the cinematic tradition of representing violence as a rather polite and sanitized affair. Peckinpah sought to realign these by bringing cinematic representations closer to what he believed were the physical and phenomenological attributes of human violence and by using those representations to explore and render as aesthetic forms the disfigurement of human potential that he took violence to emblemize.

Peckinpah's cinema, therefore, does not belong to the postmodern tradition represented in the work of Tarantino, in the Stone of *Natural Born Killers,* or in many other contemporary films which take as their essential point of reference other films and images, including the work of Peckinpah. Peckinpah, instead, was a modernist, perhaps the last modernist of the American cinema. His cinematic representation of violence did play off an established aesthetic tradition—the sanitized images of violence in earlier American films and in Hollywood Westerns in particular. But instead of imitating and recycling these images, he experienced the weight of this tradition as a burden that had to be overcome, in the interest of pursuing truth, because it was a legacy false to experience. The image, for Peckinpah, did not function as an interchangeable sign, designating only its own closed world of media-based reference. Instead, it had real-world referents that validated its aesthetic structure. This referential base in reality was defined for Peckinpah by a mix of immediately personal experiences and more distant, but still highly resonant, social events. These included, on the personal side, the chronically suppressed tension and anger in his parents' marriage, his emotional experiences with his own rage and its consequences, and his encounters with wounded and dying animals during hunting excursions; and, on the public side, the Vietnam War, the political assassinations, and other upheavals of the period. For Peckinpah, violence was not, fundamentally, an image. He would make images from it, but for him it was authentic in ways that transcended the images he fashioned and that, if those images were properly made, would validate them. As he wrote to a viewer who criticized the violence in his films, "You find it [violence] senseless in a film and I find it totally senseless in life."[57]

Like other aesthetic modernists, then, Peckinpah believed that it was necessary to shatter the old (cinema) traditions in order to purify vision and bring it into closer proximity with an ontological base. In his work, this ontology was the human propensity for aggression. Using cinema, he could fashion a mirror capable of reflecting the viewer's fallen soul back at him or her and, in the process, sustain the viewer's fascinated gaze at this disturbing mirror by aestheticizing violence in striking and original ways. Like many modernist arts, Peckinpah's thus incorporated a dialectic between truth and artifice, with the former grounding the latter and the latter making reference to the former. This is one reason Stone's attempt to recycle Peckinpah's rationale does not work in relation to *Natural Born Killers*. The imagery is not grounded in an ontology that transcends the image itself. Furthermore, in the context of the late sixties, and particularly the industry's codes governing movie content at that time, Peckinpah, as a modernist, believed that shattering the taboos surrounding the depiction of movie violence could have a liberating effect. He would show movie audiences for the first time what violence was all about.

Sadly, the liberating effects that were supposed to follow from the new, transgressive aesthetic styles proved to be very short-lived, if they occurred at all. Since Peckinpah's time, the only legacy of the graphic violence that he helped bring to cinema has been more graphic violence, and it has been perpetuated by filmmakers who, unlike Peckinpah, remain untroubled by the bloodshed on which they turn their cameras. Movie violence has proven to be a gigantic emotional and artistic dead end. Today, there is nothing left that has not been shown and nowhere stylistically for a filmmaker to go who remains interested in filming violence. Like Pike Bishop, filmmakers now need to start thinking beyond their guns, unless they wish to perpetuate a now-exhausted visual form. The form, though, had not been exhausted in Peckinpah's day, and he was resolute in his use of cinema to probe the shadow areas of human life.

If contemporary screen violence has become a debased form, the reasons why we should attend to Peckinpah's films are eminently clear and make those films especially relevant for audiences reared on the dispassionate cruelties of current filmmakers. Peckinpah was not only the last modernist of American cinema but a significant humanist as well. The cold cruelty of today's films places them in an antihumanist tradition. By deadening emotion, they constrict the realm of human experience and invalidate it. Peckinpah, by contrast, sought to affirm human potential by being candid about its everyday mutilation. His films do not deaden feeling. They are sobering accounts of loss and pain and horror. He, in turn, was shocked and disturbed by the imagery he created and the brutality it depicted. What contemporary filmmaker would weep, as Peckinpah did, when filming a scene of violence? The dialectic of tenderness and rage at the heart of his work may remain unresolved, giving his films their special edge and power, but his own capacity for suffering through and with the images and characters he created humanizes the resulting work. "If this world's all about winners, son, what's for the losers?" Junior Bonner's father asks wistfully. Peckinpah knew he saw a certain kind of truth only too clearly. Pursuing that truth may have been a losing gambit in terms of personal and career fortunes. But in doing so, in losing this way, Peckinpah left a body of work that defines the essential issues and contradictions inherent in recording violence for the camera, and that subsequent filmmakers can only replicate but not transcend. In this sense his work defines a limit point for cinema. It occupies a horizon of experience and creative expression that will not be surpassed.

Notes

Introduction

1. See Paul Seydor, *Peckinpah: The Western Films;* and Prince, Stephen, ed. *Sam Peckinpah's* The Wild Bunch.
2. Sam Peckinpah Collection (hereafter cited as SPC), *Le Devoir* interview, interviews, folder no. 96.

Chapter 1 / Peckinpah and the 1960s

1. Pauline Kael called *Straw Dogs* "the first American film that is a fascist work of art." See her review reprinted in *For Keeps,* pp. 422–426.
2. Joan Mellen, *Big Bad Wolves: Masculinity in the American Film,* p. 272.
3. Seydor, *Peckinpah: The Western Films,* pp. 309–329.
4. Kathleen Murphy, "Sam Peckinpah: No Bleeding Heart," p. 74.
5. Ibid., pp. 74–75.
6. Michael Bliss, *Justified Lives: Morality and Narrative in the Films of Sam Peckinpah,* p. 306.
7. Robin Wood, "Sam Peckinpah" in Richard Roud, ed., *Cinema: A Critical Dictionary,* p. 772.
8. Michael Sragow, "Sam Peckinpah, 1925–1984" in *Doing It Right,* ed. Michael Bliss, p. 180.

9. Aljean Harmetz, "Man Was a Killer Long before He Served a God," in *Doing It Right,* ed. Bliss, p. 173.

10. Garner Simmons, *Peckinpah: A Portrait in Montage,* p. 17.

11. Bliss, *Justified Lives,* p. 305.

12. Paul Seydor, "Peckinpah," p. 18.

13. Bliss, *Justified Lives,* p. 10.

14. John Bryson, "The Wild Bunch in New York," p. 26.

15. Simmons, *Peckinpah: A Portrait in Montage,* p. 17.

16. Ibid., pp. 25, 26.

17. David Weddle, *If They Move . . . Kill 'Em: The Life and Times of Sam Peckinpah,* p. 33.

18. Ibid., p. 23.

19. Ibid., pp. 28, 112.

20. Ibid., p. 37.

21. Bryson, "The Wild Bunch in New York," p. 28.

22. Ibid.

23. Dan Yergin, "Peckinpah's Progress: From Blood and Killing in the Old West to Siege and Rape in Rural Cornwall," p. 90.

24. See Weddle, pp. 243, 250, 251 for discussion of this.

25. Louis Chapin, "New Movie Standards: General Film Code, Not Specific Bans," p. 5.

26. "'Mature' Tag at Music Hall," p. 7.

27. "H'wood: Brave Nude World?," p. 1.

28. "Spots of Grief for Metro's 'Blow-Up' and Par's 'Sundown,' But on Whole 'C' Rating Now Stops No Chain Datings," p. 7.

29. "Urge Local Papers to Rate Pictures," p. 13.

30. "Theatre Operators and Public Require Updating on Social Point of View," p. 7.

31. *Mass Media Hearings, Vol. 9A: A Report to the National Commission on the Causes and Prevention of Violence,* p. 193.

32. "Pix Must 'Broaden Market,'" p. 1.

33. "Modern Films for Masses," p. 23.

34. SPC, Feldman memos, May 13, 1969, folder no. 46.

35. "Evans' Par Credo: Stress Story, Encourage Youth, Mix in Experience," p. 9.

36. Ibid.

37. "Youngbloods vs. Committees," p. 5.

38. "W7 Studio Ready to Give Directors Anything—Except Right of Final Cut," p. 5.

39. "Hollywood: The Shock of Freedom in Films," p. 66.

40. Gary Crowdus and Richard Porton, "The Importance of a Singular, Guiding Vision: An Interview with Arthur Penn," p. 12.

41. "Catholics and Code Watchful," p. 7.

42. See Christopher Frayling, *Spaghetti Westerns,* for a discussion of this influence.

43. Robert J. Landry, "It's Murder, Italian Style," p. 7.

44. Bosley Crowther, "A Smash at Violence," p. 10.

45. Ibid.

46. Joseph Morgenstern, "Two for a Tommy Gun," p. 65.

47. Morgenstern, "The Thin Red Line," p. 82.

48. "'Escalation' of Pix Violence Hit by Theatre Owners at Convention," p. 28.

49. Ibid.

50. "Warren Beatty 'Bonnie' Share," p. 1.

51. "'Bonnie and Clyde's' Booming Repeats," p. 3.

52. "Persevering of 'Bonnie and Clyde'," p. 5.

53. "Hollywood: The Shock of Freedom in Films," p. 73.

54. SPC, Feldman memos, letter of January 30, 1968, from MPAA's Geoffrey Shurlock, folder no. 45.

55. Ibid.

56. Ibid.

57. Ibid.

58. Ibid.

59. SPC, *Wild Bunch*—production reports, folder no. 84.

60. SPC, Feldman memos, letter of March 17, 1969, folder no. 46.

61. SPC, Feldman memos, letter of April 8, 1969, to MPAA, folder no. 46; and SPC, Feldman memos, letter of April 8, 1969, folder no. 46.

62. SPC, Feldman memos, February 9, 1968, folder no. 45.

63. SPC, Feldman memos, May 13, 1969, folder no. 46.

64. SPC, *The Wild Bunch*—Peckinpah memos, May 3, 1969, folder no. 62.

65. "'Brutal Films Pale Before Televised Vietnam'—Valenti," p. 2.

66. Ibid.

67. Crowdus and Porton, "The Importance of a Singular, Guiding Vision," p. 8.

68. *Mass Media Hearings,* p. 193.

69. "It's More Resolution than Noted," p. 5.

70. "Public Spots Deadly Parallels," p. 60.

71. Weddle, *If They Move . . . Kill 'Em,* p. 334.

72. Statistics on the riots can be found in *Report of the National Advisory Commission on Civil Disorders.*

73. *To Establish Justice, to Ensure Domestic Tranquility,* p. 51.

74. Ibid., p. 16.

75. Lou Harris, *The Anguish of Change,* p. 174.

76. Ibid.

77. Bryson, "Wild Bunch in New York," p. 28.

78. *To Establish Justice, To Ensure Domestic Tranqulity,* p. xxv.

79. Kirkpatrick Sale, *SDS,* p. 634.

80. Kenneth Keniston, *Young Radicals,* p. 248.

81. Ibid., p. 252.

82. Todd Gitlin, *The Sixties: Years of Hope, Days of Rage,* p. 6.

83. Ibid., p. 316.

84. Ibid., p. 34.

85. Keniston, *Young Radicals,* p. 252.

86. Susan Sontag, "What's Happening to America?" p. 52.

87. Martin Luther King Jr., "A Time to Break Silence" in *A Testament of Hope: The Essential Writings of Martin Luther King, Jr.,* ed. James M. Washington , pp. 233, 241.

88. Arthur Schlesinger Jr., "America 1968: The Politics of Violence," p. 20.

89. SPC, *Le Devoir* interview, interviews, folder no. 96. If Peckinpah's language occasionally seems stilted in this interview, that is a result of its translation into French for publication in Quebec and then back again into English in a translation specially prepared for Peckinpah. Upon reading the English translation, Peckinpah wrote to Andre Leroux, his interviewer, in a letter of November 30, 1975, to specially praise the interview and to compliment him for capturing aspects of his films that American critics usually ignore.

90. Ibid.

91. Ibid.

92. "Playboy Interview: Sam Peckinpah," p. 70.

93. Schlesinger, "America 1968," p. 20.

94. Yergin, "Peckinpah's Progress," p. 90.

95. Quoted in Jay Cocks, "Straw Dogs," p. 86.

96. Ibid.

97. Schlesinger, "America 1968," p. 20.

98. SPC, *Wild Bunch*—response letters, statement on violence, folder no. 92.

99. Bryson, "Wild Bunch in New York," p. 28.

100. Yergin, "Peckinpah's Progress," p. 90.

101. Stephen Farber, "Peckinpah's Return," p. 8.

102. SPC, *Wild Bunch*—response letters, statement on violence, folder no. 92.

103. Farber, "Peckinpah's Return," p. 8.

104. "Catholics Mild Re 'Wild Bunch,'" p. 13.

105. "Press Violent About Film's Violence," p. 15.

106. Farber, "Peckinpah's Return," p. 9.

107. Ibid.

108. SPC, general-misc., letter of August 27, 1969, folder no. 175.

109. "Press Violent About Film's Violence," p. 15.

110. SPC, correspondence-misc., folder no. 61.

111. P. F. Kluge, "Director Sam Peckinpah, What Price Violence?" pp. 52–53.

112. SPC, *Pat Garrett*—crank letters, letter of March 20, 1974, folder no. 16.

113. SPC, *Pat Garrett*—crank letters, letter of April 24, 1974, folder no. 16.

114. SPC, *Pat Garrett*—crank letters, letter of May 3, 1974, folder no. 16.

115. Ibid.

116. F. Anthony Macklin, "Mort Sahl Called Me a 1939 American," p. 23.

117. Farber, "Peckinpah's Return," p. 9.

118. Carl Oglesby, "Liberalism and the Corporate State," p. 22.

119. See, for example, Tom Hayden, "The Ability to Face Whatever Comes," *The New Republic,* pp. 16–18.

120. King, "A Time to Break Silence," p. 240.

121. Herbert Marcuse, *One-Dimensional Man,* p. 10.

122. Songtag, "What's Happening to America?" p. 51.

123. "Playboy Interview," p. 192.

124. Bryson, "Wild Bunch in New York," p. 26.

125. Farber, "Peckinpah's Return," p. 9.

126. SPC, *The Killer Elite*—script notes, folder no. 21; *The Osterman Weekend*—script meeting notes, folder no. 115.

127. Jan Aghed, "Pat Garrett and Billy the Kid," p. 65.

128. Ibid.

129. See Seydor, *Peckinpah: The Western Films,* pp. 302–303.

130. "Playboy Interview," p. 192.

131. Ibid.

132. Ibid.

133. Macklin, "Mort Sahl Called Me a 1939 American," p. 23.

134. SPC, *Convoy*—script notes, September 21, 1977, folder no. 23.

135. SPC, BBC radio interview, March 9, 1982, interviews, folder no. 96.

136. SPC, *Le Devoir* interview, interviews, folder no. 96.

137. Wood, "Sam Peckinpah," p. 772.

138. David Steigerwald, *The Sixties and the End of Modern America,* p. 95.

139. SPC, *Straw Dogs*—final shooting script, folder no. 21; SPC, *Straw Dogs*—memos, folder no. 53.

Chapter 2 / Aestheticizing Violence

1. Bryson, "Wild Bunch in New York," p. 25.

2. Jeff Millar, "Peckinpah Gets Nonviolent (Off Screen)," p. 1.

3. "Playboy Interview," p. 68.

4. SPC, *Wild Bunch*—response letters, statement on violence, folder no. 92.

5. SPC, *Wild Bunch*—response letters, May 13, 1969, folder no. 92.

6. SPC, *Wild Bunch*—response letters, statement on violence, folder no. 92.

7. SPC, *Wild Bunch*—response letters, September 3, 1969, folder no. 92.

8. Weddle, *If They Move . . . Kill 'Em,* p. 99, 333.

9. SPC, *Alfredo Garcia*—daily log, folder no. 45.

10. SPC, *Junior Bonner*—daily shots, folder no. 19.

11. Nat Segaloff, "Walon Green: Fate Will Get You," in Pat McGilligan, ed., *Backstory 3: Interveiws with Screenwriters of the 1960s,* pp. 143, 135–156; and author's telephone conversation with Paul Seydor, July 22, 1997.

12. Ernest Callenbach, "A Conversation with Sam Peckinpah," p. 10.

13. Weddle, *If They Move . . . Kill 'Em,* p. 271.

14. Ibid., pp. 9, 356; and David Bordwell, *The Cinema of Eisenstein,* p. 266.

15. Michael Glenny and Richard Taylor, eds., *Eisenstein. Volume 2: Towards a Theory of Montage,* p. 122.

16. SPC, *The Wild Bunch*—correspondence, letter of April 4, 1968, folder no. 35; and "Playboy Interview," p. 192.

17. SPC, general-misc., letters of December 30, 1968, and June 23, 1969, folder no. 127.

18. SPC, general-misc., letters of February 28, 1980, and March 25, 1980, folder no. 175.

19. SPC, *Cross of Iron*—script notes, letter of February 5, 1976, folder no. 26.

20. SPC, Feldman memos, October 29, 1967, folder no. 45.

21. Farber, "Peckinpah's Return," p. 11.

22. SPC, *The Wild Bunch*—correspondence, letter of March 19, 1968, folder no. 43; and Weddle, *If They Move . . . Kill 'Em,* p. 331.

23. Crowdus and Porton, "The Importance of a Singular, Guiding Vision," p. 9.

24. Ibid.

25. Ibid., p. 5.

26. Simmons, *Peckinpah: A Portrait in Montage,* p. 19.

27. Bryson, "Wild Bunch in New York," p. 28.

28. Seydor, "Peckinpah," p. 20.

29. Ibid., p. 271.

30. See, for example, Weddle, *If They Move . . . Kill 'Em,* p. 356.

31. Weddle, *If They Move . . . Kill 'Em,* p. 355.

32. SPC, *Wild Bunch*—editing, folder no. 40.

33. SPC, *Wild Bunch*—editing, folder no. 40.

34. Simmons, *Peckinpah: A Portrait in Montage,* p. 102.

35. SPC, *Straw Dogs*—shooting script, folder no. 21.

36. SPC, *Straw Dogs*—editing, folder no. 44.

37. Ibid.

38. SPC, *Straw Dogs*—shooting script, folder no. 21.

39. SPC, *Straw Dogs*—editing, folder no. 44.

40. Ibid.

41. Bliss also sees *Straw Dogs* as a film that studies male brutality toward women without endorsing it. See *Justified Lives,* p. 142.

42. See "Playboy Interview," p. 68; and Weddle, *If They Move . . . Kill 'Em,* pp. 419–424.

43. Bliss offers an excellent discussion of the psychological implications of the editing of this scene in *Justified Lives,* pp. 169–174.

44. Richard Whitehall, "Talking With Peckinpah," p. 174.

45. Weddle, *If They Move . . . Kill 'Em,* pp. 114–115.

46. Seydor discusses the discrepancies between the historical record and Peckinpah's version of events in *Peckinpah: The Western Films,* pp. 382–383, n. 13.

47. "Press Violent About Film's Violence," p. 15.

48. Farber, "Peckinpah's Return," p. 8.

49. SPC, *Wild Bunch*—response letters, May 13, 1969, folder no. 92.

50. Bryson, "Wild Bunch in New York," p. 28.

51. Kluge, "Director Sam Peckinpah," p. 53.

52. SPC, *Le Devoir* interview, interviews, folder no. 96.

53. Review of *The Wild Bunch* in *The Nation,* vol. 209, July 14, 1969, p. 61.

54. Sherwood Ross, "Blood and Circuses," p. 1095.

55. Arthur Knight, "Violence Flares Anew," p. 21.

56. Morgenstern, "The Bloody Bunch," p. 85.

57. Charles Higson, "The Shock of the Old," p. 36.

58. Anthony DeCurtis, "What the Streets Mean: An Interview with Martin Scorsese," p. 211.

Chapter 3 / Melancholy and Mortality

1. Mellen, *Big Bad Wolves,* pp. 270, 302.

2. "Playboy Interview," p. 68.

3. Ibid., p. 70.

4. Ibid., p. 68.

5. Ibid.

6. SPC, correspondence-misc., folder no. 1.

7. Robert Ardrey, *The Territorial Imperative,* p. 5.

8. Ardrey, *The Social Contract,* p. 255.

9. Ibid., p. 279.

10. Ardrey, *African Genesis,* p. 348.

11. Ibid.

12. Yergin, "Peckinpah's Progress," p. 90.

13. *Mass Media Hearings Vol. 9A,* p. 55.

14. Schlesinger, "America 1968," p. 20.

15. Quoted in Weddle, *If They Move . . . Kill 'Em,* p. 12.

16. "Playboy Interview," p. 68.

17. SPC, ABC network interview transcript, interviews, folder no. 96.

18. Ibid.

19. "Press Violent About Film's Violence," p. 15.

20. Weddle, *If They Move . . . Kill 'Em,* p. 12.

21. This interview is excerpted in the documentary *Sam Peckinpah: Man of Iron,* BBC television (1992).

22. Walter Kaufmann, *Tragedy and Philosophy,* p. 34.

23. Miller, "In Defense of Sam Peckinpah," p. 13.

24. The former British film censor Enid Wistrich points to this capability in discussing the special qualities of cinematic violence in *'I Don't Mind the Sex, It's the Violence': Film Censorship Explored,* p. 94.

25. Dorothy G. Singer and Jerome L. Singer, "TV Violence: What's All the Fuss About?" p. 30.

26. Ibid.

27. See Richard E. Goranson, "The Catharsis Effect: Two Opposing Views," in Lange et al., eds., *Mass Media and Violence,* pp. 453–459.

28. George Comstock, "New Emphases in Research on the Effects of Television and Film Violence," in *Children and the Faces of Television,* p. 130.

29. Antonin Artaud, *The Theater and Its Double,* p. 31.

30. Ibid., p. 83.

31. Ibid., p. 31.

32. Ibid., p. 82.

33. Ibid., pp. 101, 102.

34. See William Blum, "Toward a Cinema of Cruelty," pp. 19–33.

35. Artaud, *The Theater and Its Double,* p. 98.

36. Haejung Paik and George Comstock, "The Effects of Television Violence on Antisocial Behavior," pp. 516–546. For a slightly different view, see Richard B. Felson, "Mass media effects on violent behavior," p. 103–129.

37. Goranson, "The Catharsis Effect," p. 456; Eli A. Rubinstein, "Television Violence," in Palmer and Dorr, eds., *Children and the Faces of Television,* p. 120.

38. Surgeon General's Scientific Advisory Committee on Television and Social Behavior, *Television and Growing Up: The Impact of Televised Violence,* 1972.

39. Seymour Feshback, "The Role of Fantasy in the Response to Television,", pp. 71–85; "Reality and Fantasy in Filmed Violence" in Murray et al., eds., *Television and Social Behavior,* pp. 318–345; "The Stimulating Versus Cathartic Effects of a Vicarious Aggressive Activity," pp. 381–385; "The Drive Reducing Function of Fantasy Behavior," *J,* pp. 3–11. For a procatharsis view, see also Gary A. Copeland

and Dan Slater, "Television Violence and Vicarious Catharsis," pp. 352–362; Sidney A. Manning and Dalmas A. Taylor, "Effects of Viewed Violence and Aggression: Stimulation and Catharsis," pp. 180–188; Ann Roth Pytkowicz, Nathaniel N. Wagner, and Irwin G. Sarason, "An Experimental Study of the Reduction of Hostility Through Fantasy," pp. 295–303.

40. Feshback, "The Catharsis Hypothesis and Some Consequences of Interaction with Aggressive and Neutral Play Objects," pp. 449–462.

41. Leonard Berkowitz and Russell G. Geen, "Film Violence and the Cue Properties of Available Targets," pp. 525–530.

42. Albert Bandura, Dorothea Ross, and Sheila A. Ross, "Vicarious Reinforcement and Imitative Learning," p. 605.

43. Ibid., p. 606.

44. Ibid.

45. Bandura, Ross, and Ross, "Imitation of Film-Mediated Aggressive Models," pp. 3–11.

46. Leonard Berkowitz and Edna Rawlings, "Effects of Film Violence on Inhibitions against Subsequent Aggression," pp. 405–412.

47. Ibid., p. 411.

48. Robert A. Baron, "Magnitude of Victim's Pain Cues and Level of Prior Anger Arousal as Determinants of Adult Aggressive Behavior," pp. 236–243; Glenn S. Sanders and Robert Steven Baron, "Pain Cues and Uncertainty as Determinants of Aggression in a Situation Involving Repeated Instigation," pp. 495–502.

49. D. Caroline Blanchard, Barry Graczyk, and Robert J. Blanchard, "Differential Reactions of Men and Women to Realism, Physical Damage, and Emotionality in Violent Films," pp. 45–55.

50. Ibid., p. 51.

51. Wayne Wilson and Randy Hunter, "Movie-Inspired Violence," pp. 435–441.

52. See Dolf Zillmann, "Excitation Transfer in Communication-Mediated Aggressive Behavior," pp. 419–434; and P.H. Tannenbaum and D. Zillmann, "Emotional Arousal in the Facilitation of Aggression Through Communication," in Leonard Berkowitz, ed., *Advances in Experimental Social Psychology*, pp. 149–192.

53. Victor R. Cline, Roger G. Croft, and Steven Courrier, "Desensitization of Children to Television Violence," pp. 360–365.

54. Vernon Reynolds, "Comments on Papers by Flynn and Bandura," in M. von Cranach et al., eds., *Human Ethology*, p. 363.

55. Bandura, "Psychological Mechanisms of Aggression," in Cranach et al., *Human Ethology*, p. 318.

56. Ibid., p. 331.

57. Ibid., p. 323.

58. Jason Jacobs, "Gunfire," p. 40.

59. Comstock, "New Emphases in Research and the Effects of Television and Film Violence," p. 130.

60. John Fraser, *Violence in the Arts,* p. 66.

61. Wistrich, *'I Don't Mind the Sex, It's The Violence',* p. 103.

62. *Mass Media Hearings,* p. 43.

63. Yergin, "Peckinpah's Progress," p. 92.

64. Weddle, *If They Move . . . Kill 'Em,* p. 367.

65. Wood, "Sam Peckinpah" in Roud, ed., *Cinema: A Critical Dictionary,* p. 774.

66. Quoted in Marshall Fine, *Bloody Sam: The Life and Films of Sam Peckinpah,* p. 153.

67. Seydor, *Peckinpah: The Western Films,* p. 168.

68. SPC, *The Wild Bunch,* Feldman memos, folder no. 46.

69. See Seydor, *Peckinpah: The Western Films,* pp. 138–139; and Bliss, *Justified Lives,* p. 126.

70. Kauffmann, "Straw Dogs," p. 24.

71. Kael, "Peckinpah's Obsession," pp. 425–426.

72. Mellen, *Big Bad Wolves,* pp. 302, 303.

73. "Playboy Interview," p. 68.

74. Ibid.

75. Weddle, *If They Move . . . Kill 'Em,* p. 400.

76. See "Playboy Interview," p. 72; Lewis Grover, "Sam Peckinpah in Mexico," p. 46; and Macklin, "Mort Sahl Called Me a 1939 American," p. 25.

77. SPC, *Straw Dogs*—promotion, folder no. 65.

78. Ibid.

79. SPC, *Straw Dogs*—editing, folder no. 44.

80. Rory Palmieri, "*Straw Dogs:* Sam Peckinpah and the Classical Western Narrative," p. 40.

81. SPC, *Straw Dogs*—editing, folder no. 44.

82. SPC, *Straw Dogs*—memos, to Melnick from Peckinpah, March 15, 1971, folder no. 53.

83. SPC, *Straw Dogs*—promotion, folder no. 65.

84. Mellen, *Big Bad Wolves,* p. 304.

85. Lawrence Shaffer, "*The Wild Bunch* versus *Straw Dogs,*" p. 133.

86. Kael, "Peckinpah's Obsession," p. 425.

87. Mellen, *Big Bad Wolves,* p. 304.

88. Bryson, "Wild Bunch in New York," p. 27.

89. SPC, *Straw Dogs*—editing, folder no. 44.

90. SPC, *Straw Dogs*—memos, July 26, 1970, folder no. 53.

91. SPC, *Straw Dogs*—editing, memo of June 16, 1976, folder no. 44.

92. Fraser, *Violence in the Arts,* p. 116.

93. SPC, *Alfredo Garcia*—misc. production notes, letter of September 12, 1974, folder no. 69.

94. Bryson, "Wild Bunch in New York," p. 28.

95. SPC, misc. correspondence, letter of September 9, 1973, to Robert Ardrey, folder no. 1.

96. SPC, *Alfredo Garcia*—preview cards, folder no. 59.

97. Miller, "In Defense of Sam Peckinpah," p. 10.

98. SPC, *Le Devoir* interview, interviews, folder no. 96.; and SPC, *Alfredo Garcia*—advertising and publicity, letter of June 27, 1974.

99. SPC, *Alfredo Garcia*—preview cards, folder no. 59.

100. SPC, *The Killer Elite*—script notes, folder no. 21.

101. Ibid.

102. SPC, *Pat Garrett*—crank letters, letter of May 3, 1974, folder no. 16.

103. SPC, *Alfredo Garcia*—production (misc.), statement of August 28, 1974, protesting the German censorship of *Alfredo Garcia,* folder no. 69.

104. SPC, *Straw Dogs*—promotion, folder no. 65.

105. SPC, *Cross of Iron,* letter of January 7, 1977, folder no. 62.

106. Ibid.

107. SPC, audiotape of *Osterman* story conference, September 26, 1982.

108. Ibid.

109. SPC, *Osterman*—meeting notes, folder no. 115.

110. SPC, audiotape of *Osterman* story conference, September 26, 1982.

111. Ibid.

112. SPC, *Osterman*—editing, folder no. 72.

113. SPC, *Cross of Iron,* letter of December 14, 1976, folder no. 62.

114. Simmons, *Peckinpah: A Portrait in Montage,* p. 204.

Chapter 4 / Interrogating Violence

1. Brecht quoted in Frederic Ewin, *Bertolt Brecht: His Life, His Art, and His Times,* p. 373.

2. Robert Phillip Kolker, *A Cinema of Loneliness,* p. 53–54.

3. Fine, *Bloody Sam,* p. 304.

4. Artaud, *The Theater and Its Double,* p. 79.

5. Fraser, *Violence in the Arts,* p. 112.

6. Artaud, *The Theater and Its Double,* p. 79.

7. Bertolt Brecht, *Brecht on Theatre,* p. 192.

8. Ibid., p. 78.

9. Artaud, *The Theater and Its Double,* pp. 82–83.

10. Kluge, "Director Sam Peckinpah," p. 49.

11. "Press Violent About Film's Violence," p. 15.

12. SPC, *Wild Bunch,* Feldman memos, August 5, 1968, folder no. 45.

13. SPC, *Straw Dogs* final shooting script, folder no. 21.

14. Northrop Frye, *Anatomy of Criticism,* p. 41.

15. Farber, "Peckinpah's Return," pp. 8, 9.

16. Cocks, "Peckinpah: Primitive Horror," p. 87.

17. See, for example, Seydor, *Peckinpah: The Western Films.*

18. SPC, *Wild Bunch*—preview cards, folder no. 65.

19. Paul D. Zimmerman, review of *Straw Dogs, Newsweek,* p. 87.

20. SPC, *Straw Dogs*—promotion, folder no. 65.

21. Ibid.

22. "Playboy Interview," p. 68.

23. SPC, *Straw Dogs*—editing, folder no. 44.

24. Ibid.

25. Quoted in Fine, *Bloody Sam,* p. 260.

26. Quoted in Simmons, *Peckinpah: A Portrait in Montage,* p. 207.

27. Quoted in Seydor, *Peckinpah: The Western Films,* p. 228.

28. Cocks, "Peckinpah: Primitive Horror," p. 87.

29. SPC, *Pat Garrett*—crank letters, letter of June 17, 1974, folder no. 16.

30. SPC, *Straw Dogs*—production notes, memo of April 21, 1971, folder no. 61.

31. SPC, *The Getaway*—editing, folder no. 36.

32. The dark glasses are one of many self-referential elements in the film. They are a tribute to Peckinpah, on whose mannerisms actor Warren Oates modeled aspects of Benny.

Chapter 5 / A Disputed Legacy

1. SPC, *The Killer Elite*—script notes of March 14, 1975, folder no. 21; and SPC, *The Killer Elite*—script notes, folder no. 21.

2. Ibid.

3. SPC, *The Killer Elite*—script notes, note of January 20, 1975, folder no. 21.

4. SPC, *The Killer Elite*—legal, folder no. 34.

5. SPC, *Cross of Iron*—script notes, January 31, 1976, folder no. 26; and SPC, *Cross of Iron*—script notes, folder no. 26.

6. SPC, *Cross of Iron,* letter of December 14, 1976, folder no. 62.

7. Ibid.

8. SPC, *Convoy*—cutting, folder no. 32; and SPC, *Convoy* editing notes of August 3, 1977, folder no. 32.

9. SPC, *Convoy*—memos, letter of August 17, 1977, folder no. 72.

10. SPC, *Osterman*—meeting notes, September 28, 1982, folder no. 115.

11. SPC, correspondence—Lucien Ballard, letter of November 4, 1982, folder no. 5.

12. SPC, misc. correspondence, letter of November 4, 1982, folder no. 59.

13. SPC, *Osterman*—editing, memo of February 26, 1983, folder no. 72.

14. Ibid.

15. Ibid.

16. SPC, *Alfredo Garcia*—production (misc.), statement protesting the German censorship of *Alfredo Garcia,* folder no. 69.

17. SPC, *Le Devoir* interview, interviews, folder no. 96.

18. SPC, *Le Devoir* interview, interviews, folder no. 96.

19. Truffaut, *Hitchcock,* p. 311.

20. SPC, *Le Devoir* interview, interviews, folder no. 96.

21. Ibid. The awkwardness of the wording here is due to a translation from French, in which language the interview was originally published. The English retranslation was specially prepared for Peckinpah who wanted to read the interview upon its publication. After reading the text, he wrote that he considered this an especially fine interview.

22. Ibid.

23. Ibid.

24. Ibid.

25. SPC, *Alfredo Garcia*—production (misc.), statement protesting German censorship of *Alfredo Garcia,* folder no. 69.

26. Slotkin, *Gunfighter Nation,* 352.

27. SPC, *Wild Bunch*—preview cards, folder no. 74.

28. SPC, *Alfredo Garcia*—preview cards, folder no. 59.

29. SPC, *Le Devoir* interview, interviews, folder no. 96.

30. SPC, *Straw Dogs*—promotion, reply to a British article on *Straw Dogs,* folder no. 65.

31. SPC, *Straw Dogs*—promotion, letter of January 5, 1972, folder no. 65.

32. SPC, *Wild Bunch*—response letters, letter of May 13, 1969, folder no. 92.

33. SPC, *Alfredo Garcia*—production (misc.), letter of September 12, 1974, in reply to the potential banning of *Alfredo Garcia* by the Swedish Censorship Board, folder no. 69.

34. SPC, *Le Devoir* interview, inteviews, folder no. 96.

35. Ibid.

36. Kolker, *A Cinema of Loneliness,* p. 49.

37. See, for example, Tony Williams, "Space, Place and Spectacle: The Crisis Cinema of John Woo," pp. 67–84.

38. James Greenberg, "Western Canvas, Palette of Blood," p. 26.

39. SPC, *Straw Dogs*—editing, July 8, 1971, folder no. 44.

40. SPC, *Straw Dogs*—editing, folder no. 44.

41. SPC, *Alfredo Garcia*—daily log, folder no. 45.

42. Manohla Dargis, "Sleeping with Guns," p. 21; and Patricia Holland, "Thrills and Bills," p. 36.

43. One critic has used this term to describe contemporary pop cultural violence. See James B. Twitchell, *Preposterous Violence.*

44. Rob Tannenbaum, "Stallone," p. 86.

45. Fraser makes this point in *Violence in the Arts,* p. 66.

46. Gitlin, "Thrills and Kills," p. 247.

47. See the discussion in Chapter 2.

48. Stephen Pizzello, "*Natural Born Killers* Blasts Big Screen," p. 38.

49. Ibid.

50. Bailey, "Bang Bang Bang Bang, Ad Nauseam," p. 28.

51. Pizzello, "*Natural Born Killers* Blasts Big Screen," p. 54.

52. SPC, interviews, folder no. 96.

53. Ibid.

54. SPC, *Pat Garrett*—crank letters, folder no. 16.

55. SPC, *Alfredo Garcia*—production (misc.), statement protesting the German censorship of *Alfredo Garcia,* folder no. 69.

56. Ibid.

57. SPC, *Major Dundee,* undated letter, folder no. 18.

Bibliography

Archive

Sam Peckinpah Collection (SPC), Margaret Herrick Library, Academy of Motion Picture Arts and Sciences, Los Angeles, California. The collection contains over ninety boxes of material that includes the production records of Peckinpah's films, film scripts, and his voluminous correspondence. The collection is organized by topic (e.g., *Straw Dogs*—editing; *Cross of Iron*—script notes), and each topic typically contains several folders of material.

Other Works Consulted

Aghed, Jan. "Pat Garrett and Billy the Kid." *Sight and Sound* 42, no. 2 (Spring 1973), p. 65.

Ardrey, Robert. *African Genesis.* New York: Atheneum, 1961.

——. *The Social Contract.* New York: Atheneum, 1970.

——. *The Territorial Imperative.* New York: Atheneum, 1966.

Artaud, Antonin. *The Theater and Its Double,* trans. Mary Caroline Richards. New York: Grove Press, 1958.

Bailey, John. "Bang Bang Bang Bang, Ad Nauseam." *American Cinematographer* (December 1994), p. 28.

Bandura, Albert. "Psychological Mechanisms of Aggression." In *Human Ethology,* ed. M. von Cranach et. al., p. 318. New York: Cambridge University Press, 1979.

Bandura, Albert, Dorothea Ross, and Sheila A. Ross. "Imitation of Film-Mediated Aggressive Models." *Journal of Abnormal and Social Psychology* 66, no. 1 (1963), pp. 3–11.

———. "Vicarious Reinforcement and Imitative Learning." *Journal of Abnormal and Social Psychology* 67, no. 6 (1963), p. 605.

Baron, Robert A. "Magnitude of Victim's Pain Cues and Level of Prior Anger Arousal as Determinants of Adult Aggressive Behavior." *Journal of Personality and Social Psychology* 17, no. 3 (1971), pp. 236–243.

Berkowitz, Leonard and Russell G. Geen. "Film Violence and the Cue Properties of Available Targets." *Journal of Personality and Social Psychology* 3, no. 5 (1966), pp. 525–530.

Berkowitz, Leonard and Edna Rawlings. "Effects of Film Violence on Inhibitions Against Subsequent Aggression." *Journal of Abnormal and Social Psychology* 66, no. 5 (1963), pp. 405–412.

Blanchard, D. Caroline, Barry Graczyk, and Robert J. Blanchard. "Differential Reactions of Men and Women to Realism, Physical Damage, and Emotionality in Violent Films." *Aggressive Behavior* 12 (1986), pp. 45–55.

Bliss, Michael, ed. *Doing It Right.* Carbondale: Southern Illinois University Press, 1994.

———. *Justified Lives: Morality and Narrative in the Films of Sam Peckinpah.* Carbondale: Southern Illinois University Press, 1993.

Blum, William. "Toward a Cinema of Cruelty." *Cinema Journal* 10, no. 2 (Spring 1970), pp. 19–33.

"'Bonnie and Clyde's' Booming Repeats," *Variety,* February 14, 1968, p. 3.

Bordwell, David. *The Cinema of Eisenstein.* Cambridge: Harvard University Press, 1993.

Brecht, Bertolt. *Brecht on Theatre,* trans. John Willett. New York: Hill and Wang, 1979.

"'Brutal Films Pale Before Televised Vietnam'—Valenti," *Variety* (February 21, 1968), p. 2.

Bryson, John. "The Wild Bunch in New York." *New York* (August 19, 1974), p. 26.

Callenbach, Ernest. "A Conversation with Sam Peckinpah." *Film Quarterly* 17, no. 2 (Winter 1963–1964), p. 10.

"Catholics and Code Watchful," *Variety* (November 23, 1966), p. 7.

"Catholics Mild Re 'Wild Bunch,'" *Variety* (July 9, 1969), p. 13.

Chapin, Louis. "New Movie Standards: General Film Code, Not Specific Bans." *Christian Science Monitor* (September 23, 1966), p. 5.

Cline, Victor R., Roger G. Croft, and Steven Courrier. "Desensitization of Children to Television Violence." *Journal of Personality and Social Psychology* 27, no. 3 (1973), pp. 360–365.

Cocks, Jay. "Peckinpah: Primitive Horror." *Time* (December 20, 1971), p. 87.

———. "Straw Dogs." Review in *Time* (December 20, 1971), p. 86.

Comstock, George. "New Emphases in Research on the Effects of Television and Violence." In *Children and the Faces of Television,* eds. Edward L. Palmer and Aimee Dorr. New York: Academic Press, 1980.

Copeland, Gary A. and Dan Slater. "Television Violence and Vicarious Catharsis." *Critical Studies in Mass Communication* 2 (1985), pp. 352–362.

Cranach, M. von, et al. *Human Ethology: Claims and Limits of a New Discipline.* Cambridge, MA: Cambridge University Press, 1979.

Crowdus, Gary and Richard Porton. "The Importance of a Singular, Guiding Vision: An Interview with Arthur Penn." *Cineaste* 20, no. 2 (Spring 1993), p. 12.

Crowther, Bosley. "A Smash at Violence." *New York Times* (July 30, 1967), p. 10.

Dargis, Manohla. "Sleeping with Guns." *Sight and Sound* 7, no. 5 (May 1997), p. 18–21.

DeCurtis, Anthony. "What the Streets Mean: An Interview with Martin Scorsese." In *Plays, Movies, and Critics,* ed. Jody McAuliffe, p. 211. Durham: Duke University Press, 1993.

"The Drive Reducing Function of Fantasy Behavior." *Journal of Abnormal and Social Psychology* 50, no. 1 (1955), pp. 3–11.

"'Escalation' of Pix Violence Hit by Theatre Owners at Convention," *Variety* (September 27, 1967), p. 28.

"Evans' Par Credo: Stress Story, Encourage Youth, Mix in Experience," *Variety* (February 21, 1967), p. 9.

Ewin, Frederic. *Bertolt Brecht: His Life, His Art, and His Times.* New York: Citadel Press, 1969.

Farber, Stephen, "Peckinpah's Return." *Film Quarterly* 23, no. 1 (Fall 1969), p. 8.

Felson, Richard B. "Mass Media Effects on Violent Behavior." *Annual Review of Sociology* 22 (1996) p. 103–129.

Feshback, Seymour. "The Catharsis Hypothesis and Some Consequences of Interaction with Aggressive and Neutral Play Objects." *Journal of Personality* 24 (1956), pp. 449–462.

———. "The Role of Fantasy in the Response to Television." *Journal of Social Issues* 32, no. 4 (1976), pp. 71–85.

Fine, Marshall. *Bloody Sam: The Life and Films of Sam Peckinpah.* New York: Donald I. Fine, Inc., 1991.

Fraser, John. *Violence in the Arts.* New York: Cambridge University Press, 1976.

Frayling, Christopher. *Spaghetti Westerns.* London: Routledge and Kegan Paul, 1981.

Frye, Northrop. *Anatomy of Criticism.* Princeton, NJ: Princeton University Press, 1973.

Gitlin, Todd. *The Sixties: Years of Hope, Days of Rage.* New York: Bantam Books, 1989.

———. "Thrills and Kills." *Dissent* (Spring 1991), p. 247.

Glenny, Michael and Richard Taylor, eds. *Eisenstein. Volume 2: Towards a Theory of Montage.* London: BFI, 1994.

Goranson, Richard E. "The Catharsis Effect: Two Opposing Views." In *Mass Media and Violence: A Report to the National Commission on the Causes and Prevention of Violence,* eds. David L. Lange, Robert K. Baker, and Sandra J. Ball, pp. 453–459. Washington, DC: U.S. Government Printing Office, 1969.

Greenberg, James. "Western Canvas, Palette of Blood: The Films of Sam Peckinpah." *New York Times* (February 26, 1995), p. 19–26.

Grover, Lewis. "Sam Peckinpah in Mexico." *Rolling Stone* (October 12, 1972), p. 46.

Harmetz, Aljean. "Man Was a Killer Long before He Served a God." In *Doing It Right: The Best Criticism on Sam Peckinpah's 'The Wild Bunch',* ed. Michael Bliss, p. 173. Carbondale: Southern Illinois University Press, 1994.

Harris, Lou. *The Anguish of Change.* New York: W. W. Norton, 1973.

Hayden, Tom. "The Ability to Face Whatever Comes." *New Republic,* pp. 16–18.

Hersh, Seymour. *My Lai 4: A Report on the Massacre and Its Aftermath.* New York: Random House, 1970.

Higson, Charles. "The Shock of the Old." *Sight and Sound* 5, no. 8 (August 1995), p. 36.

Holland, Patricia. "Thrills and Bills." *New Statesman and Society* (April 22, 1994), p. 36.

"Hollywood: The Shock of Freedom in Films," *Time* (December 8, 1967), p. 66.

"H'wood: Brave Nude World?" *Variety* (August 23, 1967), p. 1.

"It's More Resolution than Noted," *Variety* (July 3, 1968), p. 5.

Jacobs, Jason. "Gunfire." *Sight and Sound* 5, no. 10 (October 1995), p. 40.

Kael, Pauline. "Peckinpah's Obsession," in *For Keeps,* pp. 422–426. New York: Dutton, 1994.

Kauffmann, Stanley. "Straw Dogs." Review in *New Republic* (February 19, 1972), p. 24.

Kaufmann, Walter. *Tragedy and Philosophy.* New York: Anchor Books, 1969.

Keniston, Kenneth. *Young Radicals.* New York: Harvest, 1968.

King, Jr., Martin Luther. "A Time to Break Silence." In *A Testament of Hope: The Essential Writings of Martin Luther King, Jr.,* ed. James M. Washington, pp. 233, 241. San Francisco: Harper and Row, 1986.

Kitses, Jim. *Horizons West.* Bloomington: Indiana University Press, 1969.

Kluge, P. F. "Director Sam Peckinpah, What Price Violence?." *Life* (August 11, 1972), pp. 52–53.

Knight, Arthur. "Violence Flares Anew." *Saturday Review* (July 5, 1969), p. 21.

Kolker, Robert Phillip. *A Cinema of Loneliness.* New York: Oxford University Press, 1980.

Landry, Robert J. "It's Murder, Italian Style," *Variety* (February 8, 1967), p. 7.

Macklin, F. Anthony. "Mort Sahl Called Me a 1939 American." *Film Heritage* 11, no. 4 (Summer 1976), p. 23.

Manning, Sidney A. and Dalmas A. Taylor. "Effects of Viewed Violence and Aggression: Stimulation and Catharsis." *Journal of Personality and Social Psychology* 31, no. 1 (1975), pp. 180–188.

Marcuse, Herbert. *One-Dimensional Man.* Boston: Beacon Press, 1966.

Mass Media Hearings, Vol. 9A: A Report to the National Commission on the Causes and Prevention of Violence. Washington, D.C.: U.S. Government Printing Office, 1969.

"'Mature' Tag at Music Hall." *Variety* (March 29, 1967), p. 7.

Mellen, Joan. *Big Bad Wolves: Masculinity in the American Film,* New York: Pantheon, 1977.

Millar, Jeff. "Peckinpah Gets Nonviolent (Off Screen)." *Los Angeles Times Calendar* (May 21, 1972), p. 1.

Miller, Mark Crispin. "In Defense of Sam Peckinpah." *Film Quarterly* 28, no. 3 (Spring 1975), pp. 10, 13.

Mills, C. Wright. *The Power Elite.* New York: Oxford University Press, 1956.

"Modern Films for Masses," *Variety* (April 17, 1968), p. 23.

Morgenstern, Joseph. "The Bloody Bunch." Review of *The Wild Bunch* in *Newsweek* (July 14, 1969), p. 85.

———. "The Thin Red Line." *Newsweek* (August 28, 1967), p. 82.

———. "Two for a Tommy Gun." Review of *Bonnie and Clyde* in *Newsweek* (August 21, 1967), p. 65.

Murphy, Kathleen. "Sam Peckinpah: No Bleeding Heart." *Film Comment* 21 (1985), p. 74.

Murray, John P., Eli A. Rubinstein, and George A. Comstock, eds. *Television and Social Behavior: A Technical Report to the Surgeon General's Scientific Advisory Committee on Television and Social Behavior.* Washington, D.C.: U. S. Government Printing Office, 1972.

Oglesby, Carl. "Liberalism and the Corporate State." *Monthly Review* 17, no. 8 (January 1966), p. 22.

Paik, Haejung and George Comstock. "The Effects of Television Violence on Antisocial Behavior: A Meta-Analysis." *Communication Research* 21, no. 4 (August 1994), pp. 516–546.

Palmer, Edward L. and Aimee Dorr, eds. *Children and the Faces of Television.* New York: Academic Press, 1980.

Palmieri, Rory. "*Straw Dogs:* Sam Peckinpah and the Classical Western Narrative." *Studies in the Literary Imagination* 16, no. 1 (1983), pp. 29–42.

"Persevering of 'Bonnie and Clyde'," *Variety* (March 20, 1968), p. 5.

"Pix Must 'Broaden Market'," *Variety* (March 20, 1968), p. 1.

Pizzello, Stephen. "*Natural Born Killers* Blasts Big Screen with Both Barrels." *American Cinematographer* (November 1994), p. 38.

"Playboy Interview: Sam Peckinpah," *Playboy* 19, no. 8 (August 1972), p. 70.

"Press Violent About Film's Violence," *Variety* (July 2, 1969), p. 15.

Prince, Stephen, ed. *Sam Peckinpah's* The Wild Bunch. New York: Cambridge University Press, 1998.

"Public Spots Deadly Parallels," *Variety* (May 12, 1968), p. 60.

Pytkowicz, Ann Roth, Nathaniel N. Wagner, and Irwin G. Sarason. "An Experimental Study of the Reduction of Hostility through Fantasy." *Journal of Personality and Social Psychology* 5, no. 3 (1967), pp. 295–303.

Report of the National Advisory Commission on Civil Disorders. Washington, D.C.: U.S. Government Printing Office, 1968.

Reynolds, Vernon. "Comments on Papers by Flynn and Bandura." In *Human Ethology: Claims and Limits of a New Discipline*, ed. M. von Cranach et al., p. 363. New York: Cambridge University Press, 1979.

Ross, Sherwood. "Blood and Circuses." *The Christian Century* (August 20, 1960), p. 1095.

Roud, Richard, ed. *Cinema: A Critical Dictionary*. Norwich, Great Britain: Fletcher and Son, Ltd., 1980.

Rubinstein, Eli A. "Television Violence: A Historical Perspective." In *Children and the Faces of Television*, eds. Edward L. Palmer and Aimee Dorr. New York: Academic Press, 1980.

Sale, Kirkpatrick. *SDS.* New York: Random House, 1973.

Sanders, Glenn S. and Robert Steven Baron. "Pain Cues and Uncertainty as Determinants of Aggression in a Situation Involving Repeated Instigation." *Journal of Personality and Social Psychology* 22, no. 3 (1975), pp. 495–502.

Schlesinger, Jr., Arthur. "America 1968: The Politics of Violence." *Harper's Magazine* (August 1968), p. 20.

Seydor, Paul. "Sam Peckinpah." *Sight and Sound* 5, no. 10 (October 1995), p. 20.

——. *Peckinpah: The Western Films: A Reconsideration.* Urbana: University of Illinois Press, 1997.

Shaffer, Lawrence. "*The Wild Bunch* versus *Straw Dogs.*" *Sight and Sound* 41, no. 3 (Summer 1972), p. 133.

Simmons, Garner. *Peckinpah: A Portrait in Montage.* Austin: University of Texas Press, 1982.

Singer, Dorothy G., and Jerome L. Singer. "TV Violence: What's All the Fuss About?" *Television and Children* 7, no. 2 (1984), p. 30.

Slotkin, Richard. *Gunfighter Nation.* New York: Atheneum, 1992.

Sontag, Susan. "What's Happening to America." *Partisan Review* (Winter 1967), p. 52.

"Spots of Grief for Metro's 'Blow-Up' and Par's 'Sundown,' But on Whole 'C' Rating Now Stops No Chain Datings," *Variety* (May 31, 1967), p. 7.

Sragow, Michael. "Sam Peckinpah, 1925–1984." In *Doing It Right: The Best Criticism on Sam Peckinpah's 'The Wild Bunch',* ed. Michael Bliss, p. 180. Carbondale: Southern Illinois University Press, 1994.

Steigerwald, David. *The Sixties and the End of Modern America.* New York: St. Martin's Press, 1995.

"The Stimulating Versus Cathartic Effects of a Vicarious Aggressive Activity." *Journal of Abnormal and Social Psychology* 63, no. 2 (1961), pp. 381–385.

Surgeon General's Scientific Advisory Committee on Television and Social Behavior. *Television and Growing Up: The Impact of Televised Violence.* Washington, D.C.: U.S. Government Printing Office, 1972.

Tannenbaum, P. H. and D. Zillmann. "Emotional Arousal in the Facilitation of Aggression Through Communication." In *Advances in Experimental Social Psychology*, vol. 8, ed. Leonard Berkowitz, pp. 149–192. New York: Academic Press, 1975.

Tannenbaum, Rob. "Stallone." *US* no. 233 (June 1997) pp. 85–86.

"Theatre Operators and Public Require Updating on Social Point of View," *Variety* (March 6, 1968), p. 7.

To Establish Justice, to Ensure Domestic Tranquility: The Final Report of the National Commission on the Causes and Prevention of Violence. New York: Praeger, 1970.

Truffaut, Francois. *Hitchcock.* Rev. ed. New York: Simon and Schuster, 1984.

Twitchell, James B. *Preposterous Violence.* New York: Oxford University Press, 1989.

"Urge Local Papers to Rate Pictures," *Variety* (March 22, 1967), p. 13.

"W7 Studio Ready to Give Directors Anything—Except Right of Final Cut," *Variety* (June 25, 1969), p. 5.

"Warren Beatty 'Bonnie' Share," *Variety* (August 7, 1968), p. 1.

Weddle, David. *If They Move . . . Kill 'Em: The Life and Times of Sam Peckinpah.* New York: Grove Press, 1994.

Whitehall, Richard. "Talking with Peckinpah." *Sight and Sound* 38, no. 4 (Autumn 1969), p. 174.

Williams, Tony. "Space, Place and Spectacle: The Crisis Cinema of John Woo." *Cinema Journal* 36, no. 2 (Winter 1997), pp. 67–84.

Wilson, Wayne, and Randy Hunter. "Movie-Inspired Violence." *Psychological Reports* 53 (1983), pp. 435–441.

Wistrich, Enid. *I Don't Mind the Sex, It's the Violence: Film Censorship Explored.* London: Marion Boyars, 1978.

Wood, Robin. "Sam Peckinpah." In *Cinema: A Critical Dictionary,* ed. Richard Roud, p. 772. Norwich, England: Fletcher and Son, Ltd., 1980.

Yergin, Dan. "Peckinpah's Progress: From Blood and Killing in the Old West to Siege and Rape in Rural Cornwall." *New York Times Magazine* (October 31, 1972), p. 90.

"Youngbloods vs. Committees," *Variety* (January 10, 1968), p. 5.

Zillmann, Dolf. "Excitation Transfer in Communication-Mediated Aggressive Behavior." *Journal of Experimental Social Psychology* 7 (1971), pp. 419–434.

Zimmerman, Paul D. "Straw Dogs." Review in *Newsweek* (December 20, 1971), p. 87.

Index